6⁰⁰

the Search for God

the Search for God

CHRISTIANITY — ATHEISM — SECULARISM — WORLD RELIGIONS

HANS SCHWARZ

AUGSBURG PUBLISHING HOUSE
Minneapolis, Minnesota

THE SEARCH FOR GOD

Contents

PART II

A SEARCH FOR ULTIMATES

PART III
GOD'S SELF-DISCLOSURE IN
THE JUDEO-CHRISTIAN TRADITION

Preface

Mankind has surely come a long way. From cave-dwellings to lunar landings and from a food-gathering society to modern agribusiness extends a continuous upward-slanting line of almost dazzling progress. Barely a century ago most people did not even dream of the many gadgets that we take for granted, such as color television, dishwashers, vacuum cleaners, and snowmobiles. Yet at the point where modern technological society has reached the pinnacle of success, we have become remarkably uncertain—uncertain about the future, about our own being, and about life in general. The famous post-eras (post-Christian, post-industrial, post Constantinian, *etc.*) are indicative of our state of mind. We feel that the old accustomed ways of life have gone, but we are very unsure how to map out what lies ahead of us, or even to name it.

In part, this feeling of uncertainty is fostered by the very fact of progress. Over the centuries progress has accelerated at an even faster pace. Whether we consider scientific research, fashions, or even theological movements, in each case one trend is ever more rapidly being replaced by a new one. One might even get the impression that there is nothing steady or directive except the movement of rapid change itself. While many of us still find excitement in modern life by being constantly on-the-go, others, especially among the young, wonder what the meaning of all this rushing should be. In generations past, young people hardly dared to question the values of their elders and accepted them, at the most with slight modifications, as binding for themselves. But this is

9

no longer the rule. Too many have grown up in a throw-away and pack-and-leave culture, in which nothing seems to be of lasting value, that they have become suspicious of all inherited norms. So young people drop out of society for longer or shorter periods to discover on their own a valid reason for life and a basis for living. This kind of emancipation of the adolescents and the young adults is characteristic for the emancipation of society in general.

For large segments of society historical ties are either non-existent or where they still exist they carry with them hardly any spiritual and moral obligations. Consequently, modern mobile man must become self-reliant unlike anybody in the generations before him. But this self-reliance is at the same time characterized by uncertainty, doubt, and a basic mistrust in traditional spiritual values. Often the feeling is even indicated that in a thoroughly technological society we should not waste our time indulging in spiritual values at all, since modern technological life betrays a rational mastery of the world and must be approached in a profoundly rational way. Yet again we notice that especially the young are disenchanted with such a sober prospect. They feel reason alone is not the answer to the deepest questions of life. While they are frequently disillusioned with the answers provided by Christianity, since it has often failed to create a more human world, they are seeking spiritual values from within themselves or in other religions. Should this indicate that in the long run man cannot live by bread alone?

Of course, the mood of self-reliance paired with a distrust in traditional spiritual values does not only affect doubters and unbelievers. It is too sweeping a movement not to affect many Christians and to challenge their very self-understanding. While it was still relatively easy for the first Christian communities to adhere to their beliefs, since they could still be optimistic about making inroads into the dilapidating Greco-Roman culture, things are different with present-day Christians. The claim made repeatedly that we live in a post-Christian era is not very conducive to engender an optimistic attitude. Church buildings are no longer regarded as citadels symbolizing the conquest of the earth and pointing to the heavenly future. Our technological and rationalistic society is so earth-bound that it regards them rather as relics of the past. Even the more conservative church members cannot escape the massive onslaught of an ever increasing secularization of all facets of life. The term Sunday-morning Christians shows that Christian faith is more and more edged out of our lives. Many church members live their everyday life as practical atheists, restricting their religious ties to special sacred occasions. No wonder that the basic questions of life: What shall I do? Whom shall I trust? and What is life all about? are no longer questions that are reserved for doubters and unbelievers. The foundations are shaking for everybody. Confronted with this deep spiritual crisis and in part representing it, more and more "solid Christians" have become insecure and wonder whether their basic presuppositions are still tenable.

Thus the fundamental questions concerning God gain prime importance: Is there a God? And if he can be ascertained, how can we assure ourselves of his presence? Yet in an age in which geographical, ethnic, and religious boundaries are crumbling, the question is often pushed further: Is there any difference between the way other religions know God and the way we know him? In other words, in an age of increasing global solidarity, the question must be posed whether there is still a justifiable distinctness between faiths of different believers?

This book does not attempt to cover all the areas that these questions touch upon. Nor will every reader find all the answers he is looking for in a particular area covered in this book. The terrain described with the simple title *The Search for God* is too vast and too complex to be covered by one person and in one book. Yet learning from many others, the attempt was made to provide a representative cross-section of the issues involved and to indicate that the conclusions reached do not result from ignorance.

In the first part the book addresses itself to the question that haunts many today: Is there a God? We look at the rise of modern atheism and the phenomenon of a rapidly increasing process of secularization, and discern some of the ways in which today's theology attempts to answer the God question. Naturally we must also turn to the question whether God's existence can be plausibly demonstrated or at least made intelligible.

In a second part we concern ourselves with man's continual quest for an ultimate and integrative foundation of his life. After reviewing some of the prevalent -isms that are frequently used to gain a perspective of life, we turn our attention to the religious scene. To understand religion we look at some theories of its origin and familiarize ourselves with basic concepts used in most religions. We ponder the question whether there is a progression discernible either within a particular religion or from one type of religion to another. Finally we ask ourselves how the Christian faith comes to stand in the context of world religions.

Having scrutinized both reason and religion concerning their possibilities and insights for a viable and contemporary notion of God we focus our attention in the third part on the Judeo-Christian tradition and its understanding of God. We attempt to trace the main facets of its development and show what kind of God confronts us through this tradition. We also ask ourselves to what extent such a God is compatible with and can give guidance to the secular world in which we live. If someone wants to study further in an area mentioned he may consult the material cited in the footnotes or in the selective bibliography.

At this point I want to express my gratitude to the various publishers for their generous consent to allow reprint of the passages quoted. The material contained in this book was presented many times in lectures and discussions with colleagues, students, pastors, and non-theologians. Some readers will perhaps discover in the familiarity of this or that phrase that they have unknowingly contributed to this book through their questions, criticism, or suggestions. Particularly I want to mention here my students at the Pontifical Gregorian University in Rome during the second semester 1973/74 who in a remarkably ecumenical and Christian spirit discussed the entire manuscript and provided valuable criticism. Parts of this book have been presented as special lectures in the summer of 1974 at the following schools in the Philippines: Silliman University (Dumaguete City), Central Philippine University (Iloilo City), and Union Theological Seminary (Cavite/Manila).

My special thanks go to my colleague, James Schaaf who undertook the thankless task to improve my style. His wife Phyllis who typed the several drafts of the manuscript with unfailing speed and accuracy surely deserves thanks too. I must also again thank Ronald Grissom for helping with proofreading and compiling the indexes. Of course, any inadequacy of the text, which the discerning reader will detect, is still solely my responsibility. Finally, I must thank my wife for her continued patience and endurance while I was writing the manuscript. However, I would like to dedicate this book to the one whose excited "Daddee! Daddee!" brought joy and happiness into my life when I returned from the library for hurried lunch and supper visits, my daughter, Krista Barbara.

HANS SCHWARZ

Columbus, Ohio

The Search for God

In the 16th century man could afford to make his troubled conscience the main object of his concern. Though the first thunder clouds heralding a new age were looming on the horizon, man lived a fairly sheltered existence. The earth was still considered a solid ground to stand on and beyond the sky man thought of God being in control of earthly affairs. But soon the sentiment changed. Through the Copernican-Brunoic shock man realized that the earth he inhabited was not the center of the universe but only a tiny planet of a larger solar system. Even the uniqueness of mankind remained no longer unchallenged. The revolutionary spirit of this time can be largely attributed to such men as the Italian philosopher Giordano Bruno who radicalized Copernicus' recent theory of a heliocentric world view. In pantheistic fashion Giordano Bruno advocated infinity as the new deity and proposed the existence of innumerable other mankinds and other earth-like planets.[1] Bruno's ideas proved so earthshaking that he got in trouble with Protestants and Catholics alike, and finally in 1600 Roman authorities burned him at the stake. But the ideas he disseminated could not be extinguished that easily. Western man felt that he had lost his unchallenged place in the universe, and it gradually has become a commonplace that he, and the earth he inhabits, are part of a larger evolutionary process of cosmic dimensions.

Seers, such as the 19th century philosopher Friedrich Nietzsche, have told us with prophetic clarity that the world has become cooler, that empty space breathes at us, that the bottom has been

13

removed from beneath our feet and that we are falling into infinite space.[2] While Nietzsche observed that this cosmological upheaval had profound theological implications, namely that God is dead, that God remains dead, and that we have killed him in abandoning an earth-centered world view, it has only been recently that the quest for God gained momentum in more traditionally minded quarters of Christianity. We have been used to the idea of God for such a long time that most Christians have not until very recently raised the question with utmost seriousness whether the world view demonstrated through our technological mastery of the world and the belief in God's very existence as presupposed in our Christian faith are compatible. Some people are already telling us that we might as well get used to the idea that there is no divine agent beyond ourselves whose presence we can assert, or whose guidance we may expect. If we want to address ourselves seriously to the question of the compatability or even necessity of God for our modern consciousness, we must first of all deal with the question whether there is a God at all.

PART I

GOD OR NO GOD

The question concerning the existence of God must be answered on two levels, on a practical and on a theoretical. The first and most obvious concern must be to investigate whether God is somewhere experienced as a living reality. If the result of this part of our investigation ends in the negative, it would be futile to continue the inquiry on a theoretical level and ask whether his existence can be demonstrated. We can learn here from Antony Flew's parable of the two explorers. After two explorers discover a clearing in the jungle, one asserts that there must be a gardener to tend the plot. Since the other explorer disagrees, they set up an ever more refined machinery to prove the existence of such a gardener. When finally through the mechanical setup the gardener is reduced to invisibility, intangibility, and elusiveness, the skeptic rightly wonders how such a gardener differs from an imaginary gardener or even from no gardener at all.[3]

1.

Is God Alive?

If we want to obtain a significant answer to our question whether God is alive, we should not proceed from mere assertion to logical proof, but rather ask whether the experience of God is present in the life of people. In surveying mankind we soon notice that most people still do believe in a divine agent(s) beyond themselves. Yet we also see that within less than fifty years almost one-third of the world's population has surrendered to political and philosophical ideologies that avowedly disclaim any divinity beyond man. For instance, Roger Garaudy observed rightly that there are hundreds of millions of people who find in Communism their hope and meaning for life.[4] It would be naive to ignore such a large number of people in our search for answering the question whether God is alive. But how does it happen that atheism which is at the basis of Communist ideology is spreading so rapidly?

1. The atheistic solution.

Atheism has such a long tradition that the Psalmist already witnesses to it when he states: "The fool says in his heart, 'There is no God'" (Ps. 14:1). But in antiquity an atheist was not taken seriously. He was considered a fool, an exception, and treated as such. When the Greek philosopher Anaxagoras, for instance, declared that the sun was an incandescent stone somewhat larger than the Peloponnesus, he was accused of impiety or atheism and forced to leave his hometown Athens. Others were punished more severely.

16

For instance, when Socrates was indicted for "impiety" in 399 B.C. on grounds that he had corrupted the young and neglected the gods during worship ceremonies ordered by the city and had introduced religious novelties, he was sentenced to death and was condemned to drink the hemlock within twenty-four hours. But Socrates' position and that of other atheists was far from being atheistic in the modern sense. What was meant by impiety or atheism in ancient Greece is spelled out by Plato in his *Laws:* Any citizen who does not offer sacrifices at the public temples, but possesses a shrine in his private dwelling house, is guilty of sin against piety[5].

This means that atheism was not understood as a radical negation of divine agents, but as an attempt to curb the advancement of one kind of worship or religion at the expense of another. Thus labeling someone an atheist, as was also done with the Stoics and Pythagoreans, did not imply that these people did not believe in any deity and did not perform cultic acts, but that they did not believe in the right deity and did not perform the right cultic acts. Modern atheism, however, is different from that of antiquity. It is a sweeping movement which does not reject just one particular deity or one particular cultic act, but all deities and all acts of worship. What is the reason for such a change of mind?

a. *Roots of modern atheism.*

Modern atheism, including Marxism, seems to be so intimately connected with our heritage that it might not be wrong to claim that modern atheism is an offspring of Judeo-Christian faith. But how can this claim be substantiated?

In Judeo-Christian faith there occurred an unprecedented centralization of everything divine into Yahweh, the one power, who is at the same time the father of Jesus Christ. "I am the Lord your God, who brought you out of the land of Egypt, out of the house of bondage. You shall have no other gods besides me" (Ex. 20:2f.) was Yahweh's demand of the Israelite nation. Though the actuality of other gods was conceded many times in the Old Testament, they could not measure up to the one God, and were often ridiculed (Isa. 37:19; 1 Kings 18:27). Thus the Israelite community worshiped only Yahweh and no other deities (Jos. 24:15ff.). Whenever the worship of other gods was mentioned, it was understood as a sinful act or, to draw a parallel with Athens of Greek antiquity, it was impiety. Yet in contradistinction to the local cults of Greek antiquity, Yahweh was not a tribal god. The creation accounts in

Genesis unmistakably advanced the conviction that the God who has chosen Israel was also the creator of the world to whom all other powers succumbed. The prophets also saw God's reign extended even over those foreign nations who threatened Israel's existence (cf. Isa. 14:24-27; 18:1-7). The seers of the apocalyptic movement finally completed the circle. In their attempt to periodize history, they claimed that the God who set all history into action would also bring it to a final conclusion as foreshadowed in the events of the day. The radicality of Judeo-Christian monotheism, however, came to a climax in the New Testament where it was asserted that there is only one way of salvation, only one way of coming to terms with God, and this is via Jesus Christ (cf. John 14:6; Acts 4:12).

The concentration of everything divine into one power, God, and the accessibility of this one power only through one means, his incarnation in Jesus Christ, proved in the long run to be a fatal blow to the traditional metaphysical pluralism.[6] There were no longer holy places, holy people, or holy ceremonies. Though Christianity made concessions in proclaiming holy places as centers of pilgrimages, and saints as mediators, and certain ceremonies as bringing about salvation by their very performance, confidence in non-Godly powers was shaken. Even these holy places, persons, and ceremonies no longer enjoyed independent status. They were understood as functioning as holy and efficient only through God's permission. Thus the world could lose the sacred character it once possessed and could become more and more profane.

Parallel to this desacralization of the world went a spiritualization of God. Since the divine quality was banned from more and more "sacred" objects, God and the world were seen as more and more radically disjunctive entities. God was understood as the sole divine agent over and above the world. Once God was relegated to this position, it became extremely difficult to express convincingly that he still has bearing on the secular world below him. This dilemma became especially evident in the traditional definition of a miracle that, under the influence of Anselm of Canterbury and Thomas Aquinas, had prevailed in Roman Catholic thinking until fairly recently.[7] According to this thinking, a miracle had occurred if a certain phenomenon, e.g. the healing of a sick person, could not be sufficiently explained by assuming only natural causes. This meant that God's working in the context of a miracle was conceived of as an action separate from the workings of other (secular) powers. The conclusion was almost unavoidable that God is not the sole agent of all processes; he interferes only at specific, unusual points through miraculous actions. That the occasions for these interferences must become fewer and fewer, as our knowledge of the world increases, is demonstrated by the decreasing number of actual miracles admitted by the Roman Catholic Church. Gradually God has become so transcendent that in more and more cases the world makes good sense without reference to him. God has become relegated to a sphere which has no bearing on our everyday lives.

Another instance that illuminates the danger of radical monotheism as proposed in the Judeo-Christian faith was the controversy between Calvinists and Lutherans concerning the Lord's Supper. Calvin insisted that the divine could not really be contained in the finite. The divine was thought of as so much apart from the world that its real presence in this world could not be admitted. Luther, however, less inhibited by philosophical reasoning, maintained that the divine could easily dwell in the finite if it so desired. Though during the Reformation period the argument concerning the Lord's Supper remained undecided, it has become clear that Calvin's view is much more attractive to the modern mind. Modern science set free by the desacralization of the world in turn radicalized and absolutized this process of liberation. It has explored and reproduced the cause and effect sequence within the world to such an extent that no divine agent ever becomes necessary. The godlessness of the world, once intended by Judeo-Christian faith, has turned into a world without God and without faith. The all-decisive question, however, is whether this subsequent exclusion of God is a necessary consequence of Judeo-Christian faith. An analysis of the history of modern atheism and a sampling of its contemporary representatives may help us find an answer to this question.

b. *History of modern atheism.*

One of the earliest traces of modern atheism can be seen in Niccolo Machiavelli's treatise *The Prince*.[8] Sobered by the intrigues of power-thirsty men in Renaissance Florence, this Italian statesman and writer suggested in 1513 in this treatise that to be successful a prince cannot be bound in his actions by traditional moral and religious beliefs. Though he must uphold them and show outward conformity with them, two other factors, personal success and blind fate, largely determine the course of history. Though a statesman can recognize some fateful constellations and take necessary measures to avoid their consequences, his actual virtue lies in his own success. He must adapt himself to ever-changing situations and while he should prefer to obey the good, he should not avoid evil if circumstances force him into doing it. Machiavelli therewith advanced the conviction that some people, namely those in leading positions, are no longer subjected to the religious precepts of God. They are in certain cases free to determine their own future without allegiance to a divine agent.

A factor which unintentionally increased this sentiment to an actual distrust in the precepts of God were the Crusades. Through the Crusades men became acquainted with Islam and this was for many the first confrontation with the claim of a religious truth other than that of Christianity. The result was often skepticism about their own Christian faith, or at least the secret concession that they might not have the sole truth. This sentiment is best summed up in Gotthold Ephraim Lessing's famous *Parable of the Rings*. This parable, contained in his dramatic poem *Nathan the Wise* (1779), states that a father once had three sons.[9] He wanted to give them a precious ring, but since he did not want to prefer one son above the others, he made exact duplicates of the original ring. The question that Lessing poses is, who has the original ring. The only criterion is the way the three sons act. But, perhaps, Lessing concedes, none of the three sons, Islam, Christianity and Judaism, has the original ring. It might well be that the true ring has already been lost. Underlying this religious relativism or skepticism is the motif of the three imposters, Moses, Jesus, and Mohammed, which is already contained, though in a slightly different way, in Giovanni Boccaccio's *The Decameron* or the *Ten Days' Work* (ca. 1350).[10]

There are two more factors which perhaps more than those already mentioned tended to undercut the supremacy of Judeo-Christian monotheism. The first is the influence of Aristotelian philosophy. Through the mediating function of Arabian philosophers, such as Avicenna and Averroes, Aristotelian philosophy was introduced to the West in the 13th century. Its timeless idea of the world being emanated from God in a continuous process had caused problems for the Muslim religion. To avoid an outright clash between the truth expressed through Allah's revelation in history and the monistic speculation of Arabian Aristotelianism, Muslim philosophers resorted to the axiom of a twofold truth.[11] This axiom suggested that the images and parables of Allah's revelation in the Koran provide one way of arriving at the truth, while the other way is through timeless philosophical speculation. Though both truths seem to contradict each other, the philosophical truth will coincide with the historical if properly interpreted. Imported into Christianity, the idea of the twofold truth aroused most controversy when it was applied to the understanding of immortality. Aristotelian philosophy denied the Christian hope for an individual resurrection. If affirmed that together with everyone else man would participate after death in the world soul and thus enjoy a kind of collective immortality. The church rightly saw that this idea was incompatible with Christian faith and rejected Averroism at this point. But it could not reject Aristotelian philosophy completely, because it was already too widespread and scholastic theology felt that it needed its framework to express the truth of Christianity. Thus one arrived at the fateful compromise that no teacher of philosophy was allowed to touch an explicitly theological issue. This meant that what was true in philosophy needed no longer be true according to Roman Catholic faith and vice versa.

The other factor which in the long run undercut the supremacy of Judeo-Christian monotheism is found in neo-Platonic philosophy. Unlike Aristotelianism, neo-Platonism was received quite favorably by the church. From the first Christian Apologists up to Augustine, Dionysios the Areopagite, and Anselm of Canterbury, neo-Platonism was considered quite compatible with Christian faith. Up to the Renaissance period Christian monotheism was often thought to be expressed best with neo-Platonic categories, i.e., God as the ultimate reality, and man being endowed with an immortal soul. In the Renaissance period, however, a decisive shift occurred which placed primary emphasis on neo-Platonic philosophy. Together with the efforts to return to the original sources, the antiquity of Platonic philosophy gained new attention. It was believed that there was a straight ascending line of thought from the old pagan theologians, such as Zoroaster, Orpheus, and Hermes, to Plato and Plotinus, and finally to Dionysios the Areopagite, the acme of Platonic discipline and the pillar on which Christian theology could safely rest.

Especially Marsilio Ficino, the founder and leader of the Platonic Academy of Florence, proposed the idea of a primal religion common to all mankind which now found its expression in Christianity. He underscored this in his *Theologia Platonica* (1469-1474) where he stated "that the perverse minds of many persons who do not easily yield to the authority of the divine law alone, should be satisfied at least by Platonic arguments that are brought to the aid

of religion." [12] Though Ficino was a devout Christian who wished
to avoid any scandal in the church, his ideas could prove dangerous
for the Christian faith. First, they failed to consider that Christian
faith is not a timeless philosophic system, but grounded in historic
revelation. [13] Second, they made the persuasiveness of the Christian
faith largely dependent on philosophic arguments. But what would
happen if people refused to be convinced by these philosophical
arguments? Would Christianity collapse, because it had abandoned
the proclamation of God's self-evidencing word in favor of philosophical persuasion? Yet these dangers did not become immediately
evident.

As late as the 17th century, the Cambridge Platonists carried on
the philosophical tradition of the Florentine Academy. [14] Ralph
Cudworth, one of its most well-known representatives, attempted to
refute all atheism and materialism in his classic *The True Intellectual System of the Universe* (1678). He also introduced the term
theism into the European history of thought and proposed a unity
between science, religion, and Christian revelation as the true
remedy against atheism. [15] Herbert of Cherbury, often considered
the father of English deism, continued this trend in postulating
the unity between faith and knowledge. Yet in his book *De Veritate*
(1624) he did no longer advance the specific Judeo-Christian faith,
but a natural religion consisting of five basic notions, common to
all religions and also in accordance with reason. These five basic
notions were (1) there is a supreme diety; (2) worship is due to
this deity; (3) virtue conjoined with piety is to be, and has always
been held to be, the chief component element of divine worship;
(4) a horror of evil deeds has always been native to the souls of
men; wherefore they have not been unaware that vices and crimes
ought to be expiated by penance; and (5) there are reward and
punishment after this life. [16] Though Herbert of Cherbury laid with
this approach the foundations for later deism, he was not yet critical
of the Christian faith. He only wanted to prove that religion can be
based on solid arguments of reason.

Almost a century later appeared Anthony Collins' *A Discourse of
Free-thinking* (1713). Again his approach is apologetic claiming
that "Ignorance is the foundation of *Atheism,* and *Free-Thinking* the
Cure of it." [17] He still conceded two sources of religious knowledge
for man, reason as the course commonly agreed on, and the Scriptures as the source of the specific Christian expression of religion.
While he showed in his *Discourse of Grounds and Reasons of the*

Christian Religion (1724) that many of the Old Testament prophecies were fulfilled in a different way than the New Testament makes us believe, he claimed that their fulfillment is still compatible with reason, not in their literal form, but in their spiritual meaning. Though this can be, and at his time has been understood as an attack on the truthworthiness of the Christian faith, Collins was neither agnostic nor atheist. He simply tried to show that in the Christian tradition faith does not demand a sacrifice of the intellect.[18]

The sentiment toward Christian faith, however, changed radically in the subsequent period of the Enlightenment. Pierre Bayle, one of the forerunners of the Enlightenment, was in his heart a devout Reformed Christian.[19] But he was no longer convinced that reason and religion could be synthesized. He thought that the deists had been fairly naive at this point. For him the human mind cannot always arrive at definite results in relating faith and reason. Since Bayle had lost his own brother as a victim of the persecution of the Huguenots, it was difficult for him to understand intellectually that a wise, just, and benevolent supreme being could rule the world in ultimate harmony. Yet he was open enough to concede that faith in the Christian God is not the result of superstition or ignorance but a gift of God. Having escaped the Huguenot persecution, in which the Catholic authorities had mercilessly attempted to wipe out Protestantism in France, he also wondered whether atheists must necessarily be morally inferior. He argued that most pious people would not admit that they would act immorally once they had abandoned their belief in divine vengeance in the hereafter. Therefore he concluded that morals and religious conviction need not belong together. Even atheists can be good and responsible citizens. As aforementioned, Bayle was a good Calvinist. But his importance lay on a different level, in voicing the destruction of the harmony between reason and religion and in giving atheists an equal status as citizens. This indicates the trend the Enlightenment took.

The most influential stream in the Enlightenment period was a kind of mechanistic materialism. All events, whether spiritual or physical are reduced to the mechanical interactions of matter. This, of course, meant that any kind of religion, whether natural or revealed, had to be eliminated. The main spokesman for this trend was the French physician Julien Offray de La Mettrie.[20] In his treatise *L'Homme machine* (1748), he explained man according to strictly mechanistic principles. He claimed that soul, spirit, and substance can be reduced to physiological constellations. The soul, for instance, results from a certain way the body is organized, and the higher development of the reasonable human soul is due to the bigger and much more complex structure of the human brain. Baron d'Holbach in his book *Système de la nature* (1770) gave this materialistic atheism a systematic touch.[21] All causal relationships are simply relationships of motion and man is entirely a machine. This means that free will is non-existent, the soul is a false notion, and all the arguments for the existence of God are totally wrong. Holbach declared, for example, that to believe in the immortality of the soul is as naive as to expect that a clock broken into a thousand pieces could be glued together and again chime the hours.

Already La Mettrie's writings caught many by surprise. Holbach's *Système,* however, despite its inconsistencies, had sensational impact on public opinion and was even challenged by Voltaire whose deism appeared conservative in comparison. The final point, though only of episodic character, occurred in November 1793, when in the course of the French Revolution, Christianity and all other beliefs in God were officially abolished and the New Republic was declared atheistic. A festival of reason was celebrated in the Cathedral of Notre Dame. Now the century-long process had reached its climax and it had become evident that reason and faith could not form a harmonic unity. Reason always tended to become autonomous and replace the faith to whose aid it had once been called. However, the supremacy of reason at the expense of faith marked the starting point of modern atheism.

c. *Contemporary atheism.*

Contemporary atheism has primarily been shaped by three men, Ludwig Feuerbach, Karl Marx, and Nikolay Lenin. In his book *The Essence of Christianity* (1841) the German philosopher and former student of Hegel, Ludwig Feuerbach, indicated the line modern atheism would take, when he reduced Christianity to anthropology. He claimed that only man could have religion, because only for him it is possible to be conscious of himself and to objectify his own self.[22] According to Feuerbach religion is the "solemn unveiling of man's hidden treasures, the revelation of his intimate thoughts, the open confession of his love-secrets." [23] In other words, predicate and object of theology is man's imagination, and the religious objects, such as eternal life, God's goodness, and the like are projections of his own desires. If man had no desires, despite his fantasy, he would have no religion and no gods. Since the predicates which man confers upon God are anthropomorphisms, Feuerbach concluded that God, as their subject matter, is an anthropomorphism too. He declared: "If love, goodness, personality, etc., are human attributes, so also is the subject which thou presupposest, the existence of God, the belief that there is a God, an anthropomorphism—a presupposition purely human." [24] Since God is an expression of man's desires, man does not have any feelings toward God he would not also have toward man. "The yearning of man after something above himself is nothing else than the longing after the perfect type of his nature." [25] Religion, in short, is the true characteristic of man. It shows the feeling of man's imperfections and the desire to overcome them. But religion does not indicate that man would have cognitions of anything or anyone beyond himself.

Karl Marx continued the program of modern atheism started by Feuerbach. This becomes evident in his *Theses on Feuerbach* (1845), where he claimed: "Feuerbach starts out from the fact of religious self-alienation, the duplication of the world into a religious, imaginary world and a real one. His work consists in the dissolution of the religious world into its secular basis." [26] Once Feuerbach had completed this important task, Marx faulted him for overlooking the fact that the chief thing still remained to be done. The religious projection and contradiction of the actual human situation demands a removal of the factors that make this projection necessary. According to Marx, Feuerbach was still too "pious." He had not recognized that the "religious sentiment" is not a truly anthropological phenomenon which makes man truly human. It is a *social product* and belongs to a particular form of society.[27]

The phrase *"man makes religion, religion does not make man"* [28] takes on an entirely different meaning for Marx than it did for Feuerbach. For Marx religion is the self-consciousness and self-feeling of man who either has not yet found himself or who has already lost himself again. Thus the abolition of religion as the illusory happiness is required in order to gain real happiness. The demand to give up the illusions is the demand to give up a condition which needs illusions. "The criticism of religion is therefore *in embryo the criticism of the vale of woe*, the *halo* of which is religion." [29] Religion is the opiate of the people and is a tool of the capitalists to comfort the suppressed working class with the prospect of a better beyond. Yet Marx demands that the working class should establish its happiness here on earth instead of projecting it into an imaginary beyond. Therefore "criticism of religion ends with the teaching that *man is the highest essence for man*, hence with the *categoric imperative to overthrow all relations* in which man is a debased, enslaved, abandoned, despicable essence." [30] Marx is not satisfied with philosophers like Feuerbach, who have only interpreted the world in various ways. The task is to change the world.[31] Marx went back to men like La Mettrie and Holbach, representatives of the atheistic wing of the French Enlightenment, to assert that religion is not beneficial, but wrong and detrimental to man's own happiness.

Nikolay Lenin, founder of Bolshevik Communism and by far the greatest single driving force behind the Soviet Revolution of October, 1917, attempted to carry out the Marxist legacy of happiness through revolution. According to Lenin fear of the blind forces of the capitalist socio-economic system is at the root of modern religion.[32]

> The impotence of the exploited classes in their struggle against the exploiters just as inevitably gives rise to the belief in a better life after death as the impotence of the savage in his battle with nature gives rise to belief in gods, devils, miracles, and the like. Those who toil and live in want all their lives are taught by religion to be submissive and patient while here on earth, and to take comfort in the hope of a heavenly reward. Those who live by the labor of others are taught by religion to practice charity while on earth, thus offering them a very cheap way of justifying their entire existence as exploiters and selling them at a moderate price tickets to well-being in heaven.[33]

Thus religion is the opiate of the people and "a kind of spiritual booze in which the slaves of capital drown their human image, their demand for a life more or less worthy of man." Small wonder that Lenin was quite confident that religious belief was a "delirium" that was rapidly being thrown "into the rubbish-barrel" by the progressive economic development ushered in through Marxist revolution.[34] Though Lenin projected that religion would automatically wither away once the economic conditions were changed, it was believed to be such a menace for man that Marxists could not just wait for its collapse or simply further its process of decay through anti-religious propaganda. Marxist revolutionaries were urged also to take active steps to change the socio-economic conditions so that the workers could be freed from their belief in a life beyond the grave and could be rallied to a genuine struggle for a better earthly life and for the "creation of a paradise on earth." [35] Though Lenin officially condoned freedom in religious matters,[36] things were different as far as the party was concerned. He felt that ignorance and obscurantism in the form of religious beliefs of party members must actively be combatted. And one of the main reasons for organizing the Marxist party was "to carry on a struggle against every religious bamboozling of the workers." [37] For party members the ideological struggle is not a private affair but the affair of the whole party, of the whole proletariat.

Of course, we might question whether such militant atheism can be justified. We could also point out that both in Russia and in the other Communist countries, two generations of active anti-religious propaganda have not wiped out religious dedication. Yet regardless of those objections the unanswered question still looms ahead of us whether Feuerbach and Marx were right when they labeled religion a projection of the human mind. Natural science of the 19th century at least seems to back up their atheistic claims. While in the 17th century such an eminent scientist as Isaac Newton still found that the most beautiful system of sun, planets, and comets could only proceed from the counsel and dominion of an intelligent and powerful Being, this sentiment was widely lost in the 19th century. When the French mathematician and astronomer Pierre Laplace had finished his monumental five volume work *Mécanique céleste* (1799-1825) he wrapped up the issue in his famous reply to Napoleon's inquiry where in his system there was the proper place for God: "Sir, I do not need this hypothesis." God was no longer necessary within a scientific world-view.[38] The world made sense without any reference to God. Not even the hypothesis of the creator seemed necessary any longer. In 1842 the German physicist J. Robert Mayer formulated the first law of thermodynamics or the law of conservation of energy which says that within an energetically isolated system the amount of energy neither increases nor decreases.[39] This law made it possible to endow the world with the attribute of eternity. Provided that the world is an energetically isolated system it has no beginning and no end. It is eternal. Thus the starting point of a first creation and the God hypothesis of a first creator are obviously obsolete.

Finally Charles Darwin wrote his two epoch-making books *On the Origin of Species* (1859) and *The Descent of Man* (1871). Following the ideas of Darwin, the origin of man could now be explained as being part of the total evolutionary process within our world. There was nothing peculiar to man or to his ideas; they were only products of the evolutionary process out of which they originated. Thus, a completely homogeneous world view in atheistic terms seemed unavoidable. The destiny of religion in general and of the Christian God in particular seemed to be decided. The German zoologist and enthusiastic follower of Darwin, Ernst Haeckel, summed up this sentiment in his book *The Riddle of the Universe* (1899).[40] In an uncompromising monistic attitude he asserted the essential unity of organic and inorganic nature. As the highest animals have evolved from the simplest forms of life, so the highest human faculties have evolved from the "soul" of animals. Such cherished ideas as the immortality of the soul, the freedom of the will, and the existence of a personal God were discarded. Haeckel suggests that those who still want to believe in God, should believe in a gaseous vertebrate—gaseous, because God is adored as "a 'pure spirit' without a body," and a vertebrate because of our anthropomorphic conception of God. In other words, Haeckel tells us that God is an impossibility, a contradiction in itself.

Man in the 19th century felt fairly comfortable in a world without God, especially since Darwin's evolutionary theory made him believe in perpetual progress. Yet for many this feeling has changed considerably in the 20th century. Friedrich Nietzsche already cautioned us, "How shall we, the murderers of all murderers, comfort ourselves?" . . . "Wither are we moving now?" [41] Existentialist philosophy, largely portraying the existential feeling of man confined to himself, has also painted a vividly sobering picture of heroic, self-relying man who claims that he no longer needs the God hypothesis. For instance, Martin Heidegger discovers death as the dominating category. Being is being toward death and man is suspended over nothingness. He is thrown into existence and is admonished not to resort to past experience, but to be open for the unknown future. Jean-Paul Sartre's view of man's predicament is not less sobering. Man has challenged and killed the gods. Therefore he can no longer resort to authorities outside himself to determine his life. He is doomed to freedom. Man lives in an antagonistic world depending solely on himself and on his unwarranted decisions. The conclusion is evident: Everything originates without reason, drags through life by weakness, and dies through chance. This attitude surely has lost the optimism of the 19th century.

It would be shortsighted, however, to interpret the feelings of 20th century man as being solely pessimistic. Especially Marxists remind us that the picture of the world is not to be painted with dark and threatening colors, but in bright and promising tones. The French Marxist Roger Garaudy, for instance, claims that Marxism, which is also 20th century atheism, is essentially *humanist.* "It starts, not from negation, but from affirmation; it affirms the autonomy of man and it involves as a consequence the rejection of every attempt to rob man of his creative and self-creative power." [42] Garaudy then attempts to distinguish a political atheism, prevalent in the 18th century, from the scientific atheism, dominant in the 19th century, and the present humanist atheism. In describing this humanist atheism we are not surprised that Garaudy finds its roots already in Marx who had advocated the radical emancipation of man. Perhaps to attain such a "humanist" goal, one has to work on a political and a scientific level too and cannot relegate them as easily to past centuries as Garaudy suggests. Professorships of scientific atheism in the German Democratic Republic at least seem to indicate that scientific atheism is not yet a thing of the past.

Garaudy shows that unlike existentialism for Marxism the meaning of life and of history is not the creation of the individual man, but the meaning of history is the work of men in the totality of their history. The difference from existentialism becomes especially clear when Garaudy claims that this meaning already exists before us and without us, because the realities of the past must be taken into account for the operation of our present initiatives. Nevertheless for Garaudy this meaning of history "is still an open question, for the future still has to be created even though its creation must start from the conditions inherited from the past." [43]

Ernst Bloch, the German counterpart of Garaudy, betrays a similar realistic optimism about the future. Our journey moves irresistibly ahead toward "that secret symbol" toward which our dark, seeking, difficult earth moves since the beginning of time. [44] In his monumental work, *Das Prinzip Hoffnung (The Principle of Hope)* Bloch is more explicit about "that secret symbol" or the goal of history. That which shines into everybody's childhood and that which nobody has yet entered is now named "home" *(Heimat).* [45] Yet again it is man himself, working, toiling, recreating, and sur-

passing the given, who is at the root of history and who also provides its goal. The future of hope, therefore, once thought to be
a property of God has been taken into our own hands.[46] In describing this goal Bloch talks about "the Utopian Omega of the fulfilled Moment, the Eschaton of our immanence, the illumination
of our incognito." [47] The attainment of such concrete Utopia needs
no God, because it inspires toward its own progress and toward
its own concretization. Since Bloch recognizes the close similarity
between the future-directed Christian faith that concerns itself
with the ultimate liberation and salvation of man and the aspira-
tions of Marxist ideology, he even invites Christians to join in with
Marxists in the realization of this goal. He says: "When Christians
really are concerned with the emancipation of those who labor and
are heavy-laden, and when Marxists retain the depths of the Kingdom of Freedom as the real content of revolutionary consciousness
on the road to the becoming true substance, the alliance between
revolution and Christianity founded in the Peasant Wars may live
again—this time with success." [48]

The prospect of Christians and Marxists living side by side, working for the realization of the same common goal is certainly intriguing. But can we accept this invitation without abandoning
ourselves? Too grave seem to be the differences between this radically secularized version of Christian faith and Christian faith of
Judeo-Christian tradition. For instance, both realize the inhibiting
power of our past. But unlike Marxism, Christian faith trusts and
reckons with the promise of God that those who trust in him will
not be held accountable for this past. Unlike Marxism, Christian
faith also knows that building Babylonian towers to storm the heavens and to demote God does not result in the unity of mankind but
in its disunity. Unity of mankind is only brought about through
a reversal of Genesis 11 at Pentecost. Both Marxism and Christian
faith are deeply concerned about the future in its anticipatory and
its ultimate sense, yet only Christian faith concedes that he who
brought this world into existence will also bring about final destiny.
While scientific atheism has claimed that the world makes perfectly good sense without the "God hypothesis," "humanist" atheism
has extended this claim to say that man and his destiny make perfectly good sense too without the "God hypothesis." However, at
this point of our investigation we do not yet want to settle the question whether atheism might be a true consequence of Judeo-Christian monotheism, and whether there might be an ascending and

consequent development from polytheism to monotheism and finally to atheism.

2. The non-religious solution.

There have also been voices raised within Christendom that did not bewail the increasing secularization of life and the ensuing restrictions for religion. They declared that this process caused by Judeo-Christian faith does not at all affect our Christian faith in God. Christian faith is so radically different from "religion" that it even necessitates the death of "religion."

a. *Barth's fight against religion.*

Unlike any other leading theologian of the 20th century, Karl Barth attempted to free Christian faith from the fatal embrace of modern atheism by pointing to theology's own task. We are theologians, he declared, and as theologians we are summoned to talk about God.[49] But to talk about God is different from talking in a raised voice about man.[50] "The Gospel is not a religious message to inform mankind of their divinity or to tell them how they may become divine. The Gospel proclaims a God utterly distinct from men."[51] Of course, Barth admits that God's revelation is present in a world drenched with religion, but this does not mean that revelation is the confirmation of religion. Religion is unbelief. It is the one great concern of godless man.[52] The divine reality offered and manifested to us in revelation is replaced in religion "by a concept of God arbitrarily and wilfully evolved by man." . . . "It is the attempted replacement of the divine work by a human manufacture." In religion man does the talking instead of God; man takes something for himself instead of accepting a gift. He reaches out and ventures to grasp at God instead of letting God act on man's behalf. Because religion is a reaching out and a grasping at God, it is opposed to revelation and "the concentrated expression of human unbelief."[53] While revelation is God's self-offering and self-manifestation through which God wants to reconcile man to himself, man tries through religion to come to terms with his own life, to justify and sanctify himself.[54] But God does not condone this self-redemptive attitude of man.

According to Barth the real crisis of religion is revelation, since there the whole religious process is reversed. God comes down to man and man no longer ventures to come to terms with God on his own. Since Christian faith has at its foundation God's self-disclosure, Christian religion is the true "religion." [55] Revelation is a strictly Christian phenomenon, because "the Christian religion is the predicate to the subject of the name of Jesus Christ" and through the name Jesus Christ it becomes the true "religion." [56] The adjective "Christian" thereby can never express "a grasping at some possession of our own. It can only be a reaching out for the divine possession included in this name." [57] In other words, the name of Jesus Christ is the one thing that "is really decisive for the distinction of truth and error" among religions.[58] The name of Jesus Christ does not stand for our own accomplishment, as do the divine projections in the world religions, but it stands for God's own doing. "Christ is not the king chosen by us; on the contrary, we are the people chosen by him." [59] This relationship between the name "Jesus Christ" and the Christian "religion" is not to be reversed. With this understanding of Christian faith, Barth can easily disregard Feuerbach's observation that, like any other religion, Christianity is a projection of the human mind. For Barth such an accusation is absolutely inadequate, since Christianity is the direct opposite of a projection. However, he concedes that, if limited to the religious sphere, Feuerbach was not wrong. Religion is a kind of projection. Barth observes an imminent questionableness of religion, since religion is never more than a reflection of what man himself is and has.[60] While atheism points to the futility of these projections, it cannot rid itself from its own inherent religious attitude. Atheism becomes a new religion, in which man is again convinced that he can master his own existence. A similar pattern is followed by mysticism, since, in a less revolutionary way, there the being of God is assumed to be dependent on man's own existence.

We cannot but agree with Karl Barth that atheism often bears religious overtones and employs salvational terminology similar to most religions.—Ernst Bloch's *Das Prinzip Hoffnung (The Principle of Hope)* may serve to illustrate the point. The neo-Marxist Ernst Bloch strips Judeo-Christian faith of its metaphysical implications and announces in typical messianic fashion the bringing to completion of the unfinished world (including mankind) as the goal of history.[61]—Barth also realizes the basic difference between man's own endeavors demonstrated in his religious behavior and God's salvific action announced in his self-disclosure. However, Barth fails to answer the question why Christian faith is more and more pushed into the role of a minority "religion" in a world once dominated by Christian thought.

b. *Bonhoeffer's non-religious interpretation and the death of God.*

At this point Bonhoeffer's program of a non-religious interpretation of the gospel becomes of prime importance. Dietrich Bonhoeffer advanced the idea of a non-religious interpretation of the gospel only in his *Letters and Papers from Prison.* Before that he largely shared Barth's understanding of religion.[62] Even in his *Letters* he could still use the term "religion" indiscriminately as denoting "Christian faith" [63] and he could say that " 'Christianity' has always been a form—perhaps the true form—of 'religion'." At the same time he also warned us of the consequences if it were discovered that the religious a priori on which Christian preaching and theology have rested for nineteen hundred years does not exist at all, that it was "a historically conditioned and transient form of human self-expression." [64] With this last remark Bonhoeffer understands religion in a much narrower sense than Barth, namely as the garment of Christianity and as a point of contact for the Christian proclamation.

The God of religion is the God who comes to help when human knowledge ends or when human resources fail. But according to Bonhoeffer it is pointless to relegate God to a realm beyond our cognitive faculties. The transcendence of God must rather be affirmed in such a way that "God is beyond in the midst of our life." [65] Similarly, it is futile to resort in our effort to rescue God to the so-called ultimate questions of death and guilt, claiming that only God can answer them.[66] Bonhoeffer affirms that the world has come of age and some day these questions can be answered without God. Even Barth's positivism of revelation, as Bonhoeffer calls Barth's "naive" affirmation of the word of God, can be of no help at this point. We must get used to the fact that we have to live in the world *etsi deus non daretur* (as if God were not), and in recognizing this, we must live before God.

> So our coming of age leads us to a true recognition of our situation before God. God would have us know that we must live as men who manage our lives without him. The God who is with us is the God who forsakes us (Mark 15:34). The God who lets us live in the world without the working hypothesis of God is the God before whom we stand continually. Before God and with God we live without God.[67]

It is God himself who lets himself be pushed out of the world. The Bible directs man to God's powerlessness in suffering because only the suffering God, the God who came to man in the humility of Jesus of Nazareth, can help us. Thus the starting point for a secular interpretation of the Gospel, Bonhoeffer surmised, will probably be the weakness of God. Here we touch on the center of Bonhoeffer's non-religious interpretation, the humanity of Christ, a point which he was already beginning to emphasize in his lectures on Christology when he stated, for instance, that even as the risen one, Christ "does not break through his incognito." [68]

In his *Letters* Bonhoeffer completely discarded the religious premise of Christianity. The Christian faith rests solely on God's self-disclosure in Jesus of Nazareth. This christocentric non-religious interpretation of the gospel with its emphasis on the humility of Christ proved attractive for both laymen and theologians. John A. T. Robinson, the former Bishop of Woolwich, brought Bonhoeffer's basic ideas to the attention of the wider public in his best seller *Honest to God*. Brought up in the English tradition, it is not surprising that Robinson first of all attacks the supernatural or theistic notion of God, in which God is seen as the supreme being whose existence can be proved. Robinson wants to escape from the theistic argument since it always includes the possibility that God might not be "out there." Thus he rejects this concept and simply posits God as ultimate reality. [69] He believes that the affirmation of God as ultimate reality is beyond a rational argument; it is an article of faith. Robinson also attempts to remove another obstacle to faith when, following Bultmann, he claims that New Testament mythology contains nothing which is of peculiarly Christian nature. As does mythology in general, New Testament mythology just represents the cosmology of a pre-scientific age. [70] Finally Robinson comes to the question whether Christian faith is religious. Similar to Bonhoeffer he asserts that the need has ceased for a God of the gaps of human knowledge or competence. [71] However, since God is ultimate reality, man's coming of age is no hindrance for our faith in God. Robinson no longer affirms God as transcendent, but as the ultimate depth of our being, as the creative ground and the reason of our whole existence. [72] Yet he still asserts that God is personal. It is in personal relationships that we find the ultimate reason of our existence better than anywhere else. Therefore, God is a personal God, a God who is ultimately love.

With these last remarks Robinson goes a decisive step further than Bonhoeffer. He no longer regards God as being apart from the world, but in taking seriously Bonhoeffer's claim that God is in the midst of us beyond, he "locates" God within our world. This endeavor does not just strive to bridge the disastrous dichotomy between God and the world; it also opens the possibility of turning God into a "worldly" phenomenon.

William Hamilton has come close to realizing this latter possibility. He also tries to come close to Bonhoeffer in stating that the traditional sovereign and omnipotent God is a difficult God to perceive or to meet. "In place of this God, the impotent God, suffering with men, seems to be emerging." [73] This impotence is substantiated in both non-Christians and Christians by a growing sentiment that God has withdrawn, that he is absent and even somehow dead. Hamilton indicates that he is unwilling to accept the traditional strictly dialectic scheme of finding God in his withdrawal and weakness. Reality and theological phraseology have become incongruous for him. "Our experience of God is deeply dissatisfying to us, even when we are believers," he claims.[74] The situation is bewildering for us, because on the one hand God seems to have withdrawn from the world and its sufferings, making him either cruel or irrelevant. On the other hand we experience him as a pressure and a wounding from which we would love to be free. If we resort to Jesus the Lord, our feelings are not much different. Still "the God of the time of the death of God and the coming in Jesus the Lord are somehow both with us." [75] Part of the problem is caused by the fact that the portion of the Christian gospel that speaks of ascension, exaltation, and the kingly office are without precise meaning today.[76] Hamilton is not ready to discard these assertions, but he finds himself unable to translate them into today's language.

Hamilton emphasizes so much the humanity of Jesus, and this means the humility of Jesus the Lord, that it becomes impossible to perceive that this finite being can be of infinite quality.[77] He realizes that this dilemma puts the Christian into a peculiar situation. He has not given up his hope for God, but he cannot verify him in his experience either. Thus he is "a man without God but with hope." Hamilton concludes: We know too little to know God now; "we only know enough to be able to say that he will come, in his own time, to the broken and contrite heart, if we continue to offer that to him." [78] Yet this hope is not one of assurance, because it may be that the theologian of today and tomorrow is a man

without faith, without hope, with only the present and therefore
only love to guide him.[79] With this remark Hamilton reminds us
of Robinson's assertion that love is at the center of our knowing
God. But what a difference between Robinson and Hamilton.[80]
Hamilton is unable to see that this love is at the center of a personal God. Love becomes a human phenomenon and thus the absence of God can evolve as Hamilton's dominant theological topic.

Paul M. van Buren in his book *The Secular Meaning of the
Gospel* arrives at similar conclusions. Again he starts with Bonhoeffer's notion of a world come of age. According to van Buren,
Bonhoeffer posed the question: "How can the Christian who is himself a secular man understand his faith is a secular way?" [81] Employing linguistic analysis van Buren first wrestles with the meaning of God. His frankly empirical method reflects the thinking
of an industrialized, scientific age and shows the difficulty of finding any meaningful way to speak of God.[82] He asserts that the objective use of the word God is wrong, because it dies the death of
a thousand qualifications. Still less valid is the non-objective use
of the word "God," for instance in talking about man when he
talks about God. It "allows of no verification and is therefore meaningless." [83] Yet van Buren maintains that the language of faith
still has meaning and that this meaning can be explained and
clarified by linguistic analysis.[84] The language of faith directs us
to the sort of situation "in which a discernment fundamental to
our whole conception of life and a response to commitment may
take place." [85] For instance, in the language of Christology there
are two languages intermixed. The one is that of straightforward
empirical observation (e.g. empty tomb), while the other is what
van Buren calls the language of a "blik," or what we might call
the "aha–" effect (e.g. he is risen).[86] Following Barth and Bonhoeffer, van Buren sees no possibility of reintroducing at this point
the cognitive approach to religious language, since it would single
out a certain area of experience as "religious." [87] There is no natural
approach to God possible.

Though Christianity must be taken seriously as a way of life,
the word "God" is no longer accessible to us. The meaning of the
gospel can only be elucidated from a consideration of the history
of Jesus of Nazareth and the things which the first believers said
about him.[88] It will then become clear that the Christian gospel
points "to the history of Jesus and of Easter" and that it invites us
"to see the world in the light of that history.[89] Van Buren is aware

that the question might be asked at this point, whether his approach does not ultimately reduce theology to ethics. Yet he appears to be content with his results and retorts: "In a secular age, what would that 'more' be? It is our inability to find any empirical linguistic anchorage for that 'more' that has led to our interpretation." [90] Regardless of his own satisfaction, we wonder whether his largely phenomenological approach to theology is not bound to reduce theology to observation of human (ethical) phenomena, although it attempts to maintain a decidedly christocentric basis.

Thomas J. J. Altizer noticed this reduction of Christian faith to phenomenological assertions and suggested a solution. Following William Hamilton, he proposes a consistent kenotic Christology. [91] Yet he rejects Barth's sentiment that a fully kenotic Christ is the result of God's omnipotence, through which God assumes the form of weakness to triumph in it. [92] For Altizer the descent of God into human flesh is final and irrevocable. Thus he speaks of the death of God as an event in history.

> We must realize that the death of God is an historical event, that God has died in our cosmos, in our history, in our *Existenz*. While there is no immediate necessity in assuming that the God who has died is the God of 'faith,' there is also no escaping the inevitable consequence that the dead God is not the God of idolatry, or false piety, or 'religion,' but rather the God of the historic Christian Church, and beyond the Church, of Christendom at large. [93]

Altizer cautions that this observation does not refer to

> an eclipse of God or a withdrawal of God from either history or the creation. Rather, an authentic language speaking about the death of God must inevitably be speaking about the death of God himself. The radical Christian proclaims that God has actually died in Christ, that this death is both an historical and a cosmic event, and, as such, it is a final and irrevocable event, which cannot be reversed by a subsequent religious or cosmic movement. [94]

While every man today who is open to experience knows that God is absent, only the Christian knows the reason for God's absence. He knows that God is dead and that this death is a final and irrevocable event. Yet we need not end in despair, since the death of God has actualized a new and liberating humanity in our history. [95]

God has actually died in Christ's own death.

> The death of God in Christ is an inevitable consequence of
> the movement of God into the world, of Spirit into flesh, and
> the actualization of the death of God in the totality of experi-
> ence is a decisive sign of the continuing and forward movement
> of the divine process, as it continues to negate its particular and
> given expressions, by moving ever more fully into the depths
> of the profane.[96]

Altizer claims to follow Barth who had already pointed out that
the "Christian idea of God is obviously a product of a fusion of
the Bible with Greek ontology, and in a large measure the distinc-
tiveness of the 'Christian God' derives from its Greek roots."[97] To
recover the original meaning of the Christian gospel, Altizer resorts
to William Blake's romantic mysticism. Blake was "the first Christian atheist, the first visionary who chose the kenotic or self-empty-
ing path of immersing himself in the profane reality of experience
as the way to God who is all in all in Jesus."[98] "The forward movement of the Incarnate Word is from God to Jesus, and the Word
continues its kenotic movement and direction by moving from the
historical Jesus to the universal body of humanity, thereby undergoing an epiphany in every human hand and face."[99] Yet this
pantheistic understanding of the salvation process leads Altizer
beyond the Christian realm, and we are not surprised to notice
that he finds close affinity between oriental mysticism and Christian
eschatology. He claims that both oriental mysticism in its yearning
for a return to the primordial unfallen oneness, and Christian eschatology in radical orientation towards the approaching end, are
found as essentially world-denying.[100] Only in negating the reality
of this world as an autonomous reality can we expect the epiphany
of the religious reality or the rediscovery of the sacred.[101]

What does Altizer's approach to the God question indicate? It
shows us that an exclusively christocentric approach paired with a
strong sentiment for dialectic expression involves certain dangers
for the attempt to speak meaningfully about God. As seen in
Altizer, the humanity of Christ is emphasized so much that Jesus
Christ becomes Jesus the man, and finally just the man. Consequently the Christian gospel loses its anchor in the life and destiny
of Jesus the Christ and assimilates itself with other expressions of
man's religious heritage. Thus the non-religious interpretation of
Christian faith tends to become a non-Christian interpretation of

Christian faith. As a student of the historians of religion, Joachim Walch and Mircea Eliade, it is nothing uncommon for Altizer to discover the category of the sacred in Christian faith. Yet it makes us wonder why he did so in executing, as he thought, the task that Bonhoeffer once had posed with his non-religious interpretation. Should this perhaps indicate that there is an essential non-transient element of religion even in Christian faith? But even this concession of a basic religiousness, common to all faiths, still does not solve the perplexing phenomenon of an ever increasing secularization.[102]

c. *The riddle of secularization.*

In arriving at the quest for God from an exclusively Christocentric approach one may interpret the immense impact of secularization in a relatively optimistic manner. Friedrich Gogarten, for instance, a lifelong friend of Rudolf Bultmann and one time professor of systematic theology, betrays a very appreciative attitude toward secularization. He claims that though in Greek culture man was thought to be secular or free towards the world, there was still a religious feeling towards the world. Even a man such as Plato could not renounce this basic religious feeling. Through Christian faith, however, the freedom of human reason over against the world was developed in an unprecedented way. The uninhibited development of modern science and technology stems from a fundamental freedom toward the world imbedded in a reasonable attitude and made possible through Christian faith.[103] Gogarten sees this freedom from the world reflected in Paul's statement that to the Christian "all things are lawful" (1 Cor. 10:23). Man is free from the world and from its inherent powers and is able to exert dominion over it.[104]

But how can Christian faith arrive at such freedom? The reason for this freedom, Gogarten asserts, is a new self-understanding of man. According to the Christian faith man is a son of God and therefore freed from the bondage to the world and even exalted as lord over the world.[105] A son does not have the ground for his being son in himself, but in his relationship to his father. Consequently man can only properly exert his dominion as lord over the world if he maintains this relationship and preserves it in the world which is of his father. Since the world gains its unity and cohesion from being created by God, man should preserve the creational aspect of the world. In so doing he will also preserve its unity and its wholeness. In his relationship to the world, man does not just enjoy freedom from the world but freedom for the world, which means responsibility to God. By exercising his responsibility for the world man acts responsively to God.

Gogarten expresses this twofold relationship in which man finds himself with the picture of son and heir. Man receives the world as a heritage from God, and the way he manages his heritage shows the understanding of his sonship.[106] The twofold freedom of son and heir is safeguarded by faith. This means that man comes to understand that the law is no longer binding for him. Once man could think that a work righteous attitude toward God was sufficient to fulfill the requirements of his sonship, and that obedience to certain rules would mean compliance with being heir of the world. But through the gospel this demanding and accusing character of the law has been changed into responsible freedom. "Modern man is no longer responsible to the world and its power as the classical man and, in a modified way, even the medieval man was. Instead, he has become the one who is responsible *for* this world." [107] The law as a sum of demands, valid once and for all, has been reduced to the responsibility of man for his world and for its being and remaining a world. This is a responsibility that has continually to be perceived and achieved anew.

Gogarten recognizes that the filial freedom which asks man to assume independent, rational responsibility through his works bears a great temptation in itself. To safeguard himself against merely advocating a new form of secularism, Gogarten now introduces the term subjectivism and the distinction between secularity and secularism. He suggests that modern subjectivism is not a matter of clearheaded, methodological, scientific research, but rather a world view which claims to be valid for everything there is.[108] While in Christian faith man is understood as a created being, in modern subjectivism man elevates himself to the source of meaning for all existence. Man has forgotten his twofold responsibility and has become the measure of all things. Secularism signifies a similar radical autonomy of man and it appears either in the form of ideologies or as nihilism.[109] Since both man and the world receive their true meaning from being related to God, their wholeness was lost, when man separated them from God. In his secularistic autonomous drive man could then opt for one of two possibilities. He could either base the concept of wholeness on his own ideas and arrive at an ideology which would soon be countered by other ideologies, or he could renounce the quest for wholeness as meaningless. In this latter case he confined himself to the visible and manipulable world and arrived at a nihilistic world view which is closed for any ultimate questions. Gogarten claims that subjectivism and secularism originated because of a wrong understanding of faith.[110] As can be seen in the warfare between theology and science, faith was not understood as a liberating but as a restricting force. Thus modern subjectivism in an attempt to rid man from these restrictive tendencies asserted man's absolute autonomy.

Together with Gogarten we must ask ourselves what man has gained through this liberation. He has become the measure and basis of all being, and therefore whatever he encounters in the world is in the last analysis a picture of himself. Gogarten is right when he concludes that "perhaps man has never been so lonely in his world, so dependent upon himself." [111] Yet Gogarten seems to fall short of advancing a convincing alternative to modern self-assertion. He accepts man as an autonomous being, while telling him at the same time that in all his autonomy, man is not lonely and forlorn, but son and heir.

Harvey Cox in his *Secular City* provides a similar positive evaluation of secularization. In following Gogarten, he asserts that "secularization should not be viewed as an example of massive and catastrophic cultural backsliding but as a product of the impact of the biblical faith itself on world civilization." [112] He also equates secularization with Bonhoeffer's concept of coming of age and shows that it gains its true impact in the urban setting. According to Cox, "secularization designates the content of man's coming of age," while "urbanization describes the content in which it is occurring." Urbanization is understood here as a "structure of common life in which diversity and the disintegration of tradition are paramount." The urban center is the place of human control, of rational planning, of bureaucratic organization, and the technological metropolis provides the indispensable social setting "for a world of 'no religion at all,' for what we have called a secular style." [113] Secularization occurs through an almost certain irreversible historical process through which society and culture are delivered from the bondage to religious control and closed metaphysical world views. Similar to Gogarten, Harvey Cox is also convinced that this liberating movement can easily change into secularism. For Cox secularism is an ideology, "a new closed world-view which functions very much like a new religion." [114]

He largely attributes the spirit of secularization to Judeo-Christian faith since there occurred a disenchantment of nature, a desacralization of politics, and a deconsecration of values. He can even call the Genesis account of creation "a form of 'atheistic propaganda.' It is designed to teach the Hebrews that the magical vision, by which nature is seen as a semidivine force, has no basis in fact. Yahweh, the Creator, whose being is centered outside the natural process, who calls it into existence and names its parts, allows man to perceive nature itself in a matter-of-fact way." [115] This has led mature secular man to tend nature and to make use of it, to assume the responsibility assigned to the man, Adam. Harvey Cox also sees the experience of the Exodus as functioning in a similar way as a liberating event. The Exodus

> became the central event around which the Hebrews organized their whole perception of reality. As such, it symbolized the deliverance of man out of a sacral-political order and into history and social change, out of religiously legitimated monarchs and into a world where political leadership would be based on power gained by the capacity to accomplish specific social objectives.[116]

Though Israel was often tempted to return to the practice of sacral politics as they had experienced in Egypt, no royal house in Israel was ever unquestionably secure on its throne. Finally, Harvey Cox understands the commandments given at Mt. Sinai, especially the commandment against idolatry, as pointing to Yahweh's essence and at the same time providing a world view without idols.

> Any deity which could be expressed in the form of an idol was *ipso facto* not Yahweh. The gods were thereby demoted. The Bible does not deny the reality of the gods and their values; it merely relativizes them. It accepts them as human projections, as 'the work of man's hand,' and in this sense is very close to the modern social sciences. It was because they believed in Yahweh that, for the Jews, all human values and their representations were relativized.[117]

Harvey Cox can even conclude that when "one recalls the ancient rabbinic saying that the next best thing to belief in Yahweh is at least not to believe in idols, then atheism might in fact be much closer to the biblical faith than the vague cultural theism of nominal Christians in the West." [118]

It is not surprising to find that Harvey Cox betrays great sympathy for Marxism and other secular revolutionary movements. While rooted in biblical faith they, unlike the church, have not made alliances with the establishment but have carried on the legitimate biblical heritage of social revolution.[119] Remembering the Israelite history, in which Yahweh had pledged allegiance to a nomadic and essentially homeless people, Cox finds no reason for deploring the increasing mobility of modern metropolitan man. Though mobility has its pitfalls, Cox asserts that our modern metropolitan nomads are open to change, movement, and newness, and thus their high mobility is no obstacle to their faith.[120] Asking him how man can encounter God in the secular society, Harvey Cox goes along with Bonhoeffer stating that the hiddenness of the biblical God is at the very center of the doctrine of God. Similar to Gogarten, he also claims that God wants man to assume responsibility over the world.[121] Thus we are summoned to accountability before God for all our actions. God meets us in our everyday work, in the events of social change in a client, a customer, a patient, or a co-worker and he also supplies us with a framework of limitations within which alone freedom takes on actual meaning.

The decisive question that must be addressed to both Gogarten and Cox is whether their interpretation of secularization is justified and whether the conclusions they have reached are correct. It is true that the big challenge to Christian faith could not have originated without the catalytic results of Judeo-Christian faith. But it is far less convincing to assume that modern secular spirit stands in direct continuity with Judeo-Christian faith. Ernst Troeltsch was closer to the truth when he pointed out that the active and creative forces of modern thinking result from extra and even anti-Reformation movements.[122] Elements of classical antiquity, amalgamated with Christianity, divorced themselves from Christianity in the period of the Renaissance. They surfaced in Anabaptist movements, Protestant sectarianism, and mystic and spiritualistic movements and finally resulted in the rational approach to the world as seen in the period of Enlightenment. It is not by accident that the *Schwärmer* and the Anabaptists of the Reformation have stronger ties to humanistic groups than to the leaders of the Reformation movement. When Luther, for instance, distinguished between the spiritual and the worldly kingdom, it is questionable whether one can describe his position as foreshadowing modern secularity. It seems more appropriate to interpret his doctrine as an attempt to bring the worldly and the secular together once again through the over-arching power of God who is at work in both kingdoms.[123] In other words, his doctrine of the two kingdoms is not a sign of the dawning secular spirit, but the reply to a dawning new spirit which manifested itself in Renaissance humanism and which wanted to rid man from ecclesiastical theonomy.

Gogarten and Harvey Cox in their attempt to bridge the chasm between the spiritual (God) and the secular (the world) stand more in the line of Luther than of Renaissance humanism. Though especially Cox seems to have abandoned the thought of a spiritual kingdom, he vehemently asserts the integrative power of God. But in claiming modern secular mood, at least in its more moderate forms, on their side, both do what Luther never dared to do— they baptize humanistic paganism. The appropriate reaction, however, should be that of Luther, when he rejected Zwingli's rationalistic interpretation of the Lord's Supper in saying: You have a different spirit. Though we cannot get rid of modern secularity, which is unintentionally furthered by Judeo-Christian monotheistic theocentrism, we should not claim it as our ally. Our everyday world is largely shaped by technology or applied science. This situation is conducive to a style of life and thought indifferent to God. Such "practical" atheism or secularity is today the commonly accepted starting point of all rational reflections. To abandon secularity would mean to renounce all technology and all rational investigation of nature. Some Protestant sects, such as the Amish, and some orthodox Jewish groups follow this path in a usually half-hearted fashion by abstaining to some extent from modern technology. Though we certainly do not want to follow these groups, we must admit that at least unintentionally they have recognized the dangers of such methodological atheism: very often it leads to an atheism in principle or to secularism. Christian faith must be asserted in constant reference to both secularity and secularism. Yet we dare not establish a treaty with either of them without denying the otherness or peculiarity of the ground of our Christian faith. But how is such an assertion of Christian faith still possible?

2.

Can God's Existence
Be Demonstrated?

The most obvious way to assert the validity of Judeo-Christian faith would be to prove the existence of the God who enabled the development of this faith. The idea that such proof could be possible has attracted many of the best minds of Western Christianity. The Apologists of early Christianity argued from the universal presence of the *logos spermatikos* or seminal *logos,* that all people have a notion of God.[1] From thereon most prominent theologians have spent considerable efforts to demonstrate through the power of human reason that God does exist.

1. God and the power of human reason.

Though the way to obtain a "proof" of God's existence has varied through the centuries, five proofs seem to have gained prime importance in the attempt to verify intellectually the ground of faith.

a. *The ontological argument.*

Anselm of Canterbury, the great theorist of early scholasticism, proposed the ontological argument in a manner still fascinating today. He writes his *Proslogium* or *Address* from the point of view of one who is "seeking to understand what he believes."[2] Anselm did not start with a blank, gradually working himself up to the notion of God, but he believed in order to understand. In other words, the notion of God is already presupposed. The question that fascinated Anselm is not that of the existence of God, but who the one is, whom we call God? Anselm arrived at an answer by asserting that God is "something-than-which-nothing-greater-can-be-thought." [3] Proceeding from this definition he claimed that such a being cannot exist in understanding alone. It must also exist in reality or otherwise it would not be the most perfect being. This is the point where most of the criticism set in against Anselm.[4] Anselm seemed to consider existence (in reality) as a property of God in analogy to his other properties and thus belonging by definition to the idea of the most perfect being. In his *On Behalf of the Fool* Anselm's contemporary Gaunilo of Marmoutier had already objected that such a procedure is illegitimate. He attempted to show this with the example of the idea of the most perfect island that is supposed to exist somewhere, though nobody has ever encountered it. Gaunilo argues that according to Anselm's logic, this island must exist both in understanding and in reality, since it is claimed to be the most excellent island.[5]

In his *Critique of Pure Reason* Kant objected in a similar way stating that the logical and the real predicate are being confused in the ontological argument. Unlike omnipotence or omniscience, *being* is not a real predicate, and the transition from existence in thought to existence in reality cannot be accomplished by simply adding another predicate to God, that of being, to make him perfect. Kant illustrated this with the example of a hundred thalers. "A hundred real thalers do not contain the least coin more than a hundred possible thalers," but "my financial position is, however, affected very differently by a hundred real thalers than it is by the mere concept of them (that is, of their possibility)." [6] The actual existence of the thalers is thus not contained in their thought, but has to be added to their thought. However, both Gaunilo and Kant did not seem to listen to the rest of Anselm's argument.[7]

Anselm was well aware that God's existence in reality is different from the existence in reality of excellent islands or of a hundred thalers. God's existence is not of a possible but of a necessary kind. Anselm argued that there are things which can be conceived of as either existing or not existing. But these things cannot be God. If God would be conceived of as not existing, existing things would be of higher quality than God and he would not be that, than which nothing greater can be thought. Anselm therefore affirmed: "You exist so truly, Lord my God, that You cannot even be thought not to exist. And this is as it should be, for if some intelligence could think of something better than You, the creature would be above its creator—and that is completely absurd." [8] Again Anselm did not consider his line of argument as an actual proof of God's existence, because he leaves open the possibility that one can deny God's existence in reality. He realized that men differ considerably in their understandings of God and thus the notion of God can be understood inadequately. For a person with an inadequate understanding of God it does not naturally follow that God exists also in reality. But he who thoroughly understands that God is that than which nothing greater can be conceived, "understands clearly that this same being so exists that not even in thought can it not exist." Since he felt that he was one of those, he concluded his investigation saying: "I give thanks, good Lord, I give thanks to you; since what I believed before through Your free gift I now so understand through Your illumination." [9] It becomes evident that Anselm's argument is not a proof in the traditional sense of the word, since it presupposes already a stand of faith concerning God's very existence and nature. [10]

Karl Barth has eloquently stated that it "goes without saying that for him [Anselm] the Existence of God is given as an article of faith." [11] And he summed up the matter well by saying that according to Anselm "God gave himself as the object of his knowledge and God illumined him that he might know him as object. Apart from this event there is no proof of the existence, that is of the reality of God." [12] The question, however, must be asked whether the presupposition of the Christian God that Anselm assumed is actually necessary for the ontological argument. In other words, need one be a Christian in order to understand who it is whom we call God? [13]

The French philosopher René Descartes seems to have omitted the Christian presupposition of the ontological argument and proceeds on strictly philosophical grounds. In his *Meditations on First Philosophy* (1662) he outlines two ways of arriving at God. In the third *Meditation* he first wonders why man has the idea of God. He is sure that this idea cannot proceed from man himself. The name God implies a substance that is infinite, immutable, independent, all-knowing, all-powerful, and by which I myself and everything else have been created. Descartes assumes that "all those attributes are so great and so eminent, that the more attentively I consider them the less does it seem possible that they can have proceeded from myself alone; and thus," . . . "we have no option save to con-

clude that God exists." Of course, Descartes remembers that he defined God as infinite substance. Since he considers man a finite
substance, man could have apprehended the idea of the infinite
substance by negating the finite. But Descartes disclaims that one
could arrive at an adequate understanding of an infinite substance
through such negative causal inference. Descartes suggests that
"there is manifestly more reality in the infinite substance than in
the finite substance, and my awareness of the infinite must therefore be in some way prior to my awareness of the finite, that is to
say, my awareness of God must be prior to that of myself." [14] It
is only through God's perfect and infinite nature that I realize my
imperfection and my finitude. Thus the idea of God is the most
completely true, the most completely clear and distinct of all ideas
that are in me. Or to put it in Tillich's terminology: God as the
ultimate reality exists by necessity and because of its ultimate reality it imparts to us our reality and our existence.

In his fifth *Meditation* Descartes follows even more closely Anselm's argument, yet without reference to him. He argues that
though one cannot think of a mountain without a valley it does not
follow that valleys and mountains must be in existence. Our thinking only indicates that mountain and valley, whether existent or
non-existent, are inseparably conjoined with each other. However,
Descartes asserts, in thinking of God as sovereignly perfect, we
"cannot think Him save as existing; and it therefore follows that
existence is inseparable from Him, and that He therefore really
exists." Of course, Descartes knows that God's necessary existence
might be brought about by my thinking it as necessary. But the
surprising thing is, we hear Descartes say, that we cannot think of
God as lacking existence, i.e. to think of this sovereignly perfect
being as devoid of complete perfection. Descartes admits that one
cannot think a triangle either except to think that the sum of its
three angles are not greater than two right angles and that its
greatest side subtends its greatest angle. But these necessary assertions of its essence leave it open whether a triangle exists at all. This,
however, is different with God. Though we think of him and his
essence as clearly and distinctly as of the said triangle, Descartes
asserts that he "cannot think of anything, save God alone, to the
very essence of which existence pertains." [15] Thus there is nothing
more evident than that there is a God, that is to say, a sovereign
being, and that of all beings he alone has existence as appertaining
to his essence. Descartes does not suggest that at all times we must

conceive of the idea of God. Yet each time we allow it to occupy the mind, we find ourselves necessarily constrained to ascribe to him all perfections, including that of existence.[16] This conclusion is the weak point in Descartes' argument.

In recent times fewer and fewer people seem to feel compelled to think the idea of God, because for more and more people the world makes good sense without reference to God. Yet Descartes was not yet aware of this rapidly growing sentiment. This is substantiated by his own concluding remarks after having "proved" the existence of God. Descartes reasoned:

> The certainty and truth of all knowledge depends on knowledge of the true God, and that before I knew Him I could have no perfect knowledge of any other thing. And now that I know Him, I have the means of acquiring a perfect knowledge of innumerable things, not only in respect of God Himself and other intelligible things, but also in respect of that corporeal nature which is the object of pure mathematics.[17]

For Descartes God still served as the guarantor of our and the world's reality. Yet at least since Isaac Newton scientists became more and more used to explaining nature's phenomena without reference to God. Newton himself was the first to establish a self-consistent and self-sufficient celestial physics, free from an all-embracing God-relatedness, and free from an all-embracing man-relatedness, yet without sliding into the paths of atheistic materialism. For Newton the laws of nature no longer have man or God as their starting point. They describe relations between specific natural phenomena that have been generalized as mathematical concepts and are applied to explain other natural phenomena.[18] Does it follow from this autonomy of science that not only Descartes' ontological argument, but also the traditional cosmological argument, which we will discuss next, are no longer valid?

b. *The cosmological argument.*

The cosmological argument starts with the observation that there seems to be no cause without a reason. But to assume from the possibility of an infinite regress that there is always a cause prior to an affect seems to be unsatisfying. Thus many philosophers and theologians postulate a first uncaused cause by concluding from the existence of the world to the cause of its existence.

While Plato in his *Laws* argued that the first source of change and movement has set itself into motion and in turn sets into motion a second thing, and this second thing still a third and so on,[19] Aristotle changed the idea of such a self-originated motion. Considering the problem of how motion came into being, Aristotle rejected Plato's idea of a world soul that moves itself and then in turn moves other objects. He regarded such a world soul as secondary, since it would claim the actuality of motion as secondary to potency. Thus that which is moved and also moves other things cannot be primary but must be intermediate. Only that which moves without being moved can be the true prime cause or the unmoved first mover.[20] Such first cause will be something eternal, since it is actuality and not a potentiality which at some point has not yet been actualized, and it is substance, because "everything that changes is something and is changed by something and into something."[21] To avoid the conclusion that there might be a re-action from the moved unto this first mover, Aristotle assumed that there is no physical contact between both. The first kind of spatial motion which the first mover produces is engendered by the heavens which are to be moved by the objects of thought and desire. Since the heavens and the world of nature depend on such first principle of motion, the first mover exists by necessity and its mode of being is good as far as it exists by this necessity.

Thomas Aquinas not only wrote an extensive commentary on Aristotle's *Metaphysics (Commentary on the Metaphysics of Aristotle)*, but in his *Summa Theologiae* (1266-73) he adopted Aristotle's cosmological argument with some significant modifications. Four of his five ways to prove the existence of God are devoted to the cosmological argument.[22] The first and most obvious way according to Thomas is based on change. We observe that some things in the world are in process of change. Anything that is in process of change is being changed by something else. If it could change itself, it would already contain actually and potentially that within it toward which it moves. Since it is still moving toward something, it can only potentially contain the goal toward which it moves, and the actuality must be caused by something outside. In other words, in order to change something, the cause of change always comes from outside of the object to be changed. Though we can push back the chain reaction of cause and effect further and further, we must stop somewhere, otherwise there would be "no first cause of change, and, as a result, no subsequent causes. If we exclude the possibility of a first cause of change, which is not changed by anything else, then there would be no intermediate causes, which are caused by something prior to them and, in turn, cause something subsequent to them. Thomas now postulates such a first cause and identifies it with God.

The second way in Thomas' argument concerning the existence of God goes very much like the first one and is based on the nature of causation. Thomas claims: "In the observable world causes are found to be ordered in series; we never observe, nor ever could, something causing itself, for this would mean it preceded itself, and this is not possible." Thomas assumes that such a series of causes and effects must stop somewhere where it reaches a first cause, for if there were no first efficient cause, there could be no intermediate causes and thus no causation at all. Again Thomas equates this first cause with God.

The third way in Thomas' argument is somewhat different and is based on the distinction between what must be by necessity and what need not necessarily be. Thomas observes that in our experience things can be or cannot be; there is no necessity about their existence. Yet if everything were like this—that it springs up and then dies away—then once upon a time there was nothing. "But if that were true there would be nothing even now, because something that does not exist can only be brought into being by something already existing." From the fact that there are things now Thomas concludes that not everything is of the quality that it could be or could not be. In other words, "there has got to be something that must be." [23] This necessary thing cannot owe the necessity of its existence to something else, but owes it to itself and thus in turn causes other things to be. Again Thomas equates this first necessary cause of existence with God.

The fourth way in Thomas' argument again is somewhat different and is based on the gradation observed in things. Thomas states that some things are found to be more good, more true, more noble, and so on, and other things less. All these comparative terms describe approximations to a superlative, the best, the truest, the noblest, and so on. The things which contain all these superlatives are the things most fully in being. We might expect that Thomas would now employ the ontological argument and claim that the one thing most perfect must by necessity exist. But he again uses a cosmological argument and works with the assumption of a first cause: When many things possess a common property (e.g. varying degrees of goodness), then the one most fully possessing it can cause others to participate in it. If such causative superlative would not exist, there would not be these properties. Therefore Thomas concludes that there is something "which causes in all other things their being, their goodness, and whatever other perfection they have. And this we call 'God'." [24]

All these cosmological "proofs" of the existence of God boil down to the observation that no finite being thus far observed has the cause of its existence in itself. Therefore the conclusion is reached that there must be an infinite being which is the cause of all finite beings and of itself. Yet is such conclusion justified on logical or phenomenal grounds? Immanuel Kant, one of the keenest critics of all proofs of God's existence, answered with an emphatic "No"! He did not take the issue as lightly as Bertrand Russell who simply stated that "if everything must have a cause, then God must have a cause. If there can be anything without a cause, it may just as well be the world as God". . . . "There is no reason why the world could not have come into being without a cause; nor, on the other hand, is there any reason why it should not have always existed." [25] Kant, however, rightly called the cosmological argument the most natural and "the most convincing not only for common sense but even for speculative understanding." [26] Yet Kant also demonstrated the limits of the cosmological argument in his fourth antinomy of pure reason. He showed that neither on the basis of experience nor on the basis of pure reason alone can it be decided whether there is a supreme cause of the world or whether such cause is non-existent.[27]

In his actual criticism of the cosmological argument Kant again affirms that to infer a cause from observing the contingent only applies to the observable world, but it has no meaning whatsoever outside this world.[28] Thus the principle of causality must be restricted to our observable world. Kant recognizes that in the cosmological argument this principle is precisely employed to enable us to advance beyond the observable world. Yet he objects that any inference from an impossibility of an infinite series of causes to a first cause is not justifiable within the world of experience, and it is still less justifiable beyond this world in a realm into which this series can never be extended. Kant therewith emphasizes that our experience and logic are confined to the realm in which we live, to our space-time continuum. There is no way logically to transcend this realm and attain any degree of certainty. Kant also reminds us of the dilemma that we have faced with the ontological argument when he states that the logical necessity of a prime cause does not necessitate its reality.

c. *The teleological argument.*

However, human mind thought of still other ways to "prove" God. There is for instance the teleological argument which to some extent runs like the cosmological argument though in the opposite direction. From the beauty, harmony, and expediency of the world, the conclusion is reached that there must be a highest intelligence that once arranged the world so perfectly and still governs it this way.

The harmony within the world can best be observed in the growing organisms or in the ecological harmony of the animate and inanimate world. Already in Greek antiquity these observations led men such as Anaxagoras to the assertion that there must be a world intelligence that functions as the ordering power of the universe.[29] Even the skeptic Cicero of ancient Rome could not but praise the beauty of the world and the marvelous regularity of its motions.[30] Centuries afterwards the German biologist and neo-vitalistic philosopher Hans Driesch still assumed a whole-making causality within the organic world.[31] This *entelechy*, as he called it, is not contained in space and time but acts in it. It works teleologically in transforming a mere sum of equipotentialities into the wholeness of a mature organism. Similarly it leads to restitution in lower animals, for instance, when the tail of a salamander grows back after it has been cut off. In plants the same *entelechy* leads to adaptation. When plants are removed from warm climate and are placed into a cooler environment they protect themselves with a hairy film. Hans Driesch considered each living organism in its undisputable wholeness as the most obvious result of this *entelechy*.

Before agreeing too readily with Driesch we should also remember Charles Darwin's assessment of natural adaptation when he said: "I cannot think that the world, as we see it, is the result of chance; yet I cannot look at each separate thing as the result of Design."[32] Perceiving design and beauty in nature is only half of the truth. Immanuel Kant again seemed right in his evaluation of the teleological argument. He asserted that this proof which presents the world to us as an immeasurable stage of variety, order, purposiveness, and beauty, must be mentioned with respect. "It is the oldest, the clearest, and the most accordant with the common reason of mankind. It enlivens the study of nature, just as it itself

derives its existence and gains ever new vigor from that source." [33]
In talking about harmony, purposiveness, and harmonious adaptation, however, this physico-theological proof, as Kant called it, only
refers to the form of the world and not to its substance. Thus Kant
suggests that in analogy to us observing a human artist who shapes
beautiful artifacts out of raw materials, we could at best arrive at
an architect of the world, but not at its creator. [34] If we want to
prove the existence of an all-sufficient primordial being, according
to Kant, we would then have to resort to the cosmological argument. Since we have already noticed that he reduces the cosmological argument to its ontological presupposition, we are not surprised when he arrives at the conclusion that the teleological
argument serves only as an introduction to the ontological argument. He finally sums up his criticism by saying,

> the physico-theological proof of the existence of an original
> or supreme being rests upon the cosmological proof, and the
> cosmological upon the ontological. And since, besides these
> three, there is no other path open to speculative reason, the on-
> tological proof from pure concepts of reason is the only possible
> one, if indeed any proof of a proposition so far exalted above
> all empirical employment of the understanding is possible at
> all. [35]

Kant did not only demonstrate the interdependence of the three
arguments of the existence of God thus far reviewed, but he also
pointed to a dangerous moment in the teleological argument, namely that the God therewith proved would only be a world architect.
This idea of a world architect received hardly any attention in the
Middle Ages. Thomas Aquinas, for instance, only in his fifth and
last way to prove the existence of God emphasized the goal-direct-
edness and orderliness of nature. [36] In the period of the Enlightenment, however, the teleological argument did not only lead to
the assumption of a world architect, but even more mechanically
to that of a divine watchmaker. Gottfried Wilhelm Leibniz already
indicated this transition with his idea that God has created the
best of all possible worlds. Of course, Leibniz rejected the concept
that even the greatest artistic masterpieces of our limited mind
could be set in parallel to the least productions and mechanisms
made by divine wisdom. He also asserted that between the human
and the divine artifacts there is not merely a difference of degree
but one of kind. [37] It follows from the perfection of the supreme

author of all things that the order of the whole universe is the most perfect, and that each living entity or *monad*, as Leibniz calls it, represents the universe according to its point of view and that it has all its perceptions and desires as thoroughly well-ordered as is compatible with the rest.[38] Leibniz concludes that "this perfect agreement of so many substances which have no communication with one another can come only from their common cause." Thus there is "a new and surprisingly clear proof of the existence of God." [39]

Though Leibniz attempted to demonstrate the foresight and perfection of God, again his argument considers only half of the truth. Nature is not always so complete, so well-ordered and so expedient as Leibniz' idea of a pre-established *harmony* assumes. When Teilhard de Chardin, for instance, speaks of the manifold errors and trials through which nature attained its present level, his claim coincides much better with the observable reality.

Yet the most dangerous aspect in Leibniz' argument is the idea of a *pre-established* harmony existing within creation and pre-ordained by God. In pursuing the same idea of a pre-established harmony, the Christian apologist and Archdeacon of Carlisle, William Paley, a contemporary of Kant, for instance, ventures to compare the works of nature with a watch. Though he asserts that "the contrivances of nature surpass the contrivances of art, in the complexity, subtilty, and curiosity of the mechanism," [40] It is only too tempting for minds less bound to the Christian tradition to interpret the world on a totally mechanistic basis and relegate God to the once important but now irrelevant position of the divine watchmaker. This shows us that in order to arrive at a proof of the existence of God, theologians have unintentionally furthered the argument that the world no longer needs an active God.

d. *The moral argument.*

The moral argument for the existence of God has gained new reputation through Kant. Unlike the English empiricist David Hume a generation before him, Kant did not just criticize traditional arguments for the existence of God, but also advanced as his own argument that of the moral necessity of God. Yet Kant was not the first philosopher to resort to the moral argument. The Spanish physician, Philosopher, and theologian Raymundus de Sabunde earlier advocated it in his *Theologia Naturalis Sive Liber Creaturarum* (1434-1436).[41] According to Raymundus man is a reasonable being. Yet he can neither reward nor punish himself. Thus there must be someone higher who assumes the role of distributing reward and punishment. If such ultimate retribution did not exist, human life would make no sense, since in one's personal life good and bad would not balance out.

In concluding his *Critique of Practical Reason* Kant touches the same issue when he confesses: "Two things fill the mind with ever new and increasing admiration and awe, the oftener and more steadily they are reflected on: the starry heavens above me and the moral law within me." [42] While the starry heavens show man the magnitude of the universe and his own smallness, the moral law within man endows him with dignity and personal worth. The moral law impels man to strive for the highest good in the world. But no rational being can conform in this world at any time to the moral law.[43] Kant claims that such perfection can only be attained through infinite progress beyond this life in life eternal. If we assume we could attain it already in this life, we either bend the moral law according to our inclinations, or we indulge in fanatical dreams which completely contradict our knowledge of ourselves.

Kant proceeds to show that both immortality and God must be postulated by pure practical reason. Conformity with the moral law, which is to bring about true happiness, rests on the assumption that a harmony can be obtained between nature, man's own destiny, and the moral law within him. The latter two might be able to conform, provided that man is the author of both of them. But how can they conform with the world around man? Kant observed that since man is not the cause of nature "his will cannot by its own strength bring nature, as it touches on his happiness, into complete harmony with his practical principles." If however, there is a supreme cause of nature which has a causality corresponding to the moral intention of man, such conformity could be reached. Consequently Kant assumes the existence of God as the necessary presupposition for achieving the highest good. If there is no God, as ultimate author and coordinator of man's moral drive and nature's innate possibilities, it would not make sense for man to strive for the (then unattainable) ultimate harmony. Kant readily admits that the notion of God is derived from a practical need and "it can be called *faith* and even pure *rational faith*, because pure reason alone (by its theoretical as well as practical employment) is the source from which it springs." [44] This argument for God, as the purposive integrator of man's yearning and the cause of the world, also shows that man is "the final purpose of creation," and that nature will eventually harmonize with man's happiness. Kant even asserts that without man "the whole creation would be a mere waste, in vain, and without final purpose." [45]

Johann Gottlieb Fichte, deeply influenced by Kant, again emphasized a moral order of the world.[46] He claims that everyone experiences a call to duty, which is related in its content to that of everyone else's call. The originator of this call and of its unity with all other calls endows our life with direction and also guarantees the final victory of the good. While Kant still maintained that God as the purposive integrator must be perceived as a personal agent, Fichte's idealistic notion of God is clearly pantheistic. In essence it is similar to Friedrich Schiller's comment that the world's history is the world's judgment.[47] God is equated with the driving forces of the world. He is no longer the unconditioned conditioner, but the unexplainable way the world processes present themselves. Such notion, however, indicates that the moral argument for God's existence can easily divorce itself from the Judeo-Christian faith, to the support of which it was once developed, and result in a pessimistic or at least skeptical outlook on the world processes.

e. The historical argument.

The last argument we want to mention is the historical argument or the argument from common consent. Since its basic assertion is a phenomenological one, namely that all nations at all times revered a god or gods, it hardly indicates in its outset that it wants to lead up to the God of Judeo-Christian faith.[48] Having observed that all peoples at all times worship deities or higher beings of some kind, the conclusion is then reached that there must be a reality behind this common attitude of mankind.

Though this argument might have sufficed in centuries passed, it is no longer applicable to our own time. The clearly increasing number of people who unintentionally or deliberately reject the notion of God or of any gods is one of the most bewildering phenomena of our time. In this situation the historical argument is a very dangerous one, because it could also lead to the assumption that up to a certain period man worshiped metaphysical powers. But through a process of maturation man dissolved the metaphysical world into the physical and has no longer a need for the belief in divine agents.

Having arrived at the end of our brief survey of the most prominent arguments for God's existence and having noticed in most cases their questionable nature, we must ask ourselves what these arguments actually prove. First, they prove that since the beginning of logical thought the most brilliant men of the human race endeavored to argue on a rational basis for the existence of God. The very fact of this enterprise should make anyone stop and think if he is tempted to discard the God question altogether. Beyond this point the opinions are split. Official Catholic doctrine still holds that God's existence can be proved. As recently as 1950 Pope Pius XII pronounced in his Encyclical *Humani Generis* that "human reason" . . . "by its natural powers and light can in fact arrive at true and certain knowledge of one personal God who in His providence guards and directs the world, and also of the natural law infused into our souls by the Creator." [49] This is in line with the declaration of Vatican I "that God, the beginning and end of all things, can be known with certitude by the natural light of human reason from created things." [50]

On the Protestant side, however, Kant's criticism of the proofs of God's existence left an undeniable impact. Most Protestant theologians are very hesitant to ascribe to human reason such a high faculty. But already a generation before Kant, the German pietist, philosopher, and mystic, Johann Georg Hamann had pointed out that a God whom we can grasp with our reason and whom we can penetrate with our mind, is no God.[51] Any proof of God's existence would mean either that God is on equal basis with us, i.e. part of our world, or that we are on equal basis with him, i.e. not confined to our world. Though Hamann's observation is basically right, he forgets that whenever we speak of God we are unable to grasp him completely. However, this inability does not make us refrain from using approximations or anthropomorphisms in our God language. For instance, we believe that God has disclosed himself to us in human form in Jesus Christ. Yet would it not be feasible that God has also disclosed himself to some extent to all men outside of Jesus Christ? Is Vatican I wrong when, upholding the natural knowledge of God, it quotes Paul's Letter to the Romans saying: "For the invisible things of him, from the creation of the world, are clearly seen, being understood by the things that are made." [52] Even Paul seems to concede at this point that God can be known to some degree by natural reason.

Of course, one could resort to Søren Kierkegaard who claimed that "to prove the existence of one who is present is the most shame-less affront, since it is an attempt to make him ridiculous." [53] How-ever, such a rejection of the "proofs" of God's existence seems to result from a misunderstanding of their function. The "proofs" serve either a doxological function in glorifying God through the means of reason, or they serve an apologetic function in attempting to convince doubters or unbelievers of the reality of God. But they are hardly ever intended as a means of double-checking whether God is really there.[54] This means that they always imply a prior faith decision, even if it is one of "pure rational faith" as in Kant's moral argument. The one who sets out to "prove" is already con-vinced that there is "someone" to prove. If we want to confine our-selves to a neutral ground prior to faith or prior to unbelief then Kant's critique of the first three arguments must be heeded and our result would be the ambivalent position of Kant's antinomies of pure reason. It is there that he demonstrated that as soon as we leave the ground of faith or unfaith and argue about something beyond sense experience (God, immortality, etc.) we can "prove" the pros and the cons of the argument with equal validity.

2. God—limited or limiting?

Not everybody, however, agrees with Kant's verdict that God is completely beyond sense experience once we leave the "biased" positions of faith or unfaith.

a. *God as becoming (process theology).*

Especially the representatives of process thinking will argue that God need not necessarily be thought of as the strictly uncondi-tioned agent who completely limits our reasoning to the realm of phenomena. If God is assumed as becoming and not simply as perfect, it should be possible to circumvent the alternative of faith or unfaith.

Whitehead and Hartshorne: The English mathematician and philosopher Alfred North Whitehead put forth his understanding of God in his highly influential book *Process and Reality* (1929). He is dissatisfied with both the Aristotelian notion that God is the first unmoved mover, and the "Christian" notion that God is the "eminently real." According to Whitehead, in the Western tradition both notions were fused into the idea that God is the "aboriginal, eminently real, transcendent creator, at whose fiat the world came into being, and whose imposed will it obeys."[55] Thus God was understood as a primordial tyrant fashioned in the image of the Egyptian, Persian, and Roman imperial rulers. Even the "brief Galilean vision of humility" of Jesus of Nazareth did not change this, because John lost out to Paul. "If the modern world is to find God," Whitehead claims, "it must find him through love and not through fear, with the help of John and not of Paul."[56] Assistance in this endeavor can be found in Jesus, or as Whitehead calls him, the Galilean origin of Christianity. Jesus has shown that "love neither rules, nor is it unmoved; also it is a little oblivious as to morals. It does not look to the future; for it finds its own reward in the immediate present."[57]

To attain the notion of a loving God and not of a tyrant God, Whitehead suggests that we must limit the possibilities of God. He attempts this limitation by attributing to God a primordial and a subsequent nature. In his primordial nature God is "the unlimited conceptual realization of the absolute wealth of potentiality."[58] This does not mean for Whitehead that God is prior to all creation, but that he is with all creation. Apart from God there would be no actual world, since nothing could be actualized, and apart from the actual world with its creativity, there would be no rational explanation of the ideal vision which constitutes God.[59] Thus God needs the world as its arena of actualization and the world needs God as the granter of these actualizations. This interdependence becomes even more evident in God's consequent nature. Since all things are inter-related Whitehead assumes that the world reacts to God. Thus God "shares with every new creation its actual world."[60] While in God's primordial nature all groundwork for the possible world is given, God in his consequent nature provides through a kind of feedback the weaning of his physical feelings from his primordial concepts. Therefore Whitehead describes the nature of God's subsequent involvement in the world as "the perpetual vision of the road which leads to deeper realities."[61] Since the subsequent nature is always moving on and integrates the actualities of the world into the primordial whole which is unlimited conceptual reality, God provides the binding element in the world. He confronts what is actual in the world with what is possible for it, and at the same time provides the means of merging the actual with the possible.

Both God and the world are the instrument of novelty for each other. But God and world move conversely to each other in respect to their processes. God, as primordially one, acquires in the interchange with the world through his consequent nature the multiplicity of the actual occasions and absorbs them into his own primordial integrative unity. The world, however, as primordially many, acquires in the interchange with God through his subsequent nature as integrative unity, which as a novel occurrence is absorbed into the multiplicity of its primordial nature. God and world are coaxing each other along, God being completed by the finite and the finite being completed through confrontation with the eternal. Whitehead sums up his thoughts by saying:

> "What is done in the world is transformed into a reality in heaven, and the reality in heaven passes back into the world. By reason of this reciprocal relation, the love in the world passes into the love in heaven, and floods back again into the world. In this sense, God is the great companion—the fellow-sufferer who understands." [62]

One could raise many questions against Whitehead's dipolar notion of God. For instance, the idea of creation out of nothingness is too easily discarded, and it is too easily assumed that evil will simply be destroyed instead of being punished. Yet after all the perfect though unmoved first principles we have encountered in our survey of the proofs of God's existence, Whitehead's notion of a compassionate and understanding God certainly sounds attractive.[63] Also the insistence on God's involvement in the continuous creative process [64] must find open ears by those who claim that Christianity has forgotten the necessity for creative social change. But is it really possible to circumvent Kant's *Critique of Pure Reason* so easily and introduce in highly speculative and evidently semi-Christian fashion a new interpretation of Plato's concept of a world soul? [65] Does not also the shadow of Spinoza's philosophy of identity loom behind this approach which could easily lead to an identification of God with nature's own creative principles?

Charles Hartshorne, one-time assistant to Whitehead, goes along similar lines as his former teacher. He too does not see much chance for a natural theology that advances "that Deity must be the transcendental snob, or the transcendental tyrant, either ignoring the creatures or else reducing them to his mere puppets." God must rather be conceived of as "the unsurpassably interacting, loving, presiding genius and companion of all existence." [66] Hartshorne finds such a God logically possible if we assume a middle way between the two prevalent types of theism. The first type of theism advances a purely rational approach to God. God is understood as being in all respects absolutely perfect or unsurpassable and he is considered to be in no way and in no respect surpassable or perfectible. Hartshorne sees this position represented in Thomism and in most of European theology prior to 1880. The other type of theism, or third type as Hartshorne calls it, offers a juxtaposition to the first type. It is a purely impirical approach and asserts that "there is no being in *any* respect absolutely perfect; all beings are in all respects surpassable by something conceivable, perhaps by others or perhaps by themselves in another state." Hartshorne sees this position advanced by some forms of pantheism and of atheism. Between these two types Hartshorne discovers the possibility of a mediating type of theism or, as he calls it, of a second type of theism. According to this theism

> there is no being in all respects absolutely perfect; but there is a being in *some* respect or respects thus perfect, and in some respect or respects not so, in some respects surpassable, whether by self or other being left open. Thus is is not excluded that the being may be relatively perfect in all the respects in which it is not absolutely perfect.[67]

This second type of theism asserts a God who is partly finite and partly infinite, in some parts perfect and in other parts perfectible. It is clearly distinguished from the first type which asserts an absolute God, of a tyrant type, and from the third type which advances a merely finite God. Hartshorne is aware that such notion of God as he introduces with his second type of theism could by no means be "the entire actual God whom we confront in worship," since it would still be an impersonal it and not a personal thou. Yet Hartshorne is convinced that the essence to which his human concept of a second type theism points could very well qualify God and no one else.[68] Similar to Whitehead, Hartshorne understands God as both finite and infinite, eternal and temporal, necessary and contingent. Yet this does not turn God into a partly human God, because Hartshorne affirms that God cannot be surpassed even in his perfectible traits by anyone or anything else. " 'God' is the name for the one who is unsurpassable by any conceivable being other than himself." [69] The twofold nature of God can also be compared with two poles in God, an abstract pole, which is the logical necessity that some events be actualized, and a concrete pole, fully contingent upon what happens in the universe.[70] Because of his dipolar nature, of being both necessary and contingent, neither metaphysics alone, nor all the special sciences taken by themselves can arrive at an adequate notion of God. The former would confine itself to God's necessary nature, while the special sciences would only focus upon his contingent aspect. But God is "the integrated sum of existence." [71] He is "alive" and changing together with the changes of history, whose possibilities he provides. Whenever novel events occur they change the reality of God out of which they act by adding to his reality. God and the universe are seen as interdependent and involved in significant interaction. The purpose of our life can then be understood as contributing to the concrete whole, "a contribution made meaningful, because it really affects ultimate reality." [72]

In his attempt to provide an integrative vision Hartshorne even ventures to merge Jesus' assertion that God is love with Spinoza's pantheism. He claims that we no longer have to choose between Spinoza and Jesus, because nature should not only be conceived of as God, as did Spinoza, but as God of love. If we really love humanity, we cannot be indifferent to nature upon which all our practical power depends.[73] Hartshorne then concludes:

> The ultimate ideal of knowledge and of action remains this: to deal with the world as the body of a God of love, whose generosity of interest is equal to all contrasts, however gigantic, between mind and mind, and to whom all individuals are numbered, each with its own life history and each with its own qualitative—enjoying and suffering, more or less elaborately remembering and anticipating, sensing and spontaneously reacting—natures.[74]

Though this notion of God cannot deny its Christian resemblance, Hartshorne maintains that it is found on strictly logical ground. Yet on closer examination it seems more an idealistic vision colored by rational, neo-Platonic, mystic and even existential shades.[75] Hartshorne himself, however, claims that he has disregarded all intuitive notions, and has arrived at his understanding of God on strictly logical grounds.

Cobb and Ogden: John B. Cobb, Jr., is a former student of Charles Hartshorne and also deeply influenced by Whitehead. He knows that according to Barth and Bultmann theology should be strictly void of any natural theology. Yet he wonders whether in our time an exclusive revelational theology is still the option of many.[76] He rather advocates as the starting point for theology a "Christian natural theology" in which, similar to the New Testament, faith is not seen in radical discontinuity with our usual world experience. Though taking the task of constructing a natural theology with utmost seriousness, Cobb does not feel that he would have to employ a rationality unaffected by Christian commitments.[77] The reason for this assumption is that one is unable to formulate even a Christology without employing a conceptuality that requires clarification in natural theology. When faith proceeds directly to christological formulations there are always assumptions made, for instance, about the nature of language, and about the reality of history and of nature, that are not directly validated by faith, but simply taken for granted. To make Christian faith survive and to restore it to health, we must justify the horizon in which prominent theological terms, such as God or Jesus Christ, can have their appropriate reference. This is the more urgent, since the cosmological horizons which once gave meaning to the existence of medieval and early modern man are no longer applicable.

Cobb claims that unfortunately natural theology has been identified with philosophic doctrines which rendered God as impassible, immutable, and hence unaffected by and uninvolved in the affairs of human history. Yet he sees the God depicted in the Old and New Testament and in the liturgy of the church as being deeply involved with his creation and even with its suffering.[78] Thus all along there have been serious tensions between philosophy and Christian theology. Again the philosophy of Whitehead provides for Cobb a way to escape this tension. He suggests that "Whitehead's work is obviously already Christianized in a way Greek philosophy could not have been. Hence, it proves, I am convinced, more amenable to Christian use." [79] Cobb can even call it Christian, since it is deeply affected in its starting point by the Christian vision of reality. In adopting Whiteheadian philosophy instead of developing our own philosophical framework, he claims that we would also stand in succession with the great theologians of the past, such as Augustine and Thomas Aquinas; because they did not create their own Christian philosophy. Their great contribution to philosophy lies in the fact that they adapted and developed the philosophical material which they adopted. This did not mean for them that they had to abandon their theological concern because it was precisely out of their consciously Christian convictions that they made their philosophical contribution. Cobb proposes that in a similar way our task is to examine the intrinsic excellence of any thought structure we intend to adopt and adapt, since theology is not to be distinguished from philosophy by a lesser concern for rigor of thought. Further, we should consider whether such thought structure is congenial enough to Christian faith to be transformed into Christian natural theology.

> A Christian theologian should select for his natural theology a philosophy that shares his fundamental premises, his fundamental vision of reality. That philosophy is his Christian natural theology, or rather that portion of that philosophy is his natural theology which deals most relevantly with the questions of theology.[80]

Cobb does not want us to be tied to one particular philosophy, because every argument begins with premises and the final premises themselves cannot be proved. Thus the quest for total consensus is an illusion. Though no thought system is final and though there is no human attainment of final truth we do not end up in a kind of hopeless relativism. There are always approximations of truth that are more adequate and others that are less adequate. When the theologian appeals for the justification of his statements to the general experience of mankind, he is engaged in Christian natural theology and must justify the degree of approximation to the truth attained in his statements. Without pretending that he is privileged to apprehend the reality as a whole, he can and must believe that in his witness also, somehow the truth is served. But the Christian theologian "must also witness directly to what is peculiar to his own community and to that revelation of truth by which it is constituted." [81] At this point, he is engaged in Christian theology proper, 1. in interpreting the biblical text with the assumption that the truth for man's existence is to be found in the text, 2. in reflecting on the confessions of his community as a believing participant who confesses the redemptive and revelatory power of the key events in the history of his community, and 3. in a dogmatic function of making claims of truth which are relevant to all men whether or not they are within the community.

Cobb is convinced that Whiteheadian categories will prove useful both for the formulation of a natural theology and for engaging in theology proper. According to Cobb, Whitehead's philosophy favors the Judeo-Christian concern for persons and inter-personal

relations, its monotheism, and its belief that there is meaning in
the historical process. He also finds that Whitehead's philosophy
has many points of contact with Eastern religions, especially with
Buddhism.[82] Yet Cobb does not think that we can solve our problems of religious diversity simply by adding together the beliefs
of all faiths. Though conceding that each faith apprehends the
truth, he affirms that man's final need may ultimately be met only
in one vision of reality. We can only agree with Cobb when he
concludes his *Christian Natural Theology* with the assertion that
"what the Christian dare not claim for himself or for his church,
he may yet claim for Jesus Christ, namely, that there the universal
answer is to be found." [83] In a later writing, however, Cobb admits
that the claim of finality as found in the Christian faith is proble-
matical for him and that he has arrived at more relativistic conclusions.[84] Debating the advantages of a Buddhist view of reality, he
is still convinced "that our scientific knowledge of the world can
best be fitted with our human self-awareness and with the witness
of aesthetic and religious experience in a comprehensive synthesis
that points to the reality of God." [85] He confesses that his own
beliefs allow for and suggest spiritual existence, and he could not
hold these beliefs if he did not find in them great persuasive power.
Thus the present advantage of Buddhism at the level of beliefs
may only be temporary.

Schubert Ogden, a closer follower of Hartshorne and Whitehead,
betrays a less christocentric emphasis than Cobb. He proposes, for
instance, that the "New Testament sense of the claim 'only in Jesus
Christ' is not that God is only to be found in Jesus and nowhere
else, but that the only God that is to be found anywhere—*though
he is to be found everywhere*—is the God who is made known in
the word that Jesus speaks and is." [86] Ogden not only suggests that
God can be found everywhere, but that it is possible and even
necessary to affirm the realization of authentic existence apart from
Christ. Though Christian faith or authentic existence is always "a
possibility in fact," the decisive manifestation of divine love which
enables such existence occurs in the event of Jesus of Nazareth.
In him all other manifestations of this divine love are corrected
and fulfilled. Ogden is convinced that this is also the stance of the
New Testament. Paul, for instance, in his Letter to the Romans did
not present God's original self-disclosure as something different
from his final self-disclosure in Jesus of Nazareth. The content of
these two forms of manifestation is strictly the same. Even the

church affirmed that "the word addressed to men *everywhere,* in all events of their lives, is none other than the word spoken in Jesus and in the preaching and sacraments of the church." [87]

Though Ogden emphasizes the natural element in Christian faith, he still maintains the decisiveness of the historical manifestation of the essential God-man relationship in Jesus. Ogden finds that Jesus is not an accidental occasion through which some timeless and impersonal truth can be appropriated by the intellect. Rather "the eternal Existence or Thou in whom all truth is grounded is himself personally present" in him.[88] This eternal Existence or Thou provides for us the objective ground of our ineradicable confidence in the final worth of our existence.[89] Belief in God, Ogden concludes, is unavoidable, reflectively as well as existentially, because even modern secular man, with his characteristic affirmation of life in the world in its proper autonomy and significance, has at least implicitly discovered the reality of God. Ogden therefore opts for a secular faith and like Gogarten accepts secularity as the true consequence of Christian faith.

He argues that in affirming the significance and autonomy of our life in the world, we presuppose two things. First, that the ground of our life's significance exists absolutely, relative to no cause or condition whatsoever. Otherwise the significance of our life could not be truly ultimate and the object of unshaken confidence. Secondly, to endow our life with autonomy, the ground of our life's significance must be supremely relative reality. Ogden now concludes that God as this ground of our life's significance cannot act like an impenetrable wall, but he must enjoy real internal relations to all our actions and so be affected by them in his own being. This would mean that the conception of God, more or less clearly implied in a secular affirmation of the ultimate significance and autonomy of our life, "is intrinsically two-sided or dipolar. It conceives God as at once supremely relative and supremely absolute, thereby explicating both essential elements in a secular faith in the ultimate worth of our life." [90] Traditional supernaturalism and theism, however, conceived God as monopolar. In contrast to the biblical understanding of God, it became more and more difficult to assert God's absoluteness and at the same time his meaningful relationship to anything beyond himself. Thereby Scripture's most characteristic designations of God became completely emptied of meaning. This shows for Ogden that both traditional supernaturalism and theism have in the long run prevented an adequate expression of biblical and secular faith in God. At this crucial point he sees the chance and necessity for process philosophy, because it provides a conceptuality which "enables us to conceive the reality of God that we may respect all that is legitimate in modern secularity, while also fully respecting the distinctive claims of Christian faith itself." [91]

By understanding God as infinite personal existence or creative becoming, process philosophy enables us according to Ogden to assert God's independence of the actual world without saying that he is wholly external to it. On the other hand, it also allows us to affirm his inclusion in the actual world without denying that the world in its actuality is completely contingent and radically dependent upon him as its sole necessary ground.[92] God is no longer merely the barren absolute which by definition can be really related to nothing, but he is truly related to everything in immediate sympathetic participation. Ogden is convinced that the conception of such a "temporal" God could even maintain the truth of the claim that God created everything out of nothingness. Ogden is right when he proposes that at the heart of the doctrine of *creatio ex nihilo* is the belief that God alone is the necessary ground of whatever exists or of whatever is possible, and not the conviction that God once existed in lonely isolation. Not without justification can Ogden claim that the new theism developed from process philosophy, is able to provide a fully developed conceptuality which is understandable in the present situation and which is also appropriate to the essential claims of the scriptural witness. It shows a God whose love is pure and unbounded and whose relation to his creatures and theirs to him is direct and immediate.[93] Ogden sees this love uniquely coming to expression in Jesus Christ.

Ogden recognizes that the human word of promise and demand addressed to us in Jesus Christ is infinitely more than a merely human word and it has the divine power and authority to claim our ultimate allegiance and it thereby brings our lives to their authentic fulfillment. No other promise and demand have this same divine significance.[94] Of course, Ogden realizes that such affirmation cannot be an affirmation with one's mind or one's lips, but must be asserted as a free, personal decision with one's whole heart, with the whole weight of one's existence. In other words, a purely natural theology does not suffice. There must always be a decision of faith. It is interesting that both Cobb and Ogden who emphasize so much the necessity of a natural theology ultimately arrive at this conclusion. The question, however, we must ask Ogden is whether the possibility of authentic existence can really be a natural possibility as he assumes. Is it not much more likely tied to the decision of faith to which Jesus Christ incites us? Ogden seems to overestimate the possibilities of the human self while attempting to maintain a christocentric emphasis at the same time. Consequently he is torn between the natural possibilities of man and the unnatural possibility which encounters us in Jesus Christ. The resultant "boundary existence," he advocates seems to stem from his being too indulgent to the philosophical concept of a dipolar God.

b. *God as ultimate horizon (Pannenberg).*

We have seen so far that whether we attempt to prove the existence of God or whether we follow the new theism of process theology, ultimately our own existential decision is required. The results of this decision or indecision will show themselves in a position of faith or unfaith. However, these approaches imply at the same time that man already has some kind of awareness of God before he arrives at a decision of faith. Does this mean that God can be proved after all by referring to the common presupposition of these approaches? Especially Wolfhart Pannenberg has addressed himself to this interesting phenomenon in pointing out that man has a certain world-openness which distinguishes him from all other creatures.[95]

World-openness of man: According to Pannenberg man has undergone some decisive changes during the last few thousand years. In Greek philosophy and metaphysics, for instance, man was still understood as having a definite place in the cosmos and, himself being the microcosm, he was thought of as representing the macrocosm. Man had a definite and central place in the world which in turn provided him with a shelter and a point of orientation. However, today man's attitude is no longer one of submission to the world. He attempts to break out of the natural limitations of the world and tries to master it. In his scientific and technological advancements he has realized that it is possible for him to dominate more and more facets of the world. Thus, the world is no longer conceived of as an absolute which determines man's own position. The model character of the world as advanced in technological and cosmological theories demonstrates the relativity of the world. The world has become material for human creativity and has ceased to be a shelter or a home. This transition from a cosmocentric understanding of the world to an anthropocentric one, of course, is not just a blessing for man. He is now a man without a home, because he has refused to consider the world as a shelter provided for him. He set out to provide his own shelter, an artificial world of culture and civilization. Yet this new attitude toward the world seems to express an important distinction between man and animal.

While animals have an environment, man lives in the world. Animals are highly specialized creatures who have adapted themselves to a specific environment. For instance, it would be impossible for a polar bear to live comfortably in the Sahara Desert or for a whale to live on the Himalayan Plateaus. This specialization goes hand in hand with instinctive behavior patterns through which an animal reacts to specific features in the environment in a predetermined way. For example, the summer heat causes the shedding of hair for cats and dogs. The environment is also perceived in an extremely varying degree of intensity. For some animals, for instance, eyesight is excellent while hearing is poor, for others hearing is excellent while eyesight is less developed. Man, in contrast, is much less specialized and his instinct patterns are much less restrictive. However, this also means for him that by nature he is not adapted to most situations. In most climates he cannot live comfortably without creating an artificial environment of clothes and of housing which he must then vary according to his needs. Thus he will dress warmly in cold climates and lightly in warm climates, he will heat his home in winter and cool it in the summer.

Though man still shares with animals many instinct patterns, he is less restricted by them. For instance, he is not bound to certain mating seasons, and he can also accelerate or slow down his breathing patterns at will for a certain period of time. His senses are also less prominent. They are mostly average and with the help of technological sense extensions, such as microscopes, amplifiers, or sensors he can experience the world in many different ways. Even without those aids he can approach his environment in a perspective-like manner, since his view is not dominated by the excellence or poverty of one or of several senses. Thus he experiences a forest differently if he approaches it as a lumberjack than he would do if he were a vacationer or a hunter. These perspectives do not result from an instinct or from a sense-directed biological reaction, they result from a decision. This means that man is not bound to a single way of looking at things.

Man is open for new ways of experiencing the world and he is even looking for surprises. Being able to experience the world in a selective way, he is also able to detach things so much from their environment that he can experience them "for themselves" and then put them into a certain order. Thus he comes up with certain rules and laws (of nature) which, in analogy to predetermined instinct patterns, enable him successfully to cope with his environment. The establishing, constant revision, and expansion of these orders indicates that man is always trying to go beyond his present experiences. Thus curiosity as the drive to know for knowledge's sake is something specifically human.

God-openness of man: Why is man not satisfied with the present? Why is he always reaching out for something new and unprecedented? Contemporary sentiment seems to indicate that man's creations are exercises in futility, they are like signposts on the way to something newer and bigger. More and more people realize that our present time is a period of rapid change where inventions are obsolete as soon as they hit the market and where whole life styles are subjected to at least semi-annual changes. It often seems that the only directive is the act of change, but not the content of that which is being changed. Thus sociologists talk about man without shelter who has lost his point of orientation.

Perhaps man's attempt to create his own environment and thereby to change the world resulted from an overestimation of his own possibilities. Are we to assume that similar to an animal man is not fit to live without the framework of a pre-given world and without a specific environment which an animal accepts as unchangeable? But even granted this assumption, it is simply impossible to turn back the wheel of history. Man has detached himself from the world, he has started to reflect upon it, and he is on the way to subject it to his own will. Yet why is he not satisfied with having attained a certain goal? Why is he always on the way to a beyond? We wonder if this attitude could not be explained in analogy to animal behavior.

While for an animal the environment provides the stimulus for certain reactions, the stimulus for man's creative and dominating drive must come from beyond his environment. It would be difficult to explain it as stemming from man himself, because man considers his own being as part of the environment upon which he reflects and which he attempts to dominate. Pannenberg claims that even the total available world does not suffice to provide this stimulus, since man is always striving for experiences beyond presently accessible experiences and he attempts to incorporate more and more of these facets into his constantly expanding horizon. The German sociologist Arnold Gehlen seems to have discovered a clue to this restlessness of man when he stated that the impulse of the obligation to transcend all presently available experiences is one root of man's religious life.[96] More than 1500 years ago Augustine pointed in the same direction when he stated in the opening sentences of his *Confessions:* "Thou hast made us for thyself and restless is our heart until it comes to rest in thee." [97] It is the primordial notion of God the creator that makes man seek communion with him.

But can we really conclude from man's questioning spirit and from his insatiable hunger for experience beyond experience that indeed there is a "God" out there who endows man's actions with meaning? Could it not just be that man needs religion and that the world religions witness to his need of a metaphysical dimension? Pannenberg recognizes rightly that man's striving for an infinite does not prove the reality of God, but the reality of man's finitude.[98] He also shows that man in his search for a goal of life must go beyond the available experiences to something or someone beyond this world. Yet in going beyond this world man is not just searching for a way through darkness. His very searching already anticipates a possible answer. This does not mean that there must be an answer in the beyond but, whether man realizes it or not, his very striving for experience beyond all experience presupposes that such answer is possible.

Again Pannenberg's intriguing analysis leaves us only with the phenomenal possibility but not with the phenomenal actuality of God's existence. Similar to the traditional "proofs" of God's existence, the transition from the possibility to the actuality of God's existence would require a decision of faith. The question, however, that is not yet solved at this point is whether man actually needs to make a decision of faith to ultimately ground his existence. We should not pass over the objection too lightly that only the phenomenal realm is accessible to us and that therefore we must ground our existence in a strictly immanentist way.

PART II

A SEARCH FOR ULTIMATES

The human search for an ultimate and integrative view of life expresses itself either in the secular attitudes toward life, such as positivism or relativism, or in the multitude of religious convictions, all claiming to provide an ultimate and integrative view of life. We have noticed that more and more people are discarding the traditional answers provided for them by ecclesiastical authorities, because they feel that these answers no longer apply to their increasingly complex life situations.

3.

Questionableness of the Human Situation

During the Middle Ages Western man enjoyed a relatively sheltered existence in the world. The church was conceived of as the normative institution for his conduct of life and allegiance to its rules opened for him the prospect of heavenly bliss. The 16th century not only did away with the, until then, unquestioned idea that there is only one church, but it also destroyed man's confidence that the earth he inhabited was the center of the world. The Copernician transition from an earth-centered world view to a sun-centered one deprived man of his preferred position. The thought emerged that he shared the destiny of innumerable mankinds who inhabited other planets and who like him encircled larger and more central stellar bodies in unceasing orbits.[1] Though man could still enjoy a position somewhat different than the animal world, this cherished sentiment was challenged a few centuries later by Darwin's theory of evolution. After Darwin man had lost his uniqueness; he was considered a product of evolution and closely akin to the animal world. Finally, in the 20th century man's own makeup and that of his environment has been challenged. Pharmacologists and geneticists have been telling us that they can change the biological and psychic appearance of man beyond recognition and that they can even manufacture new species of man. Technologists and futurologists also have made us aware that man's environment is rapidly disassociated from its primordial naturalness and is being turned into the artificiality of modern technological civilization.

This short review suffices to demonstrate that the essence of man's own being has more and more been called into question. But this process has not remained without consequences. The rapidly increasing number of psychiatric disorders remind us that for man this questioning is not of academic but of immensely existential nature. Thus an ultimate foundation and an integrative view of life is more necessary than ever. But the question rises at once: How can this demand be met?

1. Necessity of an ultimate foundation.

Most if not all people desire an ultimate foundation for their lives. Yet under the impact of our constantly expanding knowledge many have arrived at the conclusion that these so-called ultimates are of only relative value. New evidence will demand revisions or even abandoning of "ultimate" positions they might assume. Thus truth is most frequently relativized.

a. *Relativism.*

The standpoint of relativism is already documented in the Bible. Remembering all the messianic pretenders he had seen sinking down into oblivion and all those who went to bed knowing that they were the rulers and at daybreak discovering their friends had usurped their power, Pontius Pilate could only shrug his shoulders saying: "What is truth?" when he encountered Jesus and heard the charges made against him (John 18:38). This kind of relativism of history that Pontius Pilate betrays attained its height in the 19th century, especially through the historicism of the German philosopher and theologian Ernst Troeltsch.

Convinced that truth manifests itself in many different ways, Troeltsch did not advocate an unlimited relativism.[2] He sensed, however, that unlimited relativism seemed to be the inevitable consequence of strictly historical thinking. In historical thinking all unities of history are atomized through historical investigation so that the resulting fragments are void of all meaning and purpose in history. Furthermore, all phenomena are treated deductively as necessary consequences of their antecedents and their environment. Thus nothing new can emerge, because there is only the givenness of nature and its endless interplay of already existent forces. There is also the constant possibility of new analogies which result in a diversity of standpoints and of new judgments. Yet Troeltsch affirmed that the scientific study of history does not exclude norms. But the norms themselves always remain individual and temporarily conditioned entities throughout every moment of their existence and are at least to some degree relative. So we cannot choose between relativism and absolutism, but must see how we can combine the two. According to Troeltsch the problem is how to discern, "in the relative, tendencies toward the absolute goal." [3]

Troeltsch does not look for some natural law, but for a principle suggestive of tendencies toward a common goal.[4] In this way he does not hold that there might be a limitless number of competing values. Though on the lower levels of culture this multiplicity does exist, Troeltsch assumes that on the higher stages one is surprised to find out that man actually lives only by a few ideas. One can easily discern in Troeltsch's approach the conviction that even historical relativism is of relative character. He is certain that there must be a basic presupposition which cannot be relativized. Troeltsch calls this "ultimate" the common goal which is engendered by "the Divine Spirit ever pressing the finite mind onward towards further light and fuller consciousness." [5]

The British historian Arnold Toynbee seems to follow a similar line of thinking.[6] He declares on the one hand that one civilization after another will emerge, attain its height and then be doomed to decay through the encounter with a subsequently emerging civilization. But he also affirms that Western civilization might be able to give history a new and unprecedented turn and escape the same repetitive pattern. This means that historic patterns are not slavishly binding but open for the possibility of something new.

Already in the 17th and 18th centuries the British empiricist had advanced a very stringent relativism, especially influential for the then nascent natural sciences. John Locke, often called the father of English empiricism, vehemently attacked the concept of innate ideas, i.e. the conviction that we have certain inborn ideas and that not all our ideas are derived from sense experience, in the first book of his *Essay Concerning Human Understanding* (1690).[7] Though he asserted that all our knowledge stems from sense perception, he limited this knowledge in its extent and certainty and still allowed for religion.[8] Two generations later, however, this sentiment had changed drastically in the writings of David Hume. He radicalized Locke's approach and endeavored to rid empiricism from all its non-empirical influences. For instance, he tried to reduce the validity of truth to the validity of sense perception. He claimed that all ideas are received through our impressions of them and are then connected with each other by the principle of resemblance, contiguity in time and place, and cause and effect.[9] Hume was convinced that there are no other principles involved through which we associate ideas. He tried to prove this assertion by pointing to experience. A picture, he argued, naturally leads our thoughts to the original or to what it resembles. "The mention of one apartment in a building naturally introduces an inquiry or discourse concerning the others (Contiguity); and if we think of a wound, we can scarcely forbear reflecting on the pain which follows it (Cause and Effect)." Furthermore, he wanted to restrict all truths of reason to stating simple relationships which cover the areas of geometry, arithmetic, and algebra. These truths are valid whether or not their objects exist in the real world. "Though there never were a circle or triangle in nature, the truths demonstrated by Euclid would forever retain their certainty and evidence." Hume felt that these truths of reason entail more certainty than factual truths, because the contrary of a matter of fact is always possible. To illustrate the case, he argued *"that the sun will not rise tomorrow* is no less intelligible a proposition and implies no more contradiction than the affirmation *that it will rise."* [10] All laws of nature are consequently conceived of as laws of possibility. Hume asserted:

> Being determined by custom to transfer the past to the future in all our inferences, where the past has been entirely regular and uniform we expect the event with the greatest assurance and leave no room for any contrary supposition. But where different effects have been found to follow from causes which are to *appearance* exactly similar, all these various effects must occur to the mind in transferring the past to the future, and enter into our consideration when we determine the probability of the event.[11]

Yet Hume did not want to separate matters of fact and truths of reason as much as one might assume after listening to his line of argument. He concludes that matters of fact rest on certain conventions of experience, while truths of reason rest on certain conventions of reason. This means that the way man approaches things or ideas becomes decisive while the question is left unanswered how things or ideas really are. Thus Hume felt free to discard all metaphysics with the verdict:

> If we take in our hand any volume—of divinity or school metaphysics, for instance—let us ask, *Does it contain any abstract reasoning concerning quantity or number?* No. *Does it contain any experimental reasoning concerning matter of fact and existence?* No. Commit it then to the flames, for it can contain nothing but sophistry and illusion.[12]

Hume's judgment has had a tremendous impact on many scientists and philosophers. Often scientific or philosophical systems are regarded as having strictly model character. They express certain relationships between objects or ideas, but do not substantiate ontological claims. Einstein's theory of relativity, for instance, has recognized the interdependence of the former "absolutes" of space, time, and matter.[13] In situation ethics even moral values are relativized, since an action might be justified in one particular instance, but labeled wrong in different circumstances. Even Kant, who abhored the notion that all ideas and experiences are due to sense impression, had to concede that we cannot reach "the thing itself." We are irrevocably confined to the phenomenal world. Yet unlike Hume, Kant emphasized the importance of the observer as the noetic integrator of sense perception.

Modern science has even more upgraded the decisive role of the observer without indulging at the same time in a thoroughgoing relativism.[14] Heisenberg's uncertainty relation, for instance, permits the observer to know certain things under certain conditions to a certain degree. However, it is the task of the observer to determine beforehand which aspect of reality he wants to observe. Supported by this changing sentiment concerning the foundations of science itself, we should already ask Hume how he knew that everything depends on convention and sense perception. And further we must ask: Why do people agree on certain premises? Is it by accident, or is it because they know of the truth of the matter?

Quite often still another kind of relativism is advocated which in essence also goes back to Hume's assertion that our knowledge is derived from certain patterns of association. It is mostly represented in the life sciences suggesting that none of our actions is of ultimate significance. For instance, in psychologism as well as in biologism the idea is advanced that our reasoning is due to certain chemical reactions and psychological patterns. Thus everything is causally conditioned and there is no truth value in our reasoning or our conduct. In evaluating this extremely skeptic relativism, we must admit that drug research has shown that the human psyche can be changed to an astounding degree through certain drugs, such as alcohol, LSD, or mescaline.[15] Dale Carnegie, in his best-seller *How to Win Friends and Influence People,* has also demonstrated that our reactions largely depend on the way we encounter things or people.[16]

Yet to conclude that our reasoning and conduct can be totally explained through chemical reactions and psychological patterns seems a contradiction in itself. If it were so, how could the one who makes the assertion that they can be explained this way, claim any truth value for his argument? This shows paradigmatically the dilemma of propounding a relativistic attitude towards the conviction of an ultimate foundation. If we advocate a thoroughgoing relativism, we end up in contradicting our very goal, because we set the principle of relativism as absolute, while at the same time disclaiming that there are any absolutes. However, if we advocate a conditional relativism, we already concede the possibility of an ultimate conviction. Thus relativism is in its essence not much different from its terminological counterpart which is represented in a positivistic attitude towards ultimate truth claims.

b. *Positivism.*

The positivistic attitude of restricting our reflections to the ideas gained from sense experience has a history perhaps as long as that of relativism. The Greek atomists, for instance, reduced all reality to matter and motion. We have also noticed that prominent representatives of the French Enlightenment urged us to give up all metaphysical speculations and only focus our attention on the pure facts of science. However, it was not until the first half of the 19th century when the French philosopher Auguste Comte, under the impact of scientific progress, declared positivism to be the proper philosophical attitude of modern man.[17]

In his famous thesis of the three stages of mankind Auguste Comte proposed that the spiritual and intellectual development of man proceeded along three distinct stages. The first is the theological or fictitious phase in which man conceives of the events in nature as dependent upon the will of higher personal forces. These forces are first thought to be embodied in objects of nature (the period of fetishism), then in gods who rule over larger areas of nature (polytheism), and finally in one God who is thought to rule the whole world (monotheism). Man's mind directs itself thereby mainly to the inner nature of being and to the first and final causes of the phenomena he observes. In the second phase of human development, the metaphysical or abstract period, man replaces the anthopomorphism of the first period by more abstract forces, such as powers, inner natures, or souls. Yet it is not until the third, scientific or positive phase, that man recognizes his limitations by giving up the search after the origin and hidden causes of the universe and after a knowledge of the final causes of phenomena. By a well-combined use of reasoning and observation, he endeavors now to discover the actual laws of phenomena. He attempts to grasp that which is accessible by inward or outward sense experience and which is the actually immediately given. Though Comte himself did not exclude metaphysics totally, since he thought it could serve for aesthetic purposes, most positivists of the 19th and 20th centuries felt differently.

Opposition to metaphysics, restriction to the sensually given, trust in evolution and progress, and replacement of religion by science, art, and sociology are the main emphasis of positivists such as Herbert Spencer, Ernst Haeckel, and John Stuart Mill. In part this anti-metaphysical trend is due to the lasting influence of David Hume, who also paved the way for the positivistic confidence gained by equating sense experience with the whole of reality. Though recent neo-positivism does not share the optimistic trust in forward-moving progress, it is still convinced that anything beyond sense experience is shaky territory. Its advocators surmise that the meaning of scientific statements exhausts itself in description and further elaboration of the sensually given. There are no a priori truths which could describe a necessary and eternal structure of being. All our concepts, sentences, and even truths are agreed upon by convention, and their validity has to be continually tested by sense experience. The only a priori admitted enjoy the rank of pure hypotheses. This means that all statements concerning God, soul, prime cause, finality, and transcendence must be discarded. The problems these statements involve are pseudo-problems, since their contents have no meaning in our sense experience. Philosophy has the task solely to provide the technical rules according to which sense experience can be better understood in terms of analysis and syntax. This means that man plays certain language games, the arena of which is the world he perceives through his senses.

This skeptic attitude prevailed especially in the Vienna circle under the leadership of Ludwig Wittgenstein and in the linguistic analysis of English philosophers, such as Ayer and Flew, and in Bertrand Russell's philosophic humanism. In the preface to his *Tractatus Logico-Philosophicus,* Ludwig Wittgenstein sets the tone of this movement when he asserts: "What can be said at all can be said clearly, and what we cannot talk about we must consign to silence." [18] All that can be said is from within the world and is described by a combination of objects.[19] Although Wittgenstein denies that God reveals himself *in* the world, he feels "that even when *all possible* scientific questions have been answered, the problems of life remain completely untouched." [20] But he refuses to conceive of a way in which the question concerning the problems of life can even be phrased. There are things that cannot be put into words, he realizes. They make themselves manifest and they are what is the mystical.[21]

This kind of reasoning again betrays a basic dilemma. In presupposing the sufficiency of empirical knowledge, it erects a nonempirical absolute.[22] Yet in attempting to proceed along the lines of pure empiricism, there are, as Hans Reichenbach has pointed out, factors contained in the originally given which cannot be deduced from strict sense experience.[23] For instance, the categories of unity, identify, difference, and similarity are not just conventions. We recognize the same item for a tree as do other people, for example Australian aborigines, with whom we have never had any communication, neither immediately or in a mediated way. Yet we share with them certain (linguistic?) presuppositions.

c. Existentialism.

Similar to positivism, existentialism too presupposes that ultimate questions are beyond the grasp of mankind. Life begins and ends with existence. For Martin Heidegger, one of the pioneers of modern existentialist thought, life is being in the world. It is a being there and a being towards death. Temporality and death are constitutive factors of being there. Since in our being there we face death as the end of life, this final end of our possibilities causes anxiety as a basic phenomenon of life. Yet it would be foolish to flee from our being towards death or to cover up this characteristic feature of our being there. In so doing we would live inauthentically, and turning anxiety into fear, we would attempt to hide ourselves from us. Heidegger instead opts for resoluteness and authentic existence. He claims that we must recognize anxiety as a basic state of mind and as being there's essential state of Being-in-the-world.[24] Similarly, "*authentic* Being-towards-death can *not evade* its ownmost nonrelational possibility, or *cover up* this possibility by thus fleeing from it, or *give a new explanation* for it to accord with the common sense of the 'they'." [25] Since death is being-there's innermost possibility, "being towards this possibility discloses to Dasein [being-there] its *ownmost* potentiality-for-Being, in which its very Being is the issue." [26]

Evidently Heidegger understands being as strictly confined to this world. Though the notion that all being-there ultimately faces death could be substantiated from a phenomenological survey, Heidegger's distinction between authentic and inauthentic existence is not grounded in observing the world at hand. Contrary to his own assertions, he leaves us with the impression that the reason why we should orient our lives rather this way than that way is beyond the argument of mere phenomenology. Heidegger's opinion for authentic existence seems to be based on an "arbitrary" decision.[27]

The French existentialist Jean-Paul Sartre, who has radicalized Heidegger's approach in many ways, presents a similar picture. Again man is conceived of as a basically free agent of his destiny. In contrast to Heidegger, however, Sartre can no longer understand man's freedom as something beneficial. Man is condemned to be free.[28] There is no God, no truth, and no values, if we want to regard these terms in the traditional sense. To make it worse, Sartre depicts man living in a basically antagonistic world.[29] The others are encountered as evil, who want to infringe upon my freedom. Sartre claims that existence precedes essence and that man's essence is what has been, or in short, man's past. But there is no common essence according to which man can act.[30] Rather each man makes his essence as he lives his life. This means that he has to transcend the non-conscious level of being-in-itself and rise to the conscious level of being-for-itself. At this level he expresses lack of being, desire for being, and relation to being. Yet by his option for being-for-itself he brings nothingness into the world, since he now stands out from being and can judge other being by knowing what it is not. Sartre emphasizes that man must be-for-himself if he wants to escape from bad faith.[31] This bad faith arises if man oscillates between relying on the past and projecting himself toward the future, or what is equally bad, if he attempts to synthesize both. It is the destiny of man to venture towards the future without relying on the past or on any pre-established norms.

Sartre depicts man as existing towards the future, solely relying on himself and in continual conflict with others who in a similar way want to exist for themselves. We must ask here why man in his solitary existence should venture blindly into an antagonistic world? Would he not do much better by resigning himself to the traditional values and conventions? Of course, Sartre would say No. But besides his mere claim to do otherwise he fails to provide us with a convincing rationale for his attitude of solipsistic activism.

Albert Camus seems to have moved beyond the arbitrariness of Sartre's existentialism.[32] In his novel, *The Myth of Sisyphus* (1942), he describes the situation in which he found himself after having discovered that none of the speculative systems of the past can provide any positive guidance for human life and guarantee the validity of human values.[33] But unlike his fellow countryman Sartre, he at least poses the question of whether it makes sense to go on living, once the meaninglessness of human life is fully recognized. Camus maintains that suicide cannot be regarded as an adequate response to the experience of absurdity whereby man lives without the value supporting "standards" and ideas of the past. Suicide would only be an admission of human incapacity by cutting through the tension provoking polarity between human being and the world. Camus finds man too proud of himself to seek this easy way out. Only living in the face of his own absurdity man can achieve his full stature.

Camus, however, soon realized that man's revolt against metaphysically guaranteed directives for conduct did not really improve man's predicament. Similar to Sartre, Camus was still prompted to literary action through the injustice and cruelty of man against man. Consequently, in his philosophical essay, *The Rebel* (1951), he then arrives at the conclusion that it was the revolt against metaphysics, against human conditions as such, that led to 20th century totalitarianism.[34] Camus now rejects the metaphysical revolt and opts for an ethical revolt. He recognizes that the metaphysical revolt, while attempting to impose upon mankind a new world order, resulted in the nightmare state of power for power's sake. Yet Camus still calls for nihilism as a cathartic means. Though he does not hold that it will provide a principle for action, he is convinced that it will clear the ground for new construction in disposing of any kind of mystification by which man would try to rid himself of his radical contingency and would confer upon himself a cosmic status. How does Camus now fill this clearance —that nihilism provided for him—with positive content? Even an essentially non-metaphysical and strongly moralistic humanism must derive its directives from somewhere; otherwise it would fall prey to what Camus rightly called "metaphysical" revolution.

His last major work, The Fall (1956), seems to imply that such directives cannot come from man himself.[35] In this utterly pessimistic work Camus abandons political and social revolt in favor of a conception in which evil is no longer situated in unjust social institutions in which man is doomed to exist. Evil is now understood as stemming from the very heart of man himself. Would this indicate that man is no longer regarded sufficient to provide the ultimate directive for his own life? In his short story, "The Growing Stone" (1957), he seems to give us a clue.[36] When in the plot the French engineer D'Arrast substitutes for the exhausted mulatto ship cook and picks up the stone to fulfill the cook's vow, he does not carry the stone to the cathedral, the place where the cook had vowed he would deposit it. Instead D'Arrast carries the stone back to the little hut in which the man lives. In other words, Camus indicates that help for man can only come from human solidarity in taking upon ourselves each others' burdens. But Camus seems to assert too that such solidarity must serve a human and not a metaphysical purpose. We wonder, however, if this alternative could and even should not be bridged by suggesting that one can serve the metaphysical purpose in fulfilling a human need. If nothing comes from beyond his own sphere, how is man then able to experience "a fresh beginning of life" that D'Arrast so vividly senses? After having shown the intrinsic evil in man, we wonder why Camus is still convinced that man can become his own savior?

d. Arbitrariness of all ultimate arguments.

In reviewing these three widespread attitudes toward a unified approach of life we have noticed a final arbitrariness as their very roots. We can conclude that all our acting and our attitudes are based on arbitrary decisions which could with the same right ensue in their opposites. Even if our attitudes were similar the ensuing actions could result in opposite behavior patterns. For instance, if we would simply follow our own innermost desires, we need not coincide in our resultant actions. We could, for instance, claim that our innermost desire is to follow our sex drive and to satisfy our sexuality. The resulting attitude of sexualism would be diametrically opposed to Buddhist thinking which advocates as its innermost yearning a middle way between asceticism and sensualism.[37]

Even adopting certain values as ultimate, such as life or happiness, would lead us into blind alleys. In adopting an evolutionist attitude, for example, the biological tendency of an ever more complete adaptation to the conditions of life would be our ultimate guide. Thus we would actively foster the development of the organic world. Albert Schweitzer, for instance, advanced this attitude with his principle of reverence for life.[38] But did not Schweitzer himself demonstrate in his daily work as a physician that one has to destroy and impede certain forms of life in order to help other forms survive and grow? We must destroy and eliminate bacteria and other micro-organisms so that wounds can be healed and infections be overcome. Thus in order to foster one kind of life we must eliminate another kind unless we want to confine ourselves to the position of non-involvement. The bigger question, however, that looms in the background is: Why should we encourage the life process at all? Does not an evolutionary progression of life only increase the struggle of existence, as Arthur Schopenhauer claimed?[39] Why should we perpetuate this struggle and not simply annihilate it? The same life which is valuable for one person may appear as a burden for someone else.

Perhaps we should fare better if we abandoned all value terms and simply followed certain common principles, such as the greatest happiness for the greatest number of people or Kant's categorical imperative. When we consider the principle of the greatest happiness for the greatest number of people, we notice at once that it implies that some people will be excluded from attaining the greatest happiness. In other words, this principle is not an ultimately binding principle for everyone. This would be different with Kant's categorical imperative: "Act only according to that maxim by which you can at the same time will that it should become a universal law."[40] Kant has sufficiently demonstrated that while it will not work with such negative "values" as lying, it will work very well for everyone with such positive values as love or honor. Of course, to make the categorical imperative effective, one must presuppose that everyone wants to operate under the same common dominating rule to the exclusion of all other rules. In other words, the ultimate principle which governs our life attitude is attained by excluding other principles, or to say it more simply, through deliberate choice. Again the formative forces which influence our life style are based on arbitrary decisions which could as well have led to something else.

Of course, we could "refrain" from adopting any ultimate principles and simply accept life as it is and swim in the mainstream. But again we must honestly ask ourselves: What is the reason for swimming in this direction? And what is the reason for swimming at all? Why should swimming be preferred to drowning? From whichever way we look at our basic life attitudes, the results seem to coincide: All standpoints and systems we might adopt are standpoints and systems through our own choice. Therefore they cannot give us any ultimate orientation for our life. Yet at the same time we yearn for an ultimate foundation on which we can firmly base our day-by-day decisions. But how can we find such a basis for life and living?

2. Finitude versus infinity.

The most obvious way to find an ultimate foundation for life and living would be to look in man himself. He is the one who wants to found his life on something beyond arbitrariness. So he might attempt to escape from all the changeabilities of his environment by considering nothing but himself. Yet such striving could not bring about the desired result, because it grossly neglects man's inextricable interrelatedness with his environment.

a. Man's confined existence.

While we do not want to fall into the hands of 19th century materialists who claimed that man is what he eats,[41] we must acknowledge the findings of modern life sciences that have irrefutably documented that man is largely a result of ancestry and environmental influences. His behavior and his thought patterns are largely determined by environmental influence and ancestral heritage. In his antinomies of pure reason Kant has already shown us that as soon as we want to break out of the confinements of this world, we can only postulate and no longer prove anything; in other words, by venturing beyond this phenomenal world we have left the solid ground of experience. The same is suggested by the attempt of the English empiricists to reduce our knowledge to sense impression and to the subsequent coordination of these impressions. All our conceptual tools, including the value and world view systems they "describe," are extrapolations from experiences within our space-time continuum. Of course, many of these value and world view assertions include postulates that cannot be proved in referring to our world alone. Yet at this point we must agree with Feuerbach who claimed that all our assertions that transcend the experience of this world are projections of conditions within this world. Human predicament resembles the predicament of wild animals in our zoos. By necessity these animals are confined to their fenced-in habitations. Anything beyond their world is irrevocably removed from their immediate experience. They can dream about it, they can draw analogies, but how and if it really is, they simply cannot verify. Similarily all our attempts to transcend our inborn limitations are accompanied with the distinct knowledge that regardless how far we push back these limitations, we cannot remove them completely.

Strangely enough the same Kant, who told us in his *Critique of Pure Reason* that we are confined to the world of phenomena, in his *Critique of Practical Reason* postulated God, immortality, and last judgment. This means he advocated them as necessary factors though knowing that they strictly exceed our sense experience. Of course, these postulates are not designed to serve as logical or empirical evidence for the existence of anything or anyone beyond the world we experience with our senses. They are, however, put forth on the tacit assumption that there is something beyond ourselves and that the conditions of this beyond endow our existence with ultimate meaning. But what do we gain by adopting such a premise? We have no criterion by which we can decide to what extent the ensuing conclusions concerning the reality behind these postulates are right or which set of conclusions is the most valid one. It is again up to us to decide on the basis of our own personal preference. This shows that no matter how hard we try to circumvent a completely this-worldly existence, we always fall back on ourselves and on the environment out of which we originated. Thus it is futile for man to claim anything or anyone as having ultimate value. Our self-designed principles for life and living are as haphazard as our own existence.

b. *Man's yearning for a new dimension.*

What shall we do in this evident dilemma? Shall we simply

recognize our limitations and label the search for an ultimate foundation as an attempt in futility? After all, millions of people seem to live happily without being bothered by the quest for an ultimate foundation for their lives. Yet the impression may be misleading. Man's attitude is usually not one of confinement or resignation but of going beyond the limits of present experience. Garaudy has pointed out that even Marxism had to abandon a dogmatic materialism, that emphasized solely the mechanistic concept of reflection, and develop a dialectic materialism, a materialism of reflection and projection, to come to terms with man's self-projecting spirit.[42] Man's discoveries may not always be beneficial for him or his environment, but he is constantly projecting himself towards the future and towards the unknown. Thus it would be in obvious contradiction to the basic structure of his existence to assume, that with regard to the ultimate foundation of his life style, he would refrain from asking the ultimate "why?" question. It is exactly the always possible emergence of the "why?" questions, namely: why am I here? and: why should I go this way and not another way? that threatens man's existence.[43]

Unlike an animal, man is a being that can detach himself from his own physico-psychic structure and from his environment and reflect upon them. Thus man does not accept his present condition as something unalterably given with which he has to live. On the contrary, he wants to know why his condition is the way it shows itself to him and to what extent it can be changed. The very fact that we live in an age of rapid change shows that man refrains from being simply an administrator of the given or an advocator of the status quo. He wants to mould his future and actively transform his present existence. However, in order not to succumb to mere utopianism any such attempt must start with an assessment of the present and must give reasons why the present has become the way it is. This process demands that man asks the "why-" questions regardless of the direction in which they may be answered.

Since man is unwilling to resign from asking ultimate questions and to accept his confinement within the space-time continuum, we wonder if it is feasible that there is something beyond the phenomenologically given which serves as a kind of Aristotelian uncaused cause and which enables man to base his life-decision on a firm foundation.

Implied here is the traditional question of a point of contact

(*Anknüpfungspunkt*). In their emphasis on radical otherness of the word of God, some neo-Reformation theologians were very adamant in disclaiming any point of contact between man's existence and the illumination of man's existence through God's self-disclosure. Yet strangely enough they themselves could not entirely disregard a connecting point between the created and its creator. Karl Barth, for instance, developed an analogy of relationship (*analogia relationis*) between man and woman, portraying the relationship between man and fellow man and between man and God. He suggests that the way a man is able to conduct himself toward a woman and vice versa resembles their relationship to God. "Man can and will always be man before God and among his fellows only as he is man in relationship to woman and woman in relationship to man." [44] Though Barth claims that the analogy of these relationships is strictly derived from and through faith, we wonder if he would not admit that, regardless of his faith, man is a relational being who finds his true fulfillment only in his relationship with God to which all other human relationships witness. The neo-Reformation theologian Rudolf Bultmann, on the other hand, used Martin Heidegger's existential analysis, by many regarded as a secularized version of Christian anthropology as a reference point for his existential interpretation of the Christian proclamation.

Emil Brunner was the first neo-Reformation theologian to explicitly look for a "natural" point of contact between the word of God and secular man. Brunner asserted that the peculiarity of man's existence in contrast to the existence of any other creature, lies in him being a person.[45] As a person man is a responsible creature, a fact which Brunner finds grounded in the creation. Man's personhood shows that man was created as a creature that enjoys a special relationship to God, a creature that stands before him, and is responsible to him.[46] Of course, Brunner realizes that natural man usually is not aware that the responsibility he feels when he carries out his actions, ultimately stems from his relationship to his creator. Therefore, this "general revelation" as Brunner calls it, has no saving significance. Yet for Brunner it is of utmost importance as the presupposition of the saving revelation in Jesus Christ, because through this revelation the consequences of the responsibility man senses are illuminated.

Protestant theologians outside the neo-Reformation movement had never abandoned the search for an appropriate point of contact between the Christian message and secular man. Paul Tillich, for instance, postulates a correlation of the analysis of existence, the truth of which we discover through scientific and philosophical investigation, and the answers given to the questions implied in existence, the truth of which we encounter in Jesus Christ[47] This correlation is founded on the conviction that the universal and the incarnate logos correspond to each other and it reminds us of the concept of the seminal logos developed by the Apologists of primitive Christianity. While the analysis of existence is restricted to the observation of the phenomenally given, Tillich attempts to indicate that the phenomenally given "needs" a complementation by something or someone whose existence is beyond empirical validation.

The Swiss philosopher Karl Jaspers, though coming from a decidedly philosophical standpoint, proposes a correspondence similar to that of Tillich, namely between existence and reason. For him reason means the pre-eminence of thought which grasps that which is universally valid. Existence, on the other hand, is the encompassing in the sense of a fundamental origin, the condition of selfhood which gives content to our being. Thus Jaspers' understanding of reason is to some extent equivalent to Tillich's analysis of existence, while Jaspers' understanding of existence would be somewhat analogous to Tillich's theological answers given to the questions implied in existence. Jaspers sums up very persuasively the correspondence between reason and existence when he says: "*Existenz* only becomes clear through reason; reason only has content through *Existenz*." [48] While Jaspers rejects Christian faith with the remark that with its exclusive affirmation of Jesus Christ it has absolutized one of the many ciphers of transcendence and thereby distorted it, he nevertheless accepts transcendence when he defines *Existenz* as the unfathomable or as that which is related to transcendence.

We should also mention here the more traditional but significant approach of Langdon Gilkey who sees a paradox in the character and status of man who is both a person who thinks and decides and an object of theoretical investigation and technical manipulation. [49] The "contradictory modern picture of man as helpless patient in the backless hospital shift and yet as mighty doctor in the sacral white coat," leads Gilkey to understand this paradox of determinism and freedom with the Judeo-Christian symbols of the creatureliness of man and yet of having status as image of God. [50] He also senses in the life of modern secular man a painful void which man desperately attempts to fill, to provide meaning to his origin, his limitations, his values, and his destiny. Again Gilkey sees this emptiness originate from the exclusion of God from our lives.[51]

The sociologist Peter L. Berger also puts forth a very interesting analysis of human existence. Less inhibited by theological restrictions than most theologians, he talks about "signals of transcendence" that emerge within the empirically given human situation.[52] These "signals" are phenomena to be found within the domain of our "natural" reality, but that appear to point beyond that reality. Man's propensity for order, his joyful play, and his hope for the future are some of the phenomena that can be understood as "signals of transcendence."[53] But Berger does not go as far as the former Jesuit Michael Novak, for whom almost any human self-expression betrays religious significance.[54]

When we remember its strong emphasis on reason, we are not surprised to find forceful advocates of a "natural" point of contact in the Roman Catholic tradition. The renowned Thomist Bernard Lonergan, for instance, senses in man an unrestricted desire to know.[55] This unrestricted desire is neither diminished over the centuries nor is it paired with an increasingly unlimited capacity to attain knowledge. Lonergan then identifies the objective of this unrestricted desire with God.[56] As any theology that attempts to establish a "natural" point of contact between our world and the transcendent, Lonergan's approach is also heavily criticized, especially by Leslie Dewart, who feels that Lonergan neglects the historicity of philosophy and has canonized Thomism as a timeless philosophy.[57] Leslie Dewart instead opts for a de-Hellenization of Christian faith, since he believes that the Hellenization process of Christian faith resulted in a dangerous opposition "between God's transcendence and God's immanence" by rendering God more and more aloof of man's reality.[58] Yet Dewart's analysis of human existence is not very different from that of Lonergan. Dewart senses "an absurd, ridiculous disparity between the abstract and the concrete possibilities open to man, between what man can dream of and what he can actually bring about."[59] While Dewart recognizes that this tension stimulates man to continual progress, he asserts that progress will not remedy the generic condition of man unless it is progress in man's relation to God. Again man is seen in need of redemption to which points his yearning of closing the gap between dream and reality. Has not Immanuel Kant already postulated a similar necessity for life eternal, to close the gap between the moral law within man and the actual attainment of its precepts within man's life on earth?

Our brief sampling indicates a wide-ranging consent that human existence implies consciously or subconsciously something or someone beyond man that endows his existence with meaning and direction.[60] Yet it has also become evident that such ultimate foundation of our existence should neither be caused nor conditioned by us or the world accessible to us. Could such causation or conditioning be found, the conclusion would almost be unavoidable that this "ultimate" foundation is the result of a projection. This would mean that whenever we attempt to reach the ultimate, the possibility of a projection looms on the horizon. If there is an ultimate, then similar to a two-way mirror, the ultimate foundation can reach us in providing us with a basis for orienting our life style. But *we* cannot reach out on our own and use it for this purpose; we can never be sure that anyone or anything is on the other side. As the ultimate foundation provides something new and unexpected for us while we are unable to reach it by ourselves, we agree with Karl Heim in calling it the experience of a new dimension.[61]

The experience of a new dimension can be illustrated by the transition from one geometrical dimension to another.

TRANSITION FROM ONE DIMENSION TO ANOTHER

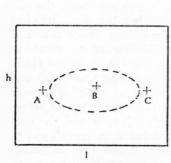

two-dimensional configuration
(e.g. plane)

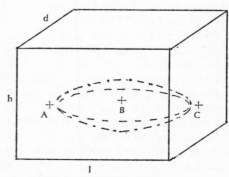

three-dimensional configuration
(e.g. cube)

For instance, if we lived in a two-dimensional configuration, such as a plane, where only length and height are existent, we could connect a point A with a point C basically two ways without touching point B which lies between them. We could go around B on the left side or on the right side. Of course, we might conjecture that there are other possibilities to circumvent B, but since we are confined to the two dimensions of a plane, we cannot actually know of any other possibilities. Yet someone occupying a three-dimensional configuration with length, height, and width could, to our embarrassment, easily demonstrate two more possibilities. He could circumvent B from above or from below. Furthermore, he would also have the possibilities which we enjoy, namely going around the left or right of B. Yet unless this new or higher dimension is disclosed to us, we do not *know* that these additional possibilities exist. Similarly, the disclosure of a new dimension could show us that there is a non-arbitrary attitude possible towards the ultimate foundation of our life style.

If there really is a new dimension beyond, above, and within our own, the decisive question is how it will relate itself to us. If it would relate itself to us in an impersonal way, we would be confronted with an ultimate foundation of our life analogous to the impersonal spheres of Greek mythology. It would determine our destiny like a fateful primordial decision without giving us any actual guidance. Obviously such a new dimension would only increase our helplessness and despair. We would no longer be confronted with our own arbitrary decision according to which we could orient our life, but without our consent there would be a pre-determined plan imposed on us without the chance of ever being changed. As we can see from Plato's and Aristotle's philosophy, this new dimension could easily herald a new era of resignation and emasculation.

However, if the new dimension would relate itself to us in a personal way, all our anxieties would be solved. This personal power could give us guidance at the present moment, enlighten our path out of the past, and show us a new future perspective. We would be able to encounter the new dimension as a personal Thou and not as a fateful decree. It would also allay us from succumbing to the heroic option of Marxist dialect that finite men must be their own Gods and their own saviors. We would be relieved from the fateful responsibility to give human history its final touch. This new dimension could give us access to an ultimate foundation of our life beyond the polarity of our either-or existence and hence beyond doubt and arbitrariness. But where can such a new dimension be encountered? Man's intellectual ability cannot give us guidance in this direction because there we are always confronted with an ultimate either-or. Yet there still is the religious sphere of man. Since this sphere is usually understood as not resulting from man's intellect, it would be the proper area to look for the disclosure of such a new dimension.

4.

The Mystery of Man's Religions I

(Origin and Structure of Religion)

Man's religious sphere is as mysterious as the meaning of the term religion itself. The Roman philosopher Cicero explained the term religion as being derived from *relegere* (to consider carefully or to reflect) and standing in contrast to *negligere* (to neglect).[1] Lactantius, sometimes called the Christian Cicero, however, thought that the term religion was derived from *religare* (to fasten or to bind to) and expresses the feeling that God has bound and fastened man to himself through the bond of piety by which we remember him as our creator.[2] Augustine, though in complete agreement with Lactantius, describes religion as a gift of God that reminds man's soul of its original and perfect nature.[3] Schleiermacher, finally, to quote one prominent theologian of our more immediate past, saw religion as the feeling of absolute dependence.[4] Yet his contemporary, Hegel, had already warned that if religion or Christianity would be founded only on feeling, namely the feeling of dependence, then a dog would be the best Christian, because he is certainly characterized most strongly by the feeling of dependence, or by the slavish obedience to the commands of his master.[5]

Though Hegel's remark is certainly an exaggeration, it shows how dangerous it is to confine religion to feeling alone. But Schleiermacher himself noticed this shortcoming, because he suggested that feeling cannot be conceived of as the exclusive root of religion. There are two sides which belong to religion, he claimed, a theoretical and a practical, and without them one would not think of religion at all.[6] A similar sentiment seems to lie behind Sir James Frazer's well-known definition of religion: "By religion, then, I understand propitiation or conciliation of powers superior to man which are believed to direct and control the course of nature and of human life. Thus defined, religion consists of two elements, a theoretical and a practical, namely, a belief in powers higher than man and an attempt to propitiate or please them."[7] Religion in its most general sense concerns itself with the relationship between man and the superhuman power(s) he believes in and feels himself dependent upon. Religious exercises, however, or the "theme" of religion, are devoted to redemption from anything or anyone that according to man might prevent him from communion with these powers. In other words, religion implies the notion of a disturbed existential union and exhibits the conviction that this union can be reestablished. This commonly accepted view might give us at least some idea in which direction we have to look for an answer concerning the origin of man's religion.

1. Origin of religion.

Man seems to be a religious being whose religions have a history as old as his own. Yet it is very difficult to uncover the origin of religion. Approximately 5,000 to 6,000 years ago man first started to entrust his thoughts and feelings to written documents. But the total history of man, which should be considered when we talk about the origin of religion is at least a hundred times older. Since this prehistoric time is immensely difficult to interpret as far as man's religious sphere is concerned, there have been several distinct theories advanced concerning the possible origin and development of religion.

a. *Animistic theory (Sir Edward Burnett Tylor).*

In 1871 in his epoch-making work *Primitive Culture,* the English anthropologist Sir Edward Burnett Tylor suggested animism as the origin of man's religion.[8] Animism, he claimed, concerns itself with souls of individual creatures, capable of continued existence after death or after the destruction of the body, and with other spirits upward to the rank of powerful deities.

> Spiritual beings are held to affect or control the events of the material world, and man's life here and hereafter; and it being considered that they hold intercourse with men, and receive

pleasure or displeasure from human actions, the belief in their existence leads naturally, and it might almost be said inevitably, sooner or later to active reverence and propitiation. Thus Animism in its full development, includes the belief in souls and in a future state, in controlling deities and subordinate spirits.[9]

Primitive men, Tylor asserts, were wrestling with two groups of questions: First, what makes the difference between a living body and a dead one? And second, what are those human shapes that appear in dreams and visions? Primitive man reached the solution that two things belong to him, a life and a phantom. They were both closely connected with the body and at death life left the body forever. The phantom, however, did not leave, because even during a man's lifetime it was separable from his body and could appear to people distant from the body. Tylor suggests that at a later step primitive man combined life and phantom as manifestations of one and the same soul. The personal soul is a shadowy human image, causing life and thought in the individual; it animates, conferring personal consciousness and volition of its bodily owner, past or present; and leaving the body far behind, it is able to flash swiftly from place to place. Tylor then expands "the general scheme of Animism . . . to complete the full general philosophy of Natural Religion among mankind." Spirits are simply regarded as personified causes and "the idea of souls, demons, deities, and any other classes of spiritual beings, are conceptions of similar nature throughout, the conceptions of souls being the original ones of the series."[10] For Tylor the conception of the human soul develops into the characters of good and evil demons, and finally ascends to the rank of deities. He concludes that in considering the nature of the great gods of the nations in whom the vastest functions of the universe are vested,

> it will still be apparent that these mighty deities are modelled on human souls, that in great measure their feeling and sympathy, their character and habit, their will and action, even their material and form, display throughout their adaptations, exaggerations and distortions, characteristics shaped upon those of the human spirit.[11]

Of course, this animistic explanation of the origin of religion proved very attractive. Deities are patterned according to elementary human experiences and serve as a pre-scientific explanation of the world. Perhaps primitive religion could have originated in this way. But one wonders if such primitive religion could have developed into a full-fledged polytheism or even monotheism. At the most, animism can lead to ancestor worship, as seen in Confucianism or in Roman and Greek religions.[12] Yet veneration of the spirits of ancestors usually occurs parallel and not antecedent to the worship of regular deities. Thus the line of development proposed by Tylor rests on shaky ground.

b. *Pre-animistic theory (R. R. Marett).*

In 1900 R. R. Marett published an essay with the title "Pre-animistic Religion" in which he suggested that primitive religion is "at once a wider, and in certain aspects a vaguer, thing than 'the belief in spiritual beings' of Tylor's famous 'minimum definition'." [13] However, Marett did not want to advance the idea that there was once a pre-animistic era in the history of religion, void of animism, but nevertheless filled with religion of some kind. While he agreed with Tylor that animism was a primary condition of the most primitive religion of mankind, he claimed that there were other conditions not less primary. In some cases, he suggested, animistic interpretations had even been superimposed on what previously had been non-animistic. He proposed that in primary religions there is a binary compound consisting of a tabu element and a mana element. The tabu element is predominantly negative in its action, being applied to many facets of the world of ordinary happenings. The mana element, however, is mainly positive in its action, being applied to something transcending the ordinary world, something wonderful and aweful.[14] Marett did not want to replace Tylor's animistic theory with the introduction of a tabu-mana complex. He suggested that mana comes close to "the bare designation of that positive emotional value which is the raw material of religion, and needs only to be moralized—to be identified with goodness—to become its essence." [15]

Marett actually advanced a dynamistic understanding of a religion where primitive man encounters a general impersonal power which must either be warded off (tabu), or which can be used to attain supernatural effects (mana). Though the phenomena of tabu and mana certainly exist, we wonder if the personal power(s) they represent are ever thought of as existing independently of their manifestations in persons or things. It is also difficult to explain convincingly how the belief in tabu and mana can ever develop into the belief in godly powers. It seems that Marett's theses lend themselves much more easily to an explanation of the origin of magic, than of religion in general.[16]

Though Marett disagrees with Frazer's idea that magic is the primitive's way to explain the world in a pre-scientific form,[17] he seems to share with him the conviction that magic develops into religion (according to Frazer, religion is the step between magic and scientific reasoning). But religion and magic seem to be equally basic to man's existence. Magic is the understanding of man that he can attain or at least gain influence upon the powers which control his life. In religion, however, man feels himself dependent upon such powers.[18] Both, the feeling of dependence upon such power(s), and the assumption that man can exert influence upon them, are co-existent in primitive religions and did not develop from each other.[19] Perhaps Marett should have heeded more his own insight that "the first chapter of the history of religion remains in large part indecipherable." [20]

c. *Original monotheism (Wilhelm Schmidt).*

While the pre-animistic and animistic theories of the origin of religion clearly suggest an evolutionary concept of man's religious development, the idea of original monotheism proceeds the opposite way. Though already advanced by critics of Tylor, such as the Scottish novelist Andrew Lang in his book *The Making of Religion* (1898),[21] the thesis of original monotheism gained its systematic form through the monumental work of Wilhelm Schmidt *(Der Ursprung der Gottesidee).*[22] Wilhelm Schmidt claimed the belief in an all-powerful highest being stood at the beginning of all religious development. Through a process of degeneration this belief was lost and man developed a mythology with many gods and spirits. Schmidt argues that this development was necessitated by the increasing specialization of man through which he needed special gods for his special enterprises. Finally Jesus Christ taught man again to believe in the heavenly father. Wilhelm Schmidt also claims that the belief in this highest god can still be traced in primitive religion. Australian aborigines, African bushmen, as well as Mongols and many other tribes believe in a highest god.

Though Schmidt's theory sounds convincing, the notion of such a highest being, undoubtedly present among most primitives, is often very vague. Many times the high god receives no special cultic attention, in contrast to spirits, powers, and demonic beings. It is also very difficult to extrapolate from a present notion of such a high god to the notion of a high god in prehistoric time. Schmidt deserves high merit in confronting us with the fact that most nations have the idea of a high god which seems to exist independently of all other religious practices. But his theory concerning the origin of religion seems to be too closely patterned according to the creation and fall stories in Genesis to have more than theoretical value.[23] Furthermore the development, if we can talk about one, has also proceeded the opposite way. For instance, in the Greek religion Zeus was not originally a high god; only gradually he emerged as the leader of the Greek pantheon. We can learn from the example of the Greek pantheon that the notion of a high god does not need to conflict with the belief in the existence of other gods. While today most historians of religion reject the thesis of an original monotheism, they are free to admit that there does exist a primitive worship of a supreme being.[24]

d. It began with drugs (John M. Allegro).

The English philologist John Allegro advanced a very interesting thesis concerning the origin of religion which because of the wide attention it received should at least be mentioned here. In his books *The Sacred Mushroom and the Cross* (1970) and *The End of a Road* (1970) he claims that religion can be explained as originating from orgiastic drug and fertility cults. Yahweh, for instance, "was himself a fertility deity, whose worship by real or simulated sexual intercourse and related rituals was an original part of the cult." [25] According to Allegro, the Greek god Zeus and the Hebrew god Yahweh derive their name from a common linguistic source which he finds in ancient Sumer.[26] All the names for god, such as Zeus, Yahweh, and even Allah, mean "the sperm of heaven." Religion namely is born out of a sense of weakness in the face of a largely hostile environment. So man is looking for something beyond himself and beyond his environment, to the sky, for something which he can tap as a creative power. From the sky then comes the creative sperm (water) which impregnates the earth and makes it yield its crops. Even in the name Jesus/Joshua, Allegro finds this fertility attitude, because it means "'the semen that heals' or 'fructifies,' the god-juice that gives life." [27] Thus Christianity, like all other religious manifestations of the Near East, was derived from a fertility cult first celebrated in ancient Sumer. Allegro finds the reason for pointing to Sumer in the fact that it was there that man first started to entrust his thoughts to written words. This means for him that Sumer encompasses mankind's whole (unwritten) history of thought.

But how is this fertility religiousness related to drugs? Allegro discovers the clue in the red-capped *Amanita muscaria* or toadstool. This mushroom contains in its cap several powerful drugs which can give users effects varying between light euphoria, extreme physical violence, or display of almost supernatural strength. According to Allegro "some users have reported having the illusion of travelling vast distances over space and time, floating free of their bodies, and enjoying unaccustomed spiritual perceptiveness." [28] Allegro finds striking similarities between the effects of this holy plant, as it was called from the earliest times onward, and the prophetic experiences in the Old Testament, and even the appearance of the son of man in Revelation 1:13-16. This mushroom, with its upshooting stem and the red canopy, even seems to depict the sexual copulation. Since mushrooms grow especially well after storms, the thought naturally followed that the heavenly deity must have brought about this miraculous fertility. This means for Allegro that Israelite cult and mythology, Yahweh worship, patriarchal legends, Exodus from Egypt, and so on are without historical value. They relate directly to the old fertility-drug cults and were "historized," and a theology was made "to hang upon the actions and words of their legendary characters as real people." [29] A similar phenomenon can be observed with Christianity.[30] In Allegro's eyes "religion is part of growing up." [31] Though growing up is a painful process, Allegro observes that "if the world survives to adulthood, the new road that stretches ahead promises far greater opportunities for the fulfillment of man's spiritual potential than could any of the old religions. At least he will be able to call his world his own." [32] Thus Allegro asks for freedom from the crumbling confinements of religion.

While the judgment might be true that Allegro's hypothesis "is unlikely to cause many sleepless nights in the theological faculties," [33] in their general implications Allegro's observations deserve some attention. 1. We agree with Allegro that fertility cults do indeed play a major role in man's religions. This is true for the Canaanite Astarte cult in Israel's neighborhood as well as for the ancient mystic-orgiastic Cybele cult. Yet to reduce all religions to fertility cults overstates the point. It would have been good for Allegro not to confine his observations in Pan-Sumerian fashion to the ancient Near East. Buddhism, for instance, would be very difficult to explain on the basis of a fertility cult. 2. Man's anxiety and fear are certainly conducive to a religious apotropaic attitude. Yet, as we will see, besides anxiety and fear there are other basic characteristics of religion. 3. As we have learned from Bonhoeffer, the sentiment that religion is only a transient phenomenon on man's way to adulthood is shared by many. Weston La Barre, for instance, who is just as critical of religion as Allegro, writes:

> Old Stone Age man had to imagine magic because he was so feeble and frightened a little animal to hunt behemoth beasts, as he had to do to stay precariously alive. And Neolithic man sorely needed religions with comforting and protective cosmic parents, because there gaped so terrifying a chasm between his needs and his knowledge of the world and of himself. But today, protected by the technical accomplishments of his many brave dead fathers, can not man know and accept his nature and his limitations with equanimity, and receive with cool confidence and gladly the legacy of his manhood, without any antic self-cozening ghost dance? [34]

Yet we must ask: Is it only a lack of maturity that religiosity did not collapse as Marxists had projected long ago and as many seemingly enlightened people in the West still prophesy? Only an understanding of the basic structure of the major world religions can answer this perplexing question.

2. Basic concepts in the world of religion.

Basic concepts in the world of religion are as plentiful as the religious scene itself. There is first of all the vast variety of means through which religious activities are expressed and then there is the variety of objects toward which these exercises are directed. [35]

a. *Means and objects of religions.*

When one surveys the means of religious exercises, it becomes evident that religion is not restricted to one particular aspect of human life or human activity. Religion pertains to the totality of human existence. All of man's senses are involved in his religious activities. He goes through certain rituals in cultic devotions, he reads divine texts or words inspired by the divine. He is summoned to certain acts and responses by prophets or holy men and he encounters the religious object through special phenomena such as unusual events which he calls miracles or signs of the divine. Man can also have visions and auditions through which the divine is mediated to him. By approaching the object of religion in these various ways, man can be very sober and have faith in the validity of his experiences or he can attempt to communicate in a state of utter ecstasy, often enhanced through the use of stimulants. His approach can also be one of extreme inwardness and result in meditation and opening up for the divine descent.

These different, yet opposite, ways are all intended to lead to one goal, the understanding that one's existence is now freed from bondage and that salvation is closer than it was before. This is partly shown in the responses to the encounter with a religious object. These responses again involve the whole human existence. Often they are of symbolic nature and result in cultic acts such as sacrifice, dramatic actions, dances, songs, and music, and other audible responses, as well as taking the form of prayer and adoration. The whole ethical sphere must also be included in the religious scene and can be understood as both means and result of the approach toward the object of religion. But what is this object of man's religious activities?

Again the possibilities we encounter are plentiful. The object of man's religious activities can be thought of as a plurality of powers, such as ghosts, demons, or angels. It can be supreme powers, such as gods, or simply an impersonal god as in Platonic philosophy. Sometimes only one supreme being is made the sole object of religious activities. In most cases, however, the objects of man's religion do not coincide with the objects of his religious acts, because there seems to be a dialectic relationship between the sacred (object of man's religion) and the profane (means and object of man's religious acts).[36] In other words the objects in nature become transparent for the actual object of religion. For instance, when a stone becomes the object of cultic devotion, this stone does not cease to be a stone or a profane object, but for those to whom this stone reveals itself as sacred, "its immediate reality is transmuted into a supernatural reality." Thus the Ka 'bah in Mecca, the cultic center of Islam, is still a stone. Yet it can become the manifestation of something other than this simple meteorite. There are many other objects that can assume this "dual" character, such as mountains, trees, water, animals, stars, thunder, fertility, and even such undifferentiated objects as earth and fire. The orders of nature must also be included, such as the lunar month, the week (still referred to in the context of Easter as the Holy Week), the solar year and its main seasons, especially summer and winter. We agree with Malinowski when he says that "to a savage all is religion, that he perpetually lives in a world of mysticism and ritualism." [37]

But hearing Martin Luther saying that worship is not restricted to one or two kinds of activities, or to one or two professions, but it is part of all activities and professions,[38] we wonder if the all-inclusiveness of religion is only true for the savage. If religion really pertains to the human existence as a whole, it is almost futile to exclude any aspect from it, or to claim that through his maturation man emancipates certain aspects of his life from the religious sphere. Thus it is extremely difficult, if not futile, to define clearly the objects and the means of religious activities, especially in functioning as a disclosure of the sacred. The whole reality of man is, at least potentially, open to the disclosure of the object of religious devotion and similarly it is being used as a means to approach or to respond to the object of religious devotion.[39] This all-inclusiveness of religion is especially well expressed in the notion of one supreme God.

b. *The one supreme God.*

The discovery that most religions contain the idea of one God, or to put it in more neutral terms, of one supreme being, came as quite a surprise to many interested in man's religions. The notion of a high god, if it would prove to be an integral part of primitive religion, would shatter the idea of a gradual evolution from animism to polydemonism, polytheism, and finally to monotheism. Of course, one can always argue that the concept of a high god is the result of missionary teaching, since the missionaries came in contact with primitive tribes and conveyed this prevailing concept.[40] However, Father Wilhelm Schmidt adduced so much evidence proving that the belief in a high god is so universal among all the peoples of the simplest cultures, that it can no longer be discarded as an echo of missionary teaching or as an irrelevant fragment of mythology. Even the idea, at one time proposed, that this highest being is a *Deus otiosus,* a god who originally created the world and who is regarded by man as its creator but who then withdrew and no longer cares about his world, is difficult to maintain.[41] On the contrary, often this highest being is believed to have instituted the ceremonies of worship or is the object of worship and even of sacrifice. It is also remarkable that outside the prescribed rites the individual spontaneously turns to the high god when in trouble or when his mind is uplifted to the one who enjoys his awe and his trust.

Often the high gods are regarded as culture heroes, as all-fathers, or as creators. This main quality enables them to give answer to the question about origin and cause, and distinguishes them from spirits, souls, and gods. Naturally they are placed in and identified with such prominent localities as sun, moon, or thunder. But Söderblom asserts that they are not derived from nature or from human life and that they constitute a "presentiment of the Creator." [42] Yet we wonder if such an evaluation can be justified? We have seen in Wilhelm Schmidt's thesis of an original monotheism that Judeo-Christian faith served for him as the glasses through which he perceived and evaluated the world of religion. We are far from standing on neutral ground ourselves knowing that even the vantage point of a dispassionate spectator shows a certain engagement. However, we realize that some observations connect the idea of a highest being much closer with human nature.

Pettazzoni, for instance, maintains that the notion of a supreme being springs from man's existential needs.[43] Similar to Söderblom, Pettazzoni rejects the idea that the phenomenology of the supreme being is exhausted by the alternatives of a supreme being who is the creator of the world and therefore a candidate for gradual inactivity, and a supreme being who is omnipresent and omniscient with the explicit vocation to interventionism.[44] Though many supreme beings, such as the Roman Jupiter or the Greek Zeus, are celestial beings, the notion of a supreme being does not just lead to the concept of a celestial being. "For many peoples the Supreme Being is not the heavenly Father, but the Mother Earth." The supreme being can be associated with either the sky or the earth. Pettazzoni asserts: "Behind the Mother Earth there is a long tradition of agricultural matriarchal civilization. The Heavenly Father is the Supreme Being typical of the nomads who live on the products of their herds; the herds live on the pastures, and these in their turn depend on rain from the sky." In more remote times, prior to agriculture and the breeding of livestock, Pettazzoni surmises, the supreme being was the Lord of the animals and the success of the hunt depended upon him. Therefore he concludes that the notion of the supreme being is always connected with that which is vital to human existence. Existential anxiety about daily living is "the common root in the structure of the Supreme Being, but this structure is historically expressed in different forms: the Lord of animals, the Mother Earth, the Heavenly Father." [45]

Though we agree with Pettazzoni's existential emphasis, we doubt that the historic progression implied in his argument can be verified. Why, for instance, did the Israelites not abandon their "sky God" Yahweh, and adopt the earth or fertility god Baal when they abandoned their nomadic existence and settled down in an agricultural setting? Though transition from the Lord of animals to a sky god and to an earth god may have some merit, there does not seem to be a necessity for a people to abandon one concept of a highest being in favor of a different one when they attain a "higher" cultural level.

As does Pettazzoni, Geo Widengren emphasizes the primal notion of a highest being which determines human destiny and is beyond bad and good. He even regards this idea of a highest being as an original feature in man's concept of god. [46] Widengren demonstrates that the belief in one god as the creator and Lord of our existence is accepted in most religions whether they originated in Australia, Africa, America, Asia, or in Europe. Since primitive religions are still widespread in Africa, we need not wonder that Widengren finds his main proof for the highest being in African religions. [47] He is not as narrow as Pettazzoni in his description of the supreme being in confining his relevance mainly to the creation of the world and to the provision of food. Though god gives rain and provides or withholds fertility, Widengren sees in him also the Lord over life and death and the one who gives well-being or who sends sickness. [48] Occasionally he is even regarded as the judge of man's doings. Thus this highest being, as the Lord over life and fertility, determines in decisive ways the existence of society and of the individual.

If the high god has such all-encompassing function the question almost necessarily arises of the manner in which the multitude of other gods and powers are related to him. Widengren offers a very plausible explanation in connecting the different qualities and functions that these other powers and deities enjoy with their origin. There is first of all a group of deities that result from a specialization or absorption process of the high god. [49] Often the high god is attributed with specialized adjectives, such as Jupiter with lightning. However, gradually this adjective may gain such momentum that it becomes an independent god, while the god originally associated with this adjective becomes suppressed in this context. Often the place of adoration can also become a second name for a high god, such as Zeus Elymnios, which means Zeus who is worshiped on the mountain Elymnion. Sometimes other gods who have been worshiped for a long time, perhaps even former high gods, lose in power and are gradually regarded as followers of the new emerging high god. For instance, in Greek religion Hades, a god of the underworld, is introduced as a brother of Zeus. Yet Homer can call Hades the "underground Zeus," [50] thereby indicating that Zeus is the supreme god.

A second group of gods is clearly associated with nature, such as gods of the earth, mountains, rivers, trees, and springs.[51] With extreme caution Widengren suggests that they could be understood as derivatives of a pantheistically conceived high god. But the belief in a pantheistic high god presupposes a great deal of abstraction at an early stage of primitive man. Hence, contrary to Widengren's suggestion, it might be more conclusive simply to refer here to man's experience of, and dependence upon, nature and to understand these gods of nature as expressions of man's fear of powers against whom he is relatively helpless.

Finally, Widengren mentions a group of gods who function as mediators between man and the highest god. Here is the place of the culture hero, as for instance Prometheus in the Greek religion.[52] Prometheus' evaluation, however, oscillates between Hesiod's description of a bringer of civilization and woe, and Aeschylus' insight that he prevents the threatening destruction of mankind, decreed by Zeus, and enabling mankind to survive, he introduces all the arts and sciences. This shows that the cultural hero can either be a trickster or a salvation-bringing mediator. In both cases man understands himself at the mercy of powers higher than himself.

Regardless of the form in which it may appear, religion always seems to imply the belief in a supreme god. That this belief has at its ultimate concern the destiny of man and to a lesser degree that of all beings between god and man is a fact not yet sufficiently explained. We might not be far off in regarding this belief as a primordial notion of man.

c. *Holiness or insanity?*

Considering the attributes conferred upon the one supreme god, it becomes clear that such a being cannot be approached in a casual way. Consequently Rudolf Otto in his classic *The Idea of the Holy* has pointed out that holiness is a basic experience of all religion. As a creature man feels himself dependent and recognizing his dependence he is overwhelmed by his own nothingness in contrast to that which is supreme above all creatureliness.[53] The feeling of dependence and of being creature ensues from an experience of the numinous. Where the presence of the numinous is not felt, there can be no feeling of dependence and creatureliness. Being confronted with the numinous, man experiences his own nothingness and begins to shudder.[54] This awe-inspiring confrontation is not just a negative experience, because man also senses the majesty and power with which he is confronted. Man realizes his own impotence and nothingness by the haunting presence of a "super power." This power is not like a threatening object; it contains energy, will, and movement. Otto shows that the dynamic of the holy can be encountered on the level of the demonic as well as on the level of the "living" god.[55] Understandably this power could easily be perceived as something threatening. But Otto emphasizes that it contains a polarity between the awe-inspiring and fascinating. The numinous does not only put man in his own creaturely place; it also allures and fascinates him.[56] In other words, man cannot escape from it.

Many Old Testament passages can be quoted to illustrate holiness as a basic concept of religion. For instance, on the flight from his brother, Jacob has the dream of an encounter with angels and with Yahweh himself. When he awakens, he reacts in typical religious fashion: "He was afraid, and said, 'How awesome is this place! This is none other than the house of God, and this is the gate of heaven.'" (Gen. 28:17). But admitting his awe and recognizing Yahweh's superior power is not the full story. Jacob does not simply run away in fear as someone might run away from a threatening enemy. He is drawn back to this place, erects a stone and pours oil on it. In other words, the experience of awe drives him to recognize the superior power in a cultic act. We could also cite Moses' encounter with the burning bush. When Moses discovers the bush, he is fascinated by the unusual phenomenon of a burning bush that does not burn up. But right away Yahweh puts him in his place and demands that Moses show respect to his majesty by taking off his shoes, for the ground on which he stands is holy (Ex. 3:5).

These examples demonstrate that it would be a gross misunderstanding to follow the Latin proverb *timor fecit deos* (fear created gods) and conclude that man creates gods as an expression of the existential fear or anxiety that dwells in him. The opposite is true. Because man has the experience of holiness as something awe-inspiring and fear-causing, he feels himself existentially insecure. His basic anxiety always presupposes outside himself a cause of this anxiety. For instance, Isaiah did not feel a certain anxiety or fear and then concluded that he had better follow Yahweh, but because he sensed that Yahweh had called him he expressed his basic existential inadequacy (Isa. 6:5). Thus a religious man is not someone who has certain existential deficiencies, but someone to whom something is holy.[57] This sentiment seems also to be substantiated by psychology.

Carl Gustav Jung, for instance, tells us that the essential processes of religious life take place not in the spirit, in feelings, or in reason, but in the unconscious. This unconscious or psychic realm of man, however, is far removed from all human volition and influence.[58] Jung fully agrees with Otto in saying that the numinous is "a dynamic existence or effect, not caused by an arbitrary act of will. On the contrary, it seizes and controls the human subject, which is always rather its victim than its creator. The numinosum is an involuntary condition of the subject, whatever its cause may be." [59] In the following Jung it seems impossible to explain the experience of the numinous as a figment of the human mind or as a projection of man's (known) desires.

William James in his Gifford Lectures, *The Varieties of Religious Experience* (1901/02), had proceeded already before Jung to claim that "whatever it may be on its *farther* side, the 'more' with which in religious experience we feel ourselves connected is on its *hither* side the subconscious continuation of our conscious life." [60] Since the subconscious is understood by James as intermediating between nature and the "higher region," he feels that the subconscious therefore can be analyzed by the scientist as well as safeguarded by the theologian who claims that the religious man is moved by an external power. Such external power, however, is not disjunctive with the visible world, since "the visible world is part of a more spiritual universe from which it draws its chief significance." James suggests that union or harmonious relation with that higher universe is our true end. The awe-inspiring and fear-causing numinous therefore seems to witness to both our sense of belonging to a higher union that exceeds the visible world and our sense of alienation from that "higher world." However, the latter, namely alienation, seemed to be underplayed by the pragmatic optimism of James. Otherwise he could have hardly stated that each religious attitude in its diversity is but a "syllable in human nature's total message," it takes the whole of us to spell out the meaning of religion completely.[61] In contrast to the positive connection between the human psyche and religion as expressed by Carl Gustav Jung and William James, we must also remember that another prominent representative of psychoanalysis, Sigmund Freud, attacked religion rather vehemently.

According to Freud religion is largely projection and "a large portion of the mythological conception of the world which reaches far into the most modern religions, *is nothing but psychology projected to the outer world.*" [62] The unclear inner perceptions of man's own psychic apparatus incite to illusionary thinking, being then projected into the world around us, and characteristically also into the future and into the beyond. Immortality, vengeance and the whole hereafter are labeled by Freud as projections of our psychic interior and as psychomythology.[63] Freud suggests that myths could very likely be regarded as distorted vestiges of wish-phantasies of whole nations and as age-long dreams of mankind in its infancy stage.[64] Freud claims that myths did not originate in heaven but on earth and were in turn projected into heaven.[65] Even the gods are largely a creation of man. Man ascribed to them everything that seemed unreachable for him or that he felt was forbidden to him. He projected into them his own human characteristics with all their evil consequences.[66] Psychologically speaking, the belief in a personal God is according to Freud ultimately nothing but the belief in an elevated father image and this desire for the father leads to religion. Hence Freud surmises that the yearning for a father can be regarded as an essential root of all religion.[67] Underlying this idea is the thesis that the primal tribe murdered the father.[68] The murder satisfied the hostility feelings of his sons against the father's patriarchal domination. However, when these feelings faded away, a void was experienced and a yearning for the father emerged. This led to the creation of gods as a rejuvenation of the father ideal and also to a new kind of patriarchal community. The father is now thought of as the creator god who will protect the tribe and raise ethical demands.[69] Of course, Freud knows that this theory cannot account for the existence of mother goddesses.[70] But this does not prevent Freud from arriving at the devastating conclusion:

While individual religions struggle with each other as to which one possesses the truth, we are convinced that the truth question of religion can be neglected completely. Religion is an attempt to master the world of senses, in which we find ourselves, by means of a wishful world which we have developed in ourselves due to biological and psychological necessities. But it cannot do the job. Its doctrines bear the imprint of the times in which they originated, the ignorant infancy stage of mankind. Its consolations do not deserve trust. Experience tells us: the world is not a children's playground. The ethical demands which religion attempts to emphasize demand a different foundation, because they are indispensable for human society, and it is dangerous to connect obedience to them with religious faith. If one wants to classify religion in the evolutionary process of mankind, then it appears to be of no permanent acquisition, but a counterpart of neurosis which individual civilized men have to go through on their way from infancy stage to maturity.[71]

Freud's theory resembles somewhat Feuerbach's idea that religion is a projection of man's desires, and it is easy to understand that it engendered considerable discussion.[72] Unlike Feuerbach, however, Freud claimed that this projection originated from the sickly mind of emerging mankind and could be traced back to some rather simple motifs, such as the murder of the ancestoral father, the Oedipus complex, and totemism as the beginning of human culture. Scholars in the history of religion like Wilhelm Schmidt found it easy to prove that these theories could not be made to agree with the material adduced by ethnology.[73] But Freud's argument does not stand or fall with ethnological arguments. The argument that religion is a projection, a projection of the psychic realm of man into the outer world cannot be proved or disproved on strictly empirical grounds.[74] Here we touch the weak point in Freud's approach, because Freud thought that he had established such proof.

However, Freud's approach is not as negative towards religion as it seems at the first glance. Freud's investigation shows us first that there is a definite analogy between religious and pathological phenomena, perhaps indicating a certain interdependence between these phenomena. But we question Freud's assumption that this discovery has thereby unearthed the origin of all religious phenomena.[75] Secondly, Freud has shown, for instance in his treatise

on the totem animal, that symbols can point out the birth of idols.
But again, is this all? Can psychoanalysis prove that this is all
that there is to symbols? Hardly. Symbols are not just fantasies that
should be overcome and abolished. They also give rise to thought;
thought about the ultimate meaning of life.[76] This brings us to
the final, critical point. In his failure to recognize the ambiguity
contained in that which he analyzes, religion becomes for him all
projection, all desire, and all wrong.[77] However, historians since
Wilhelm Dilthey have cautioned us that understanding means living with that which is to be understood. In his analyses of the
human psyche Freud is too much the "objective" observer to tolerate ambiguity. While attempting to show us how reality really
is, he distorts it and presents us only part of it. Yet in so doing
he forces us to distinguish between sickness and saintliness, and
between idol and symbol. In other words, he unintentionally tells
us that even the holiness of God does not prevent man from constructing and using Him according to his own desires. This can be
especially observed with the concepts of mana and tabu which
are also central to the idea of holiness.

d. *Mana, magic, and tabu.*

Mana is a word in the Melanesian languages, perhaps imported
from Polynesia, and denotes a supernatural invisible power that
usually rests in a strong man, such as a chief or a medicine man,
and which can also be imparted to animals, plants, and stones.[78]
The belief in a power inherent in animated and inanimated objects, which can be transferred to other men and other objects, is
characteristic of most religions. The Old Testament provides us
with many examples of the concept of mana. However, there mana
usually does not rest in a strong man, but is absorbed in God's
holiness. For instance, the Old Testament tells us that Yahweh
commanded the Israelites to use the ashes of the red cow for a
cultic cleansing ritual (Num. 19:9). The idea that Yahweh's spirit
can be imparted to Moses and then in turn to other men points
in a similar direction. Yet the understanding that he can again
withdraw his empowering spirit, indicates that in the Israelite religion this mana or power is never thought of as existing independently from Yahweh. The example of King Manasseh (2 Chron.
33:6), however, reminds us that the Israelites did not always follow
this thinking. More than once were they tempted to make use of
this power in a way independent of Yahweh's will. Then they acted

in analogy to magic practices, common to most religions, especially on a primitive level.

Magic betrays the belief in mysterious powers that when tapped in their proper way bring inevitable and predictable results. Yet magic is not born out of an abstract conception of universal powers and subsequently applied to concrete cases.[79] Each type of magic originated in its own situation and represents the spontaneous re-action of man to a particular situation. Magic is a ready-made ritual act and belief with a definite mental and practical technique which serves to bridge the dangerous gaps in important pursuits or critical situations.[80] Since it shows man's anxiety and is at the same time a means to overcome it, magic bears a very close affinity to re-ligion. Even modern man who is convinced of a rational mastery of his own existence and who discards both "primitive supersti-tion" and religious ties, still maintains his magical inclination. Amulets, talismans, and mascots are almost omnipresent, in the form of charms they dangle from bracelets, from rearview mirrors, and are worn around the neck by athletes and housewives alike. They are no longer symbols of transcendent powers but have be-come idols of secular man.[81]

The idea of tabu is related to the concepts of mana and magic and is associated with the idea of holiness. The term *tabu* perhaps comes from the Polynesian *tapu* meaning to mark exceedingly or to mark out as forbidden. It was first introduced into the English by Captain Cook who noticed its use at the Tonga Islands in 1777. Again we find many analogies to the idea of tabu in the Judeo-Christian religion. Most well-known to us are the Old Testament laws concerning clean and unclean which unmistakably imply the tabu concept. But again these *taharoth* laws are closely related to Yahweh, as the one who decreed certain things as clean and others as unclean. If people transgress these laws they are excluded from the community and from communion with Yahweh until purifica-tion is obtained (Lev. 5:2ff.). In most religions tabus are also concerned with the dead and their places of rest, with women in their menstrual flow, in the pregnancy state, and in childbed; often bride and groom are tabu until the wedding day, and certain places, such as a temple, or certain days, for instance festivals or the new moon day, are covered by tabu rules. In this manner tabu can serve to set aside certain objects that are not accessible for average man or it can simply warn people about negative influ-ences from demons and spirits, as in the case of the deceased. In other words, tabu is used to protect man's life against possible danger arising from that which is experienced as beyond man's capability. Most peoples also have some kind of buffer zone in the institution of divine kingship. While ordinary man thereby escapes the danger of coming into too close contact with these powers beyond his control, he is still able to have access to them through their royal representations.

e. *The divine kingship.*

The idea of the sacred kingship gained very dubious fame in Old Testament studies, especially through its most prominent advocates, Sigmund Mowinckel and Ivan Engnell. They attempted to understand the whole Israelite religion as having originated from one spiritual center which they saw located in the enthronement festival of Yahweh.[82] For example Engnell suggested that the idea of the divine kingship was prevalent throughout the ancient Near East. Therefore, the Israelite understanding of Passover, the Feast of Booths, the belief in the resurrection, messianism, and even essential features of the idea of religion were derived from this pattern. But it seems that the history of the Israelite religion is more complicated and many-faceted than Engnell suggested.

Many scholars even deny that a festival of the enthronement of Yahweh ever existed. Georg Fohrer, for instance, points out that an identification of God and king, which such a festival presupposes, is an unacceptable thought for Israel.[83] On the other hand we read in the Mishnah Sanhedrin that none is allowed to ride the king's horse, "and none may sit on his throne and none may make use of his sceptre. None may see him when his hair is being cut or when he is naked, or when he is in the bath-house." [84] These rules do not just express due respect for the kingly authority. Though in Israelite thinking the king is nothing apart from his election and sustenance by Yahweh, these rules make us aware that even for Israel the king is not just a human figure.

The exceptional role of the king is much more emphasized in other cultures. There the king mostly enjoys a fairly independent position and is often regarded as divine by his own office or by descent.[85] For instance, until 1945 the Japanese Emperor was considered as son of the sun and actual god, on whom the welfare of the state depended. Until the mid 19th century the Japanese Emperor was not even allowed to leave his palace, since someone might see him and thereby desecrate his holiness. Later, when he was allowed to leave his palace, people had to turn their backs to him for the same reason. Very interesting also is a custom in ancient Rome where the king was not allowed to mingle with other people or touch the ground with his feet, for fear that he would make the people or the ground he touched sacred; he had to be carried in a sedan-chair. The idea that the king is not permitted to touch the ground with his feet is also very wide-spread among African tribes. Often the tribal chief can only walk as far as a carpet or an animal skin extends. Traces of this practice can be found in the famous red carpet treatment for foreign dignitaries and, in a more "sacred" fashion, in the custom that the Pope is carried to his mass audiences, that everyone has to bend the knee before him, and that his seat is always elevated above the rest of the people. We are also reminded of the idea of sacred kingship when we hear that according to English tradition the king or the queen are anointed with oil on the day of their inauguration.

The king did not just enjoy certain privileges through his divine status. Often the idea of sacred kingship could also imply dangerous aspects for the king. In ancient Mexico, for instance, the Aztec rulers had to swear during the inauguration ceremony that they would permit the sun to shine, that they would give rain to the clouds and command the earth to bear fruit. One can easily imagine the consequences for the king if nature did not meet the expectations expressed in his oath. Similarly, in certain African religions the custom is reported of disposing of the king (chief) when his physical power diminishes, since his intercessory and protective power is then believed also to be waning away.[86] Thus those who mediate the ultimate holiness are themselves subject to fear and trembling as well as engendering it in their subjects.

5.

The Mystery of Man's Religions II

(Christianity among the World Religions)

1. A religious progression?

After our review of some of the basic concepts in the world of religion, as far as the idea of God is concerned, we must now address ourselves to the question of whether it is possible to trace some kind of historic progression in the religious development of mankind. Of course, we again will limit our observations to the consciousness of God and to his self-disclosure.

a. *Primitive religions.*

When we assume primitive religion to be the first step in man's religious development, we must guard against the misunderstanding that primitive religion would belong to a certain epoch of man's past history. Though primitive religion certainly embraces the prehistoric time (ca. 600,000 to 6,000 B.C.), it is also a contemporary phenomenon in Africa, Asia, and in certain parts of America. While a clear development from primitive religion via polytheism to monotheism is difficult to assert, it is fairly safe to maintain that no religion prior to 800 to 500 B.C. was more than a tribal religion.[1] Only from that timespan on, which Karl Jaspers called the pivotal age of history, can we trace the emergence of universal religions beyond their original tribal confinements. It can hardly be mere coincidence that within these barely 300 years a Deutero-Isaiah, a Buddha, a Lao-tzu, a Zoroaster, and even a Homer and a Plato stimulated the spiritual life of mankind. It seems that during this

116

epoch modern man emerged whom we encounter today. Man must have felt a solidarity in the basic understanding of his ultimate concerns that made him break through the tribal barriers. But not everybody participated in this new movement. Not only did primitive religions survive until today, but primitive religious concepts also survived within the universal religions themselves.

It has often been claimed that no correlation is more definite and more constant than that between a given economic level of society and the nature of the supernatural beings postulated by the tribe at large and by the religious individual in particular. But we wonder whether "the presence of true deities and gods" is dependent on explicit class and caste distinctions.[2] The unsolved phenomenon of a belief in high gods or supreme beings among primitives seems to contradict the idea of a necessary correlation between a cultural level of people and the religious beliefs to which they adhere.

A predeistic state of development, at which personal gods or demons were still unknown and only the actions of sacred powers existed, expressed through the concepts of mana and tabu, and activated through totems, holy objects, and magic rites, is also difficult to assert.[3] Mana and tabu, though basic concepts in all religions, can be regarded as an attempt to master the powers surrounding man and to coordinate them to a logically ordered system which can be theoretically explained. Thus they already betray a primitive theological explanation of the world. Magic for hunting and for battles can be traced at least to the Neo-paleolithic period[4] and shows an active and systematic "use" of the powers denoted by mana and tabu. This fairly sophisticated mastery of man's destiny led Malinowski, not without justification, to regard wizards and witches as specialists who from earliest time onward handled the art of magic, while he claimed at the same time that the sphere of religion had always been accessible to everyone.[5]

We cannot escape the impression that primitive man is really not that primitive, neither in his mastery of his world nor in the perception of his destiny. Therefore it is very difficult, if not impossible, to assert an organic development common to all primitive religions. It is as equally unwarranted to affirm that religion grew specifically out of magic, as to claim that "magic very definitely preceded religion."[6] We are in a similar dilemma concerning the origin of primitive monotheism. High gods emerge in an amazing manifoldness in primitive religions as creators, cultural heroes, god-

fathers, sky gods, and father gods.[7] One might not be wrong asserting that they represent "the highest form that abstract thinking
assumed among any aboriginal people." [8] But it is unwarranted to
perceive high gods as developments of the spirits and "souls" of
animism and polydemonism, or to see in them the influence of higher religions. Animism, polydemonism, polytheism, and the manipu-
lations of magic are not threatened by the appearance of high gods
in primitive religion. There is usually no need to transform the idea
of a high god into the highest god of a polytheistic pantheon as
Radin, for instance, assumes. It seems that all the ideas of primitive religion, high god, mana, tabu, magic, animism, and polydemonism gradually lead to, and to some extent already represent, a
personal understanding of god as the governor of man's existence
and that of the world around man.

b. *Polytheism.*

Primitive religions very seldom develop into monotheism. The
history of Latin America, Africa, and New Guinea, where primitive
religions have rapidly been supplanted by Christian faith, shows
us that in most cases the transition came too abruptly. New religions, such as cargo cult or voodoo, emerged and Messianic pretenders with clearly polytheistic persuasion arose.[9] Polytheism
seems to offer itself as the most natural transition between primitive religion and monotheism. This transition appears to coincide
with man's changing cultural achievements. When man ventured
from his hunting and fishing stage to more diverse cultural activities, we also notice a change from a more dynamistic and demon-
istic understanding of transcendent powers to a more anthropomorphic one. Man now apparently began to distinguish more clearly between the area of the power's responsibility and the power
itself. In Greek religion, in Germanic religion, and to some extent
even in the Israelite religion, for instance, we detect a polydemo-
nistic background with a plurality of object-residing powers and
a subsequent emergence of more detached powers. As soon as the
powers were detached enough from the traditional empowered
objects, they were clothed in anthropomorphic gowns. In Greek
antiquity we hear Xenophanes say that man pictures his gods according to his own likeness and consequently he reprimands Homer
and Hesiod for patterning the gods too much according to weak-
nesses of man.[10]

The emergence of the godheads' distinct and anthropomorphic

features went hand in hand with their increasing specialization. This can best be observed in Roman religion where many gods were characterized by special adjectives, such as Jupiter, the thrower of thunder, or Fortuna, the goddess of luck. Gods assume more and more a functional role,[11] similar to the saints in Roman Catholicism, where the function of one saint can even differ from one region to another. Often the multitude of gods was believed to operate under one godhead, such as the Greek Olympic gods under Zeus, or the later Roman gods under Jupiter, the god of the Emperor. Sometimes the cooperation of this polytheistic high god with specialized gods appears to resemble a monarchic or a city type of government.

As we can gather from the fate of Socrates and that of the early Christians this kind of "monotheistic" polytheism was highly exclusive. If one doubted or rejected the peculiarity of this pantheon venerated by a certain group of people, they often counteracted through persecution or even capital punishment. This shows us that polytheism already portrayed the factor of exclusiveness.[12] However, this did not introduce a static feature into polytheistic religions. Characteristics of one god could easily be merged with those of another god and even new gods could be introduced. The Roman Jupiter, for instance, could be identified with the Greek Zeus, or the Roman Minerva with the Greek Athena, and the Persian fertility goddess Magna Mater Cybele could make its successful debut on the religious scene of imperial Rome.

Yet when we come closer to our own time, polytheism does no longer seem to be compatible with the enterprising spirit of modern man. It might be tempting to explain the origin of monotheism by pointing to "founders" of world religions, such as Moses, Buddha, Jesus, Mohammed, and Zoroaster, and claim that they affirmed the power of one god, who does not tolerate any other gods besides him, so passionately that monotheism emerged. But then we must also remember the contrary evidence of Homer and Hesiod, who decisively formed Greek polytheism, and not a monotheistic religion. Although monotheism always presupposes polytheism, the latter does not always evolve into the former. For instance, since the time of Moses Israel's religion was highly monotheistic, while the neighbors of Israel, evidently untouched by this monotheism, continued to favor their polytheism.

When we consider the cultural and technological drive exhibited by those nations most clearly influenced by monotheism, we wonder whether we can deny that we are here confronted with a progress of mankind caused by spiritual factors. Admittedly, Greek and Roman polytheism led to a very high cultural level too. But the intrinsic mood demonstrated by Greek and Roman philosophy was not one of optimism, but of pessimism. Again we must refer to Xenophanes who had already discovered that the Greek gods looked much like deified men and that they themselves were subjected to the destiny of the world.[13] Stoic heroism best describes the earth-denying yet earth-bound fate of man. The only continuity is provided by the eternal recurrence of the same, by the ever-moving celestial spheres. Even Buddhism, though culturally on a high level, and, as we will see, to some extent bearing distinctly monotheistic features, does not seem to provide a stimulus for a positive conquest of the world. It advocates as one of its main goals the negation of all craving for life, and breaking out of the fatal ever-turning wheel of life with its recurrent stages of birth, death, and reincarnation. That Buddhist Japan, though open to all Western ways of thinking, still has a suicide rate unparalleled in any Western nation might also be partly attributed to this highly pessimistic and world-negating attitude. Any appreciation of life would only contradict the dominant cyclical understanding of time. Judeo-Christian faith, however, and in a similar way Zoroastrianism and Islam are world-affirming and basically future oriented. This is largely due to their monotheistic character.

c. Monotheism.

In monotheism for the first time the plurality of holy powers was conceived of as being more and more absorbed by only one god. This process opened the possibility of a thoroughgoing desacralization of the world. Once the world is no longer experienced as sacred, man can dare to subdue the earth and all the powers contained therein. Of course, the activity of the one god, who is retained, is greatly expanded and he is understood as the divine originator and grantor of all facets of life. This means that the god who provides this life is also the one who supervises its present course and who establishes its final goal. Since this god is no longer equated with anything bound to change, he is exempted from the ongoing transitoriness of history and can sovereignly decree its movement toward the goal envisioned by him. History is now freed from cyclic pessimism and endowed with divinely sanctioned linear progression. In other words, monotheism enables history to have a definite starting point, a definite course, and a definite goal. But monotheism need not necessarily lead to an upward slanting progression in which man plays a dominant role. If the one god assumes the position of a "primordial tyrant" who determines each facet of human life and who refuses to endow human activities with responsible freedom, monotheism can also lead to human passivity. This inherent danger of monotheism is best depicted in two basic strands of monotheism, characterized through salvation by law and salvation by devotion.

Salvation by law: The classic example of a monotheistic religion characterized through salvation by law is Islam. The word Islam, meaning "surrender to God's will," shows in a nutshell the prevailing attitude in this religion, submission to God's will and exact fulfillment of his laws. The whole life of the Muslim is determined by the *Shari'a* (the way) or the body of regulations which makes up the Islamic religious law. It contains all the prescriptions of Allah which pertain to man's actions, and it stands so high in rank that it has been said that Allah did not reveal himself but only his law.[14] Early Islam did not even distinguish between law and religion and therefore it is not theology which is dominant in Islamic scholarship but the study and explication of the law.[15] Since all aspects of life fall under the religious sphere, the *Shari'a* contains prescriptions concerning religious and cultic duties as well as juridical and political rules. All actions are divided into five categories:[16] obligatory, recommended, indifferent, undesirable, and forbidden. For instance: it is obligatory to wash oneself before prayer; it is recommended to start with the right side; it is indifferent whether warm or cold water is used; and it is forbidden that someone touches the water beforehand. Furthermore, the actions are evaluated according to their validity or invalidity. Of course, most of these laws are already contained in the *Qur'an* (meaning "recital"), the sacred book of Islam.

There are two main types of texts in the *Qur'an,* those which are clear and definite and those which could have more than one meaning. The texts which are clear and definite are concerned with basic beliefs, such as belief in Allah and the last day. They also contain information concerning the origin of the law and in regard to them there is no freedom of interpretation. Then there are the texts which could have more than one meaning. They "are concerned with subsidiary aspects of Islam, but not [with] its fundamentals, and have given rise to a plurality of Muslim theories and attitudes which are more or less personal points of view and are far from being obligatory." [17] Thus the *Qur'an* in the foundation of faith and the code of legislation. Since there are items contained in the *Qur'an* that can have more than one meaning we also have to consider the *Sunnah* or custom, which is the legislation given by Mohammed on matters not specifically detailed in the *Qur'an*, and traditions based on the actions and utterances of the Prophet as a human being.[18] The value of the *Sunnah* lies in the fact that it expounds specific aspects of the general principles of the *Qur'an*, either by example of action or by adding certain ceremonies not expressly described in the *Qur'an*. Of course, not everything that is contained in the *Hadith*, the tradition that embodies the *Sunnah* of the Prophet, actually goes back to Mohammed. Often its various strands were simply developed to support the traditions of certain groups within Muslim faith. But through critical studies of the *Hadith* one is still able to establish and to maintain the historical continuity between the time of Mohammed and the present by concluding what the Prophet might have said, had he been asked[19] Finally there is also discretion employed in the communal consultations concerning issues not specifically covered in the *Qur'an* and the *Sunnah*, and there is the private discretion of the individual by which decisions are reached by independent thinking. Both kinds of discretions are not binding for anyone except the individual(s) who use(s) them.[20]

Though the immense legal codes contained in the *Shari'a* are based on the idea that Allah speaks and commands while man submits and obeys, the obedience is not simply a passive or servile one. Muslim theologians assert that "Muslims conceive of their religion as a community which says 'Yes' to God and His world; and the joyful performance of the Law, in most areas of the Islamic world, is looked on as a positive religious value." [21] But when we consider the creed, the first of the five pillars of Islam (the other pillars being daily prayers, fasting, giving of alms, and pilgrimage), which is always contained in the first section of the law, we find there not only confession of Allah, of the last day, and of the resurrection, but also of Allah's predetermining will.[22] This is a clear indication in which way the undecidedness between free will and determination contained in the *Qur'an* itself has traditionally been resolved.[23] Allah is the determining factor of all facets of life. Hence it is impossible to render anything in the world as profane, and the important Judeo-Christian distinctions between church and state or ecclesiastical and worldly are missing in Muslim vocabulary.[24]

One way of breaking out of this almost demonic dominance of Allah over human life was found in Sufism. Having its roots in the more mystic strands of the *Qur'an,* this mystic and ecstatic movement gained supreme importance from the end of the ninth century onward in moulding the attitude toward life in the individual Muslim.[25] To some extent it symbolizes the victory of common man over the mighty of this earth and over the learned professors and scholars, representatives of the all-embracing law. Under Sufism common man managed to live in a world of ideas and emotions of his own construction, and had the satisfaction of seeing the powerful and the learned bow before the uncouth, saintly vagabond and beggar. Its mysticism, to some extent influenced by Christian monasticism, was largely an escape valve and provided no actual stimulus for progressive mastery of the world. Traditional Muslim education did not provide much hope either for a creative intellectual movement. It consisted mainly of memorizing prescribed texts and studying the same material generation after generation.[26] While we must acknowledge the important Islamic achievements in the area of philosophy, mathematics, chemistry, and medicine,[27] we wonder to what degree the "progress" exhibited in these achievements is analogous to the mystic escapism demonstrated in Sufism. Our suspicion is nourished when we remember that even a philosopher such as Averroes, who made a tremendous impact on Christian theology, was forced to develop a system of twofold truth to show at least outward conformity to Islamic traditionalism.[28]

In the last few centuries, however, there has been a renewed emphasis on the progressive dynamism of the *Qur'an* teachings. Muhammad Ibn Abd al-Wahhab, for instance, returned to the *Qur'an* and the traditions of early Islam while revolting against the stifling results of a strict application of the *Shari'a.* The movement engendered by him and known as Wahhabism, has been most influential in the Arab countries and in India during the last two centuries in abolishing veneration of saints and of their tombs and restoring a free interpretation of the tradition.

Muhammad Ikbal (1876-1938), the spiritual father of Pakistan, must be mentioned here too.[29] Being exposed to Western education in England and Germany, he recognized that dynamic Islamic thinking had been repressed for centuries by a strict dogmatism and covered over by pantheistic mysticism. Ikbal, in turn, advanced the idea that the *Qur'an* is a doctrine destined to further and higher development. Thus he understands man as God's administrator in this world who is compelled to develop his personality in steady combat with the powers of evil and who will finally attain perfect manhood. Of course, we notice that this is not exactly *Qur'an* teaching. It contains a good sense of Western idealistic philosophy and also shows that Nietzsche's concept of the superman was not foreign to Ikbal. The question that only history can answer is, whether Islam contains within itself enough freedom and drive to break through its intrinsic legalism and to make transition from a religion of salvation by law to a religion of salvation by invitation. Perhaps the fact that their progressive spiritual leaders must be first exposed to Western Judeo-Christian tradition before they discover a progressive spirit within Islam, serves as a partial answer.[30] Yet we should not forget that Islam already absorbed a good measure of this tradition as a result of Mohammed's encounter with peculiar forms of Judeo-Christian faith.

Zoroastrianism may serve as another interesting example of a religion characterized by salvation through law. Unlike Islam it is not dependent on Judeo-Christian influence, but, going back to the priest and prophet Zarathustra (Zoroaster according to the Greek transcription), it served as a major stimulus for developments in both Judeo-Christian faith and Islam. Zoroaster apparently lived in Eastern Iran, but the dates of his life are uncertain. While Greek writers date him 6,000 years before Plato, the Parsees themselves, as the followers of Zoroastrianism are called, date him 258 years prior to Alexander the Great. In the opinion of most scholars this later date holds more truth, and he probably lived in the sixth century before Christ.[31] In the center of his proclamation was the god Ahura Mazda or Ormuzd. He was the creator of heaven and earth, without image, and the lawgiver of the whole cosmos. Loyalty to Ahura Mazda excluded the worship of any other old Iranian gods. This strict monotheism resembles that of the Israelite religion. However, Zoroaster emphasizes the unsurmountable opposition between almighty Ahura Mazda and Angra Mainyu, or Ahriman, the manifestation of everything evil. This cleavage seems to result in a definite dualism of ethical and metaphysical nature, though Zoroaster deliberately refrains from attributing both spirits, Ahura Mazda and Angra Mainyu, to the same source or origin. Once these "gods" made their initial ethical choice they separated themselves and the world into a sphere of light and a sphere of darkness.[32] The incompatibility of both gods is for Zarathustra the basis for his ethical demands. Although the ethical demands remain mostly in the realm of social ethics, i.e. fight against evil, even against mistreatment of cattle, the actual goal of ethical realization lies in the eschaton. There will be a pleasant dwelling in green pastures for those people, including peasants and herdsmen, who adhered to the good.[33]

Characteristic for Zoroaster's doctrine is a two-fold outcome of history: an eternity of bliss and an eternity of woe allotted respectively to good and evil men in another life beyond the grave. After death the soul of the deceased has to cross the Chinvat bridge which stretches over hell, an abyss of molten metal and fire. For the good the bridge grows broader and broader for easier transit and on the other side follows ascent into heaven where the pious soul will live in eternal joy in paradise. But for the wicked the bridge grows narrower until it is like the blade of a razor and the soul falls into the abyss of hell, where there will be eternal torment and suffering. There is also some kind of intermediate state for those whose good and bad deeds are in strict balance.

Zoroastrian religion also knows of a judgment and completion of the whole world. Three thousand years after Zarathustra the Saoshyant or savior will come and bring the present world to its end. The dead will be resurrected, and both wicked and good will have to pass through a flood of molten metal. The good will pass without harm and enter the new world. The wicked will either be purified or burned, and the evil spirits will be burned. After this worldwide purification in the last days of the present crisis, Ahura Mazda's sovereignty will be complete, and together with him the good will enjoy a new heaven and a new earth. Of course, not all ideas in the Iranian religion go back to Zoroaster. Some are later developments, but most have their roots in his teachings. Similarly to Islam, Zoroastrianism betrays in its eschatological outlook a confident optimism. The good will ultimately prevail and the bad will be destroyed or at least purified.[34] Zoroaster's ethics demand from its adherents a constant battle against the evil and the evildoers.

Although many of Zoroaster's eschatological ideas evidently served as a catalyst for the emerging Judeo-Christian doctrine of an afterlife, we must bear in mind that Zoroastrianism was neither strictly dualistic nor strictly monotheistic. With regard to this life the dualistic traits in Zoroastrianism prevail, leading to a basically

pessimistic outlook on life, and emphasizing the continuous battle
between good and evil. With regard to the afterlife, however, the
monotheistic traits dominate and the outlook becomes optimistic,
believing in the eventual redemption of all people.

The pessimistic tendencies result in a cleavage between the world
and man and find expression in the idea of the "redeemed redeemer." The divine redeemer, descending in human form from heaven,
does not redeem the (bad) world, but only his own kind. He represents mankind and he is present in all men as the higher (divine)
element, which he leads back to heaven. Contrary to Christian
belief, this idea results in a hope for redemption *from* the body
and not *of* the body.[35] The influence of this thinking was especially
important for Gnostic thought, the competitor of early Christianity.
The actual goal of realization does not lie in this world, but in the
eschaton.[36] The Hellenistic mystery cult of Mithra, popular particularly among soldiers of the collapsing Roman Empire, though partly
dating back to a pre-Zoroastrian form of Iranian religion, also reinforces in part the mystic and world-denying tendency prevailing in
Zoroastrianism.

As aforementioned, the optimistic tendencies in Zoroastrianism
with their emphasis on salvation in the hereafter were influential
for the Judeo-Christian tradition. Yet they were not simply adopted
as a hope for a better hereafter. On the contrary, the Judeo-Christian tradition claimed that the eschatological realization can already
be anticipated proleptically in the present activities of the believers.
Thus the Judeo-Christian attitude toward life became not one of
futuristic hope, in being indifferent to the affairs of the world, but
one of the future-directed activism. This trait, however, is still
missing in Zoroastrianism.

Present day Parsees number in the neighborhood of 130,000 and
live mostly around Bombay, India. They are known for their active
world-openness, their enterprising spirit, and their interest in
schools and hospitals. Their obvious success as a minority group
might in part be due to the fact that they are closer to the Judeo-
Christian heritage, and therefore more open to Western ideas, than
the religions of the East in whose environment they live. Yet
they dearly paid for their rapid and thorough Westernization by
abandoning most of their religious tradition and substituting for
it the Western idea of progress without having an adequate spiritual basis.[37] It should also be noted here that only this small group
of Parsees survived in India, while in other countries Zoroastrianism

was wiped out by the more earth-centered Islam. Zoroastrian inability to anticipate the eschaton already proleptically in the present led to a ritualistic other worldly attitude and made it impossible for its adherents to engage actively in a progressive mastery of the world without abandoning the integrative religious basis.

Salvation by devotion: Does a monotheistic understanding of salvation by devotion leave more freedom than salvation through legalistic or ritualistic obedience to certain rules, and does it provide an incentive for a progressive mastery of the world? A brief review of its most characteristic manifestations may help us find an answer. The founder of the most widespread religion that is seeking salvation through devotion was the Indian Prince Siddharta Gautama who belonged to the tribe of the Sakyas and lived approximately between 560 and 480 B.C. in the northeast of India, an area which is today known as Nepal. The story goes that at the age of 29 he left home against the will of his parents, cut his hair and his beard, and became a monk to search for nirvana, the eternal, blissful peace. His sudden decision was caused by the discovery that all life was suffering and that it had to be extinguished by the extinction of man himself. Mara, the personification of evil, accompanied him on his journey and promised him an empire if he would desist from his plans. But Gautama did not give in. For years he wandered from place to place in search of a teacher who could guide him to attain supreme enlightenment. Since none could satisfy him, he finally decided to struggle alone. Together with other monks he practiced Yoga and asceticism and after years of meditation he came at the age of 35 to the conclusion that the right way to achieve nirvana lies midway between the extremes of worldly activity and strict asceticism. The rest of his life he spent preaching his newly discovered doctrine with often more than 500 disciples around him.

The center of Prince Gautama's or Buddha's (the enlightened one) teachings are the Four Noble Truths (of Buddhism) which he exemplified by his own life.[38] The first noble truth is the understanding that all life is suffering. Who attains this insight is already an *arhat,* a perfect saint. The second noble truth is the understanding of the cause of suffering. The craving for life which is fed by perceptions and feelings leads to suffering and to rebirth. Thus man must abolish this cause by eliminating four fundamental evils, sensual desire, desire to be, wrong beliefs, and ignorance. The third noble truth lies in the insight of how to attain cessation of suffering. Cessation of suffering, as a result of the cessation of craving for life, enables man to end the cycle of rebirth and reach nirvana. Finally, the fourth truth, the eight-fold way leading to the cessation of suffering and thereby achieving nirvana, consists of actual instructions for arriving at the goal outlined in the first three truths. It contains methods of concentration and meditation to subdue the self and to curb the craving for life. Yoga exercises, control of breathing, fasting, and mystic concentration are included here.

It is obvious for Buddhists that Buddha did not come into the world for the first time at 560 B.C. Like everyone else, he had undergone many rebirths, had experienced the world as animal, as man, and as god. "During his many rebirths, he would have shared the common fate of all that lives. A spiritual perfection like that of a Buddha cannot be the result of just one life. It must mature slowly throughout the ages." [39] This conviction shows us two characteristic teachings of Buddhism, the idea of reincarnation and the idealization of Buddha. Reincarnation was already a basic tenet in the Hindu religion out of which Gautama came. Through the *karma,* or the total resultant of our existence on earth, our life is continued in a new reborn form as animal, human, or god, and thus the *samsara,* or the whirlpool of existence, never ceases.

The idealization of Buddha is already present in Hinayana Buddhism, but is more prevalent in Mahayana Buddhism. This idea is enhanced through the concept of a Bodhisattva. A Bodhisattva is a future Buddha who attempts to realize the ideals of Buddhahood and who strives for the enlightenment of other sentient beings.[40] But only Mahayana envisions all its followers to become Bodhisattvas and it seeks to persuade everybody to become like Buddha, since Buddha himself wishes to help all creatures and bring them to full enlightenment. Hinayana, however, is content with the attainment of an *arhat* for its followers, because they should strive only for their own enlightenment and liberation. This brings us to the basic distinction between the two main branches of Buddhism, Hinayana, or also known as Theravada, meaning "the School of the Elders," and Mahayana.

While primitive Buddhism covers the first 100 years after Buddha's death, Hinayana Buddhism was prevalent from then until around A.D. 100.[41] Still today it is the main religion in Ceylon, Burma, Thailand, Laos, and Cambodia. Around A.D. 100 Mahayana Buddhism emerged and both strands coexisted for the next 200 years. Finally Mahayana prevailed for another 200 years until both came into conflict with Indian orthodox feeling. Nowadays Mahayana prevails over Hinayana in China, Tibet, Korea, and Japan. Since Hinayana is more concerned about individual enlightenment, it is best represented in Buddhist monasticism. Mahayana, however, is more interested in universal enlightenment and attempts to be a missionary folk religion. While adherents of Mahayana are free to admit that Hinayana may have preserved more the letter of Buddha's teachings, they insist they have better captured its spirit, but that both strands are rooted in primitive Buddhism. Their respective names, Mahayana, meaning "great vehicle," and Hinayana, meaning "small vehicle," express the idea that the larger vehicle is able to carry all beings to salvation while the smaller can carry only a few. They further convey the feeling that Mahayana can absorb Hinayana while the latter does not accept the former. Yet both forms strive for the same goal, the attainment of nirvana.

Nirvana is not simply void as sometimes has been assumed. It means first of all the extinction of all passion for life, similar to the extinction of a flame through cessation of fuel. It also is the state in which all evil passions are subdued and uprooted, and the mind regains its original purity and grace, and is altogether free from worries and other annoyances. In this latter understanding nirvana can even be equated with *samsara*. It is then no longer a transcendental entity to be reached after death or after the cycles of death and birth have ceased. In living a life of eternal becoming we already are nirvana. "All that we need do, therefore, is to find ourselves." [42] While Hinayana is more interested in the negative, world-denying side of nirvana, Mahayana conceives of nirvana more positively as a pure and undefiled reality which stands by itself. While nirvana has no cosmological functions, it comes close to the attributes of the Godhead as they are understood by the more mystical tradition of Christian thought.[43] Apart from the major division between Mahayana and Hinayana, there are many Buddhist sects, each of them emphasizing one aspect of Buddhism. Zen, for instance, emphasizes self-control, discipline, and simplicity; Shin, gratitude and brotherhood of life; Nichiren, a nationalistic viewpoint and sacrifice; and Shingon, symbolism, ritualism, and art.[44] Though the biggest difference exists between Hinayana and Mahayana, Buddhist thought always strives for tolerance and inclusiveness. And the ideal sect is one that attempts to harmonize tradition with a progressive spirit.

At first glance, Buddhism appears pessimistic and world-negating. According to Buddhist thinking, it is already futile to spend thoughts on the idea of a personal creator of the universe, because the purpose of Buddhist doctrine is to release beings from suffering and not to speculate on the origin of the world. Yet it is wrong to assume that Buddhist thought would result in radical pessimism. While reflecting a complete disillusionment with the world as it is, it shows an extreme sensitivity to pain, suffering, and any kind of turmoil, and a total dedication to the alleviation of these evil causes.[45] Buddhists also insist that the object of Buddhist life is not negation, but search for freedom from ignorance and reincarnation, since partial knowledge leads to wrong deeds or to evil *karma*. But we wonder whether a Buddhist such as Beatrice Suzuki is right when she asserts that "Buddhist life is an open war on bondage, slavery, and attachment of all kinds." [46]

There are certainly very progressive Buddhist sects, such as the Japanese sect Soka Gakkai, founded in 1930 by a Tokyo school teacher as the Value-Creating Education Academic Society, and rapidly expanding throughout Japan. Makiguchi, the founder, based the Society's program on a combination of the teachings of the Buddhist sect Nichiren Shoshu and his own theory of value.[47] He held that there are three ultimate virtues, beauty, gain, and goodness. The purpose of life is then found in the pursuit of happiness through the attainment of the three supreme virtues, which are accessible only by faith in the teachings of Nichiren.[48] The goal of the believer is to promote this type of Buddhism as the only true kind. Within fifteen years, from 1953 to 1968, the family membership of Soka Gakkai in Japan has increased from 20,000 to over 6½ million, accompanied by a similar increase in cultural and political activities. However, within Buddhism such a world-affirming movement is still an exception and it does not change the overall picture, namely that for Buddhism man is a stranger on earth.[49] His task is to regain the state of perfection which was his before he fell into this world. Thus self-denial can be adapted to highly political and capitalistic endeavors, such as the rebirth of Japan after World War II. Yet our modern technological civilization originated and is sustained through a different spirit. It regards man as born for this earth and it advocates self-preservation and continual progress as the highest goals of man. The earth is his home and his task is to treat it as such.[50]

However, Judeo-Christian faith, out of which the progressive spirit of our present technological civilization emerged, and Buddhist thought show some striking parallels, even interdependencies. Most well-known is the fact that Siddharta Buddha's conversion story was introduced to the West by Christian pilgrims and was rather popular in the Middle Ages as the novel of Barlaam and Josaphat. Though both names, Barlaam and Josaphat, are only a disguise for Bodhisattva, they made their way into the Christian calendar for saints as Saint Barlaam and Saint Josaphat, being identified as an Indian prince and a merchant respectively.[51] Of course, this incident deserves attention only as a historical curiosity.

Of more serious nature, however, is the fact that virtually at the same time as Christianity emerged, Buddhism underwent a radical reform of its basic tenets which made it more similar to Christianity than it had ever been before.[52] Lovingkindness and compassion, subordinate virtues in older Buddhism, are stressed more and more and move right into the center of Buddhist religion. Then we hear of compassionate beings, Bodhisattvas, who sacrificed their lives for the welfare of all. They remind us of Christ's sacrificial death and of his command that we should become like him, i.e. sacrifice our lives for others. Furthermore, the concept of Amida, the Buddha of Eternal Light and Infinite Life, originates as a savior figure infinite in love, wisdom, and power, again clearly resembling Christ. Though Amida as the object of faith evidently comes close to Christ, Buddhists are quick to show that unlike Christ Amida is mercy himself, who does not judge or suffer for our sins. A crucified or judging Christ is an impossible thought for Buddhism.[53]

Nevertheless, the fact is just too striking that Mahayana Buddhism, which is so analogous to Christianity and which is much more adaptable to Western thought, emerged almost in succession to the rise of Christianity. Hinayana is not completely exempted from analogies to Christian faith either. Though it rejected the idea of a savior, since everyone must save himself and no one can save another, it developed the concept of Maitreya, the coming Buddha.[54] This sudden interest in "eschatology" seems rather strange, even foreign, to primitive Buddhism. It should also be noted that the two Indian regions in which Mahayana Buddhism made its first appearance, the South of India and the Indian Northwest, were geographically in contact with the Mediterranean cultures. This has been shown in recent years through findings of huge hoards of Roman coins and by the art represented in these regions. It is also remarkable that, contrary to Hinayana, Mahayana demonstrates an openness to foreign, non-Indian influences.[55] As Edward Conze has shown, there are even occasional close verbal coincidences between Christian and Mahayana Scriptures. But there is an even more serious affinity.

The Christian mystic with his negative theology and his concept of God as ground of being, as nothingness, and as naked Godhead, and the Buddhist concept of nirvana, bear very close resemblances. Buddhism can justifiably be regarded as a special form of mysticism, in which the goal of salvation, oneness with nirvana, is basically identical with the goal of the Christian mystic, oneness with God.[56] One might also be tempted to assume that both forms strive for the same kind of world-negating self-redemption. Yet exactly at this point emerges a decisive difference. For instance, researching Meister Eckhart's teachings, Rudolf Otto discovered that Eckhart's mysticism is "colored by the Christian teaching of justification and permeated through and through by the influences of its origin, by Christian conceptions, without which it would be an almost empty contraption." [57] This emphasis on justification stemming from the experience and knowledge of God's saving activity is totally missing in Buddhist mysticism. D. T. Suzuki describes the situation most eloquently when he says:

> What a contrast between the crucifixion-image of Christ and the picture of Buddha lying on a bed surrounded by his disciples and other beings non-human as well as human! Is it not interesting and inspiring to see all kinds of animals coming together to mourn the death of Buddha? [58]

Very sensitively Suzuki noticed the fundamental difference between Christ dying vertically on the cross and Buddha passing away horizontally. The former provided the possibility of reconcilliation with God who is above and beyond ourselves, whereas Buddha showed us ways and means to attain harmonious unity with all being.

Another striking analogy, between Buddhist monasticism and the world-denying form of Christian monasticism is still unresolved. Nevertheless, we must ask ourselves to what an extent mysticism and monasticism, even of Christian persuasion, are essential components of Judeo-Christian faith. Though mysticism is always related to a particular religion and cannot survive apart from it, it is a phenomenon common in many religions and occurs in Islam as well as in Judaism (as Kabbalah) and in Christianity. Because of its esoteric, individualistic character, its representatives often come in conflict with their religious authorities. Their goal is always the same: liberation of man, or of his inner core, from the earthly situation of doom and salvation of his whole being through union with absolute and pure primal Being, or with God. Monasticism, though very widespread among most world religons too, is more flexible in its attitude toward the world and may be extremely esoteric and world-withdrawn, as in early Christian monasticism in Egypt, or very world-involved and often extremely casuistic, such as in the Society of Jesus.

The Israelite religion emerged when the Israelites left the desert and settled down in the cultured land, and Christianity spread out when Christian missionaries went into the cities of the Roman Empire. Judeo-Christian faith is both world-affirming and God-relying. As we will see later it is neither a faith based on law nor on devotion. It is a faith in salvation by invitation. God calls and man responds, God acts and man confirms. How shall these other religions then be evaluated from a Christian perspective? Are they only based on trial and error, or is there some value in them?

2. Religious truths and Christian faith.

To determine the value of religion as a God-disclosing phenomenon, we must first find out whether such a phenomenon is at all possible. After all, it is difficult to repudiate Kant's insight that our experience is confined to that within the categories of space and time, and, as we might add, of matter. Thus we are confronted with the all-decisive question whether the disclosure of God can transcend these natural limitations.

a. *Possibility of revelation.*

If there is God, we cannot reach him by our own endeavors. God is by his very "definition" that which is not confined to our space-time continuum. He is not a phenomenon of space, time, or matter and his nature is withdrawn from our sense experience. When religions talk about revelation, they usually do not want to leave the impression that revelation is only discovery of something which I already knew, or something which was hidden within me. They talk about a new and surprising experience beyond my own possibilities. In the strict sense, they never admit the possibility of a natural knowledge of God. In talking about God as the object matter of religion, revelation of God is always self-disclosure of God and not disclosure of something about God.[59] Revelation then would mean the making known to us of that which is not at our disposal (God). Yet in talking about revelation, we talk about experiences that have happened within our world and not in some transcendental realm. For instance, when the Old Testament talks about Yahweh's theophanies, it talks about his appearance in material objects, in the burning bush, in the pillar of cloud and fire, or in the tent of encounter. Revelation is the appearing within the categories of space and time of that which is not of space and time. In other words, God's self-disclosure is always self-disclosure in our world.

Of course, this transition from beyond space and time to within space and time makes revelation ambiguous to us. While it is not impossible that God, who is not at our disposal, may bring himself to our disposal, we cannot be certain that he ever did or will do so. In the same way as our world can make sense without God, it can also make sense without revelation. Kant demonstrated this 200 years ago in his antinomies of pure reason. He showed that one can logically assert both that the world has a beginning in space and time and it does not have one, that there is a necessary cause for the world's existence and that there is none. In so doing he trimmed the wings of human reason, and indicated that since human reason is the measure of all *things,* it cannot extend itself beyond the bounds of *things.* In other words, one cannot look at the world of things from outside and verify that it is really the way it appears to be. Most scientists have long recognized this and no longer pose the question what their objects of investigation, e.g. particles, waves, light, life, and the like, really are, but how they function. With regard to religion, revelation, and God, it is becoming increasingly popular to ask similar phenomenological questions, e.g. how do religion, myth, and God function? But frequently a decisive difference is assumed between a scientist asking a functional question concerning light, and, for instance, a sociologist of religion asking a functional question concerning myth in the life of people. While it is now commonly acknowledged that a scientist cannot existentially divorce himself from his object matter, since there always occurs an interaction between the scientist and his object matter, the sociologist of religion still frequently assumes that he can deal with his object matter in strictly neutral fashion. Yet is such an attitude tenable?

As soon as God discloses himself, he makes himself disposable to us within the space-time continuum.[60] This means that our attitude toward this self-disclosure, which is now "contained" in our world, already pre-decides our evaluation. We cannot divorce ourselves existentially from it and at the same time interpret it correctly.[61] The very occurrence of revelation demands and results in our existential decision of indifference, acceptance, or rejection. For instance, when Jesus, as God's self-disclosure, began his mission, he challenged his audience with the words: "The time is fulfilled, and the kingdom of God is at hand; repent and believe the gospel" (Mark 1:15). Of course, the decision of faith does not rule out reason. Anselm of Canterbury showed us that, once the initial decision of faith or rejection is made, reason has ample ground to delineate the implications of this decision. However, it is wrong and misleading to pretend that the decision of accepting or rejecting the actuality of revelation itself (not the possibility of revelation) is already based on strictly rational argument. But what does this have to say to the relationship between Christian faith and the world religions?

b. *Christian faith and the world religions.*

The argument has often been advanced that the Christian faith is the way to salvation while the world religions only show how religious truths can be distorted. Already Karl Barth's strict distinction between religion and Christian faith and his disregard for religion as man's attempt to provide his own self-redemption, comes close to this verdict. For him religions are basically man-centered and are, similar to Feuerbach's claim, projections of man's desires.

From the New Testament to Martin Luther: It is difficult, however, to find even in the New Testament much backing for this judgment. Paul, for instance, could cite Abraham, the Jewish patriarch, as the example of faith (Rom. 4:12). He certainly did not do this believing that Abraham's religion was all self-centered. On the contrary, Paul attempted to demonstrate a continuity amid all discontinuity, yet even a historical priority of the Old Testament over the New (cf. Rom. 9:11). Paul, however, was not only appreciative of his Old Testament heritage. In the famous speech on the Areopagus in Athens, he is also quoted saying that the God whom the Athenians worship as unknown, he is now declaring unto them (Acts 17:23). This is the line the Apologists of the Early Church followed when they were confronted with a multitude of religions which all claimed some kind of revelation.

The first and most biblical argument of the Apologists was that of the *logos spermatikos.* It contained the conviction that the pre-existent logos, indwelling in man, enabled pagan thinkers like Socrates already to see dimly what came later to be clearly perceived through the revelation of the incarnate logos in the person of Jesus.[62] Since the prologue of the Gospel of John shows us that this logos had already been present at the creation of the world, the Apologists concluded that it had been present too in the history of Israel, and even to some degree in paganism. The Stoics, the poets, and the historians "each man spoke well in proportion to the share he had of the spermatic logos." [63] Now that the seminal logos had come in person, in Jesus Christ, those under his guidance could find the fuller meaning of these intuitions. Thus the logos prepared the advent of the Christian self-disclosure of God and bridged the gulf between Christianity and the world religions.

Another quite common method for the Early Christian Apologists was to assert that the truth contained in paganism had come from the Old Testament. This argument had already been advanced by Jewish writers, such as Philo and Josephus, when they traced various Greek doctrines to a biblical origin.[64] Yet in attacking the pagan rituals Ambrose demonstrated that the argument from antiquity should not be slavishly followed, since it was not shameful to move to something better if this is available.[65] This leads to the third very interesting argument, that of accommodation. Christian Apologists suggested that God had accommodated himself to human weakness in the Old Testament. In a similar way the parallels between Jewish and pagan rites of sacrifices must be understood. But actually these pagan and Jewish analogies are only steps of God's pedagogical action leading up to his revelation in Jesus Christ. Thus this doctrine expresses God's love in moving mankind adequately along from paganism via Judaism to Christian faith.[66] Most of these arguments are varied throughout the centuries and applied to the relationship between Christian faith and non-Christian religions.

Luther offers a very interesting solution to our problem. Of course, he was convinced that all men know about God. The Psalmist, for instance, tells us that there are gods. But he also admonishes us to distinguish appropriately between their power and the power of the one God. God has ordained them to function as gods over other nations, without infringing upon his own sovereignty. Thereby he remains in control of all gods, because "he wants to be supreme God, a judge of all gods." [67] Luther understood the whole Decalog as an expression of the extra-biblical knowledge of God. This understanding was especially confirmed for him through Paul's assertion in Romans 1 that all heathen know that there is a God and that certain laws are commonly known.[68] In referring to Romans 1:21 Luther asserted: "The heathen know about the nature of God" and they "have through a natural instinct the feeling that there is a supreme numen." [69] But their knowledge did not arise through their own ingenuity. It was God himself who implanted in their hearts this knowledge.[70] Luther is convinced that it is man's innermost being to be religious and to have a God.[71] It is amazing what natural man can know about God. For instance, pagans know that God is almighty and all-knowing. Since they also know that he is just, they want to establish with him a dialog of intercession and response.[72] "Therefore," Luther claims, they "all know that God is our refuge, and they implore his help and support." [73] But the knowledge that God is almighty and just, a helper in need, and governor of the world does not yet touch the center of understanding God; it is only knowledge from outside.

Luther realizes that though there is a common agreement on certain features of God, God always assumes the shape we attribute to him. This projective subjectivity, according to which God becomes a projection of our God desires, is utterly helpless in thinking properly of God, since it has no corrective outside man and the world he lives in.[74] Luther, however, emphasizes that there is a big difference between merely knowing that there is a god and knowing what or who God is. He says: "The former is known by nature and is inscribed into all hearts. The latter is taught only by the Holy Spirit." [75] The actual revelation of God, which is God's self-disclosure, occurs in such a way that it strikes our hearts and makes us proceed from the knowledge of God in Jesus Christ to the knowledge of God the Father and the Creator.[76] Thus revelation always starts with the second person of the Trinity or with Jesus Christ.[77] Luther expresses this christocentricity of the full knowledge of God more clearly when he says: Christ is everywhere. "But he does not want that you grab him everywhere. Only where the word is, there you should grab him and grasp him properly.

Otherwise you will tempt God and institute idolatry. Therefore he has given us a certain way how and where we should seek and find him, namely in the word." [78] This means that there are many ways in which we can know something about God, but there is only one way, through his self-disclosure in Jesus Christ, in which we get a full "picture" of God and a corrective of our subjectivity.

Finding our way between Karl Barth and Ernst Troeltsch: In recent discussions of the relationship between Christian faith and the world religions the conclusions reached ranged from the extreme and christocentric position of Karl Barth to the historicist relativistic approach of Ernst Troeltsch. For instance, Werner Elert, from the so-called orthodox Lutheran camp, and Otto Weber, from the Barthian group, feel free to dispense with any recognition of the validity of world religions.[79] Though now pursuing a more dialectic approach toward world religions the noted Dutch historian of religions, Hendrik Kraemer in his book *The Christian Message in a non-Christian World,* still emphasized predominantly the dissimilarities between the various religions and Christian faith and called the world religions misdirected and mainly great human achievements.[80] Thus the only legitimate point of contact with them is "the disposition and the attitude of the missionary." Kraemer claimed that this is not done out of a feeling of superiority, but for Christ's sake and for the sake of these people.

Paul Althaus is much more hesitant to arrive at a strict condemnation of religions. Similar to Emil Brunner, he sees a twofold relationship between Christian faith and the world religions.[81] There are moments of truth in all religions, he asserts, and yet they stand against the truth of Christian faith as a lie.[82] Christian faith does not just introduce a new idea of God or represents a higher level of religious consciousness. It presents a new relationship with God which is documented in Christ and his coming. This is where according to Althaus the contrast to all religions becomes evident. Only as Christians do we know about the revelation of God's love, which is shown to us in Christ. Thus the passage from the world religions to the Christian faith and vice versa is never just a transition, but based on decision and change. Althaus, however, is far from assuming that the world religions are without God. Man in his human existence is always kept by God and dependent upon him and even in a distorted way, he must witness to God. The knowledge of God in its most limited expression of the ultimate dependence of man still contains a kernel of truth about the innermost connection between God and man. Yet in just knowing of a god, the worship of a god is a lie; it belies the fact that God is more than just a god.

In his systematic theology Althaus gives considerable attention to the phenomenon of religion. He is now somewhat more appreciative of the world religions, especially of the "religions of grace" in the Far East. He recognizes that religion generally has two poles, a divine and a human. It acknowledges that attesting godhead and it is concerned with the unresolved question of salvation and how to solve it.[83] Then Althaus attempts to evaluate religion in confronting it with the gospel. He realizes that it contains truth insofar as it is determined by God's primordial self-disclosure *(Uroffenbarung)* and it is a lie insofar as man in his self-centeredness perverts this primordial self-disclosure when he himself attempts to answer the question of salvation which is not yet solved there.[84] Althaus asserts that man always needs a conversion to turn from the religions to the Christian faith, since religions are not in part truth and in part a lie. They always express a holistic attitude of man in which the truth too serves the lie.

Paul Tillich goes beyond the strict dialectic form of Althaus' approach, though claiming that the relation between Christianity and the world religions is "profoundly dialectical." [85] On the one hand he calls Christianity all-inclusive and universal, and on the other hand he sees its ultimate criterion in the concreteness in Jesus as the Christ. The appearance and reception of Jesus of Nazareth as the Christ is the event on which Christianity is based and it provides in human history the decisive self-manifestation of the source and aim of all being.[86] Tillich does not opt for religious syncretism, since this would rob a particular religion of its concreteness and at the same time of its dynamic power, and he does not want a victory of one religion, since this would impose one particular answer on all other particular answers. Only in breaking through one's particularity can one experience the spiritual presence in other expressions of the ultimate meaning of man's existence and engage in a fruitful critical dialog.[87] Tillich, of course, justifies this dialogic situation in which Christian faith finds itself, since the universal logos, at work in the world at large, and the incarnate logos, manifesting itself in the church, its traditions, and its present reality, correspond with each other.[88]

It is not without importance that in his last public lecture, "The Significance of the History of Religions for Systematic Theology,"

Tillich went a decisive step further in his appreciation of world religions. Now he claims that "there are revealing and saving powers in all religions" and that

> there may be—and I stress this, there *may* be—a central event in the history of religions which unites the positive results of those critical developments in the history of religion in and under which revelatory experiences are going on—an event which therefore, makes possible a concrete theology that has universalistic significance.[89]

Tillich concedes here to the world religions considerable revelatory and redemptive power regardless of their explicit relationship to the Christ event and at the same time he has also become more hestitant to attribute to any event, including the Christ event, unmistakably universal validity.

Roman Catholic theologians, coming from a tradition that feels itself all-inclusive, often find it easier than most Protestants to arrive at a positive evaluation of non-Christian religions. This became especially evident at Vatican II where the "Declaration on the Relationship of the Church to Non-Christian Religions" stated that all peoples comprise a single community which has its one origin and goal in God whose saving power extends to all men. Therefore the Catholic Church rejects nothing which is true and holy in these religions and exhorts its members through dialog and cooperation with the adherents of the other religions to "acknowledge, preserve, and promote the spiritual and moral goods" found among them.[90]

The Roman Catholic theologian Hans Küng seems to underline and broaden the approach of Vatican II. His major concern is with the countless millions outside Christianity who are no longer poor heathen, but rather modern men in industrialized states with great and ancient cultures, such as India and Japan.[91] He does not find the dialectic approach satisfying, because it ultimately labels world religions as an expression of unbelief and godlessness. He does not feel either that the traditional Roman Catholic stand, which asserts that there is no salvation outside the church, still applies to our present problems concerning world religions. He finds the fact affirmed by Vatican II "that men can be saved outside the Catholic Church."[92]

Nevertheless Hans Küng arrives at a dialectic position, which at first looks very much like that of Paul Althaus. He argues on the one hand that though the world religions contain truth concerning the true God, they are in error. They are "an expression of estrange-ment from God and from him whom the gracious God has sent, and who is not only light but *the* Light, not only truth but *the* Truth." But Küng concedes on the other hand that "*the world religions do, though in error, proclaim the truth of the true God.*" Though they are far from God he is not far from them. They may flee from the true God but they are graciously held by him who is their God too. Thus the grace of the true God can witness itself even through false gods, and can trace the image of the true God even through its misplaced and disassociated features. Küng, however, surprises us when he uses his concept of the universal presence of God and his grace to suggest that while the church is the "extraordinary" way of salvation, the world religions are the "ordinary" way of salvation for non-Christian humanity.

> God is the Lord not only of the special salvation history of the Church, but also of that other salvation history: the univer-sal salvation history of all mankind. This universal salvation his-tory is bound up with special salvation history in a common origin, meaning and goal, and is subject to the same grace of God.[93]

With this highly universalistic approach Küng goes well beyond Vatican II. Though it was asserted at Vatican II that the Catholic Church rejects nothing that is true and holy in other religions, Küng can hardly find backing in Vatican II when he surmises that "*every* world religion is under God's grace and can be a way of salvation: whether it is primitive or highly evolved, mythological or enlightened, mystical or rational, theistic or non-theistic, a real or a quasi-religion. Every religion can be a way of salvation and we may hope that every one is." [94] Still, these assumptions do not abolish for Küng the uniqueness of Christian faith. Küng finds that this radical universalism is grounded, centered and made concrete in Jesus Christ, in whom God has spoken for all man in a unique way. Without this concretization, Küng claims, we would not know that God's love includes all men and that he desires all men to be saved and that he gave Jesus Christ as a ransom for all (1 Tim. 2:4-6). Therefore, Küng does not want the church to stop bearing witness to Jesus Christ in the sight of the world religions, to cease with the proclamation, declaration and exposition of his gospel.[95] But he insists that it should also function as the true vanguard of humanity, a living invitation and a joyful challenge to the people of the world religions.[96] He reminds us too that we should have a more relaxed attitude towards the traditional "saving of souls" as the exclusive function of the church, discovering that the salvation of mankind does not depend on us, since it is already accomplished in Jesus Christ.

Needless to say, this highly universalistic though still christocentric approach toward the relationship between Christian faith and the world religions, is attractive for those who want to engage in an appreciative dialog with representatives of these religions. But it also is often considered as pulling the rug out from underneath for those who stand on the missionary forefront in Asia and Africa. H. van Straelen, for instance, gives us an overview of Roman Catholic theologians that provides a very positive view of non-Christian religions, while pointing out that at the same time many of them show little enthusiasm for mission.[97] Eugene Hillman indicates some traces of this tension though advocating the missionary task very fervently.[98] He is not convinced that the missionary task should continue indefinitely or until every contemporary individual has been converted to the visible membership of the church. He assumes that such goal is an eschatological one. The present function of the mission, however, is to gather at least a small flock which can serve as the visible witness of the sacramental church that must be founded once for all in every nation in order to signify and "repeat" sacramentally what Christ has achieved once and for all. The mission of the church endeavors, so to speak, to erect signposts and "sacramental" bodies among all peoples as a sign of hope for all who love the coming of the Lord and as a sign of his advent. With this sacramental interpretation of the mission's task, Hillman has toned down the necessity of conversion as the goal of missionary activity.

The best synthesis from the Roman Catholic side between missionary zeal and positive appreciation of non-Christian religions is brought forth by Karl Rahner.[99] Starting with Paul's insight that non-Christians do not know God and yet worship him (Acts 17:23), Rahner is free to admit that God is greater than man and the church. Though we should be firm toward all non-Christian religions, we should at the same time be humble and tolerant.[100] There is not doubt for Karl Rahner that Christianity is the absolute religion, intended for all men. He claims that "Christ and his continuing historical presence in the world (which we call 'Church') is *the* religion which binds man to God." [101] Yet he affirms that a non-

Christian religion too contains supernatural elements arising out of the grace which is given to men as a gratuitous gift on account of Christ.

Without denying the error and depravity contained in it, "a non-Christian religion can be recognized as a *lawful* religion." [102] Such concession to the validity of non-Christian religions would witness to the fact that God is present outside the limits of the visible church. It would also suggest that every human being is really and truly exposed to the influence of divine, supernatural grace which offers an interior union with God and which demands a decision towards this grace which is reflected in the non-Christian attitude towards his "lawful" religion. Rahner understands by lawful religion "an institutional religion whose 'use' by man at a certain period can be regarded on the whole as a positive means of gaining the right relationship to God and thus for the attaining of salvation, a means which is therefore positively included in God's plan of salvation." [103] This means that the religions outside and prior to Christianity are not regarded as illegitimate from the very start, but as quite capable of having positive significance. Thus a member of a non-Christian religion is not simply labeled a mere non-Christian, but someone "who can and must be regarded in this or that respect as an anonymous Christian." [104] He already has some knowledge, however, distorted of God's grace and truth. The transition between Christian and non-Christian, or between Christians in Christendom itself, is then no longer expressed in terms of an absolute either-or, but in a gradual more or less.

Rahner's stand excludes a conversion in the traditional sense as the goal of missionary activity. In most cases the goal would rather be an explicit self-realization of one's hitherto anonymous Christian existence and an ever growing awareness of God's grace and truth. Two big questions, however, emerge in listening to Rahner's thoughtful and persuasive approach: 1. Did not Jesus' proclamation and that of the early church lead first to a decision and then to a continuous growth in grace and truth, while Rahner's approach proceeds the opposite direction? 2. Does not Rahner's approach by avoiding a clear distinction between Christian and non-Christian faiths lead to a sliding scale of Christianity in which one is never really certain whether one is already on the side of those who are saved? The latter reservation is amplified through Rahner's remark that one reason for missionary activity is that "the individual who grasps Christianity in a clearer, purer and more reflective way has, other things being equal, a still greater chance of salvation than someone who is merely an anonymous Christian." [105]

When we come to the noted British historian Arnold Toynbee, we are confronted with a very different assessment of the relationship between Christian faith and the world religions. Toynbee has abandoned a christocentric approach to the world religions altogether. He states that it is high time that all the living higher religions subordinate their traditional rivalries to reflect on their common ground. Toynbee finds this common ground first of all in human nature which is basically self-centered and which has succumbed to original sin.[106] To wrestle with original sin is the challenge in response to which all higher religions have arisen. Toynbee regards it as hardly accidental that the higher religions, as we know them today, all made their appearances within a period of less than a thousand years of one another. He assumes that it was the same human nature, with which we are confronted today, that evoked the higher religions two or three thousand years ago. Thus the higher religions have common ground in the permanence and universality of human nature and in the present state of the world. Higher religions also share a common aim, namely to emancipate individual souls that they can glorify God and enjoy him forever. Since the major religions address themselves to all men, this aim is not reserved for a privileged minority.

However, Toynbee sees two main obstacles which prevent Christianity from recognizing this common ground and this common aim in other higher religions and from being also recognized by those other religions as having these common denominators. First, Toynbee suggests that Christianity should clearly distinguish between its message and its Western gown (civilization) in which it usually presents this message. With this suggestion, Toynbee touches on that which today many missionologists demand, an indigenization of religion. He claims that often the Western gown hindered others outside our civilization from adopting Christianity.[107] Of course, it is questionable whether one can disassociate a particular form of religion so easily from its cultural environment. Toynbee's law of inverse operation, in which he suggests that the spiritual achievements and material ones proceed antithetical to each other, does not prove the case.[108]

We admit that religions often make their appearance and spread most rapidly when civilizations are in an unstable state. However, there is a clear dependence of Western progress (civilization) on Judeo-Christian faith. Without the progressive spirit of this faith, Western civilization would have been bound to a similar pessimistic cyclic pattern as are all other civilizations.[109] Thus one could predict that if missionaries would not export Christian faith together with its Western gown, Christian faith alone would be sufficient to transform the cultural and religious milieu of the respective missionary scene. If it were otherwise, Christian faith would have lost its transformative power. Of course, we do not want to imply that missionaries should advance a neo-colonialistic or imperialistic stance as they have often been inclined to do in the past. Neither should they become advocates of a modern secular spirit, since, as we have seen, this spirit is only indirectly related to the Christian faith. While a missionary can never be effective unless he is able to understand the world view of the people to whom he ministers and unless he is able to relate his message to their frame of reference, he dare not leave the impression that acceptance of his message would make no difference to the life and living of his listeners.

Second, Toynbee observes that many in East and West reject Christianity because of its traditional arrogant spirit. Thus Christianity should abandon its intrinsic and traditional belief that it is unique,[110] because out of the belief in its uniqueness follows its exclusive-mindedness and its intolerance. Toynbee does not want Christianity to renounce the idea that its own convictions are right and true. Yet it should recognize that all higher religions are also in some measure revelations of that which is true and right. Higher religions differ in the content and in the degree of the revelation that has been given to mankind through them. And they also differ in the extent to which this revelation has been translated by their followers into practice. But Toynbee claims that all religions "are light radiating from the same source from which our own religion derives its spiritual light." [111]

God is the god of all men and Toynbee can even venture to say that God is another name for love. Toynbee also mentions that in six major religions, Buddhism, Hinduism, Zoroastrianism, Islam, Judaism, and Christianity, the greatest spiritual presence known to man has a personal aspect. According to Toynbee this "personal aspect is a bond of unity which transcends the differences between the views of what the personal aspect is." [112] Though looking for a common ground, Toynbee rejects all syncretistic endeavors, since such artificial religions would fail to capture the imagination, the feelings, and the allegiance of mankind.[113] He wants religions to retain their historic identities, while becoming more and more open-minded and open-hearted towards one another. Christianity should even continue to preach its truths and ideals to the non-Christian majority of our fellow human beings and give practical examples of it in action. Toynbee also touches the essence of Christian faith when he names three points in Christian faith which he wants to be furthered: 1. The proclamation of the saving history of God in the life of Jesus Christ. 2. The conviction that human beings ought to follow the example that God has set in the history of Jesus Christ. 3. The enactment of this conviction in one's own life. When we disregard Toynbee's universalistic attitude, he seems to have captured the essence of Christian faith and he rightly scolds Christianity for its often unjustified arrogance. Considering our brief survey of world religions, we wonder, however, whether there is as much similarity between Christian faith and the world religions as Toynbee suggests.

Having started with Karl Barth we must finally come to Ernst Troeltsch as a representative of the opposite side of the spectrum. Ernst Troeltsch, Professor of Philosophy and Theology first in Heidelberg and later in Berlin, has already been introduced to us as the father of historical relativism. Yet in his book, *The Absoluteness of Christianity and the History of Religions* (1901), he still advocates the superiority of Christian faith. Among the great religions, Troeltsch contends, Christianity is in actuality the strongest and most concentrated revelation of personalistic apprehension. It is the only religion which completely broke with the limits and conditions of nature religions, and therefore

> it represents the only depiction of the higher world as infinitely valuable personal life that conditions and shapes all else. It renounces the world, but only to the extent that its superficial, natural significance clings to it and the evil in it has become dominant. It affirms the world to the extent that it is from God and is perceived by men of faith as deriving from and leading to God. And renunciation and affirmation, taken together, disclose the true higher world in a power and independence that are experienced nowhere else.[114]

Christianity even demands a decision between redemption through meditation on a transcendent Being and redemption through faithful, trusting participation in the person-like character of God, the ground of all life and genuine value. Troeltsch asserts that Christianity must be understood as both the culmination and convergence point of all developmental tendencies that can be discerned in religion.

Troeltsch is historian enough to concede that he cannot prove with absolute certainty that Christianity will always remain the final culmination point which will never be surpassed. Though Christianity is God's great revelation to man, other religions are likewise revelations of God. One cannot even rule out the abstract possibility of further revelations. There is also a power at work in every religion that provides genuine deliverance.[115] Troeltsch checks his universalistic ideas at this point by his confidence that Christianity is unlikely to be surpassed as the way of attaining deliverance from man's predicament and loving fellowship with God.

At the end of his life, however, in his lecture on "The Place of Christianity Among the World Religions" (1923) this optimism had disappeared. Though unwilling to withdraw anything he had written some twenty years earlier, he added some significant modifications. He recognized now that a religion in the several forms assumed by it, always depends upon the intellectual, social, and national conditions among which it exists.[116] This means for Christianity that from once being a Jewish sect, it has become the religion of all Europe. It stands or falls with European civilization; while, on its own part, it has entirely lost its oriental character and become Westernized and Hellenized. All our European conceptions of personality, its eternal, divine right, its progress towards a kingdom of the spirit and of God, the enormous capacity for expansion, even our whole social order and our science and art rest upon the basis of this deorientalized Christianity. With this important assertion Troeltsch has recognized Christianity as the seminal ground for our Western way of life. He also affirms that the only religion we can endure is Christianity, for it has grown up with us and has become part of our very being. Troeltsch even concludes that it could not have become the religion of such a highly developed racial group if it did not "possess a mighty spiritual power and truth; in short, if it were not, in some degree, a manifestation of the Divine Life itself." [117] Yet now he dares only to admit that it is final and unconditional for us, whereas it is quite possible that other racial groups, living under entirely different cultural conditions, may experience their contact with the "Divine Life" in quite a different way. They may themselves also possess a religion which has grown up with them, and from which they cannot sever themselves so long as they remain what they are. Therefore Troeltsch allows missionary endeavor only against "inferior religions" while between "higher religions" there should be agreement and mutual understanding instead of conversion.

Troeltsch has now abandoned Christianity as the definite culmination and convergence point of religion's evolution. Instead he asserts that all religion has .

> a common goal in the Unknown, the Future, perchance in the Beyond, so too it has a common ground in the Divine Spirit ever pressing the finite mind onward towards further light and fuller consciousness, a Spirit which indwells the finite spirit, and Whose ultimate union with it is the purpose of the whole many-sided process.[118]

We wonder if a common transcendental goal, which Troeltsch now asserts, is a more tenable position than claiming the absoluteness of Christian faith. Furthermore, Troeltsch does not seem to have emphasized enough that Judeo-Christian faith is by its very nature a historical religion. It is connected with specific historical occurrences up to and including the historical person of Jesus of Nazareth, who at the same time is the divine savior in whom Christian faith is grounded. Such historicizing of religion, of course, invites a historical consciousness. But remaining at the same time religion and not just history, it claims to transcend historical relativism. With these observations, however, we have ventured into the evaluative part of determining the relationship between revelation encountered in Christian faith and in the world religions.

Judging without being judgmental: In adequately determining the relationship between revelation encountered in Christian faith and in the world religions, it would be a gross oversimplification to abstract from all historical peculiarities and to look for a common denominator. Unlike philosophical truth existential truth is always embodied in historical forms and is never found in abstract ideas. Hence a strictly phenomenological approach seems to be unable to do justice to the intricacies of history.[119] For instance, Zeus and Yahweh are both phenomenologically speaking high gods, but they bear hardly any other resemblance. Therefore it is very difficult to maintain on a strictly empirical grounds that all religions converge toward a common goal. The very fact that primitive religions, polytheism, and monotheism coexist on the same time level, yet to some extent even in the same religion, makes it extremely difficult to talk about a religious progression in the usual evolutionary sense. Since the major religions are world religions and therefore universalistic, they have incorporated many heterogeneous elements and assimilated them into their own traditions during their individual historic evolvement and expansion. Often these adoptions were even made from other world religions.[120] Thus our search for an understanding of man's religions has led us to discover certain common elements, and also a remarkable interchange between religions, in part fostered by the increasing amalgamation of mankind. Yet does this mean that all religions will gradually overcome their distinctive claims for salvation and merge into one religious body of a global brotherhood of mankind? There is no indication of the emergence of one universal religion.[121] Even an overtly syncretistic religion such as Buddhism only adapts heterogeneous elements into its body of tradition, but is by nature unwilling to succumb its tradition to other truth claims. Contrary to Toynbee's conviction, it is not only a peculiarity of Christian faith to assert with utmost conviction the truth claim of its own religion. However, it would be over-reacting to assume that each religion, including Christian faith, has its own view of truth and is co-equal to all other religions.

Since neither believer nor unbeliever can by his own volition abandon his own position to assess objectively the religious scene, the best way for adequately evaluating the relationship between Christian faith and other religions concerning their understanding of revelation is to look for a criterion within the Judeo-Christian tradition. If revelation means God's self-disclosure, this self-disclosure would best be possible in an actual I-thou encounter. The existence of this condition is confirmed by the paradise stories in Genesis. But in relegating such an I-thou encounter with God to paradise, the biblical writers tell us that it is no longer a possibility for us.

As we will discuss more extensively later, the God-disclosive history of Judeo-Christian tradition is of much more modest beginnings. First Yahweh is encountered through dead objects, in theophanies of a burning bush and at Mt. Sinai. Of course, God himself has to interpret the meaning of these events. Eventually

God uses prophetic spokesmen, such as Moses, Amos, or Isaiah to disclose himself to Israel. At a later stage we encounter his disclosure through the medium of the written word, the Torah, and finally, though not accepted by all Jews, he discloses himself through his embodiment in Jesus of Nazareth. This incarnation of God in an actual person is not without purpose introduced as an analogy to the ideal paradisiac time (cf. John 1). Yet it is not only a recapture of the past. It is interesting that Jesus as the Christ is understood by Paul not as a parallel but as an antithesis to Adam, the first man.[122] In so doing, Paul wants to assert that that which man was initially unable and unwilling to do, to live in conformity and community with God, is now being accomplished through Jesus, the God who became man. As a real man Jesus was able and willing to live in conformity and community with God until his very end. Since Jesus has done this in our interest, or *pro nobis,* we can envision such a goal for us in claiming Jesus the Christ who has accomplished this goal on our side. Even more, we can already anticipate this goal proleptically. Thus man can feel free to approach the future confidently, since the ultimate future, eternal union with God, has been secured for him.

We are not wrong to assume that the typical Western affirmation of the world, its typical optimistic and irreversibly progressive spirit, cannot be thought of without the Judeo-Christian tradition as its source of inspiration and its sense of direction.[123] Even the Western understanding of man as a person, with inalienable human rights, is difficult to understand without the Christian conviction that man is elected by God to live as a distinctive thou in eternal conformity and communion with his creator, and that man can already now participate proleptically in this promised experience.

It would be shortsighted, however, to conclude that non-Christian religions are just a lie measured by Christian standards. It cannot be substantiated on biblical grounds that non-Christian religions do not contain any truth, that they are plagiarists in the instances in which they bear similarities to the Christian faith and that they simply express man's need for God in the instances in which they differ from the Christian faith. We agree with Friedrich Heiler that non-Christian religions too bear witness to the fact that God seeks man,[124] and not only that man seeks God. The essence of any religion, primitive, polytheistic, monotheistic, and Christian, is the communion of man with the transcendent reality experienced through God's grace. Thus Mensching is right when he sides with Otto expressing that in all religions there can be experienced a true encounter with the Holy.[125] Neither the Bible nor even Luther ever taught that God was confined to the Old and New Testament covenant community whereas outside this community there was a godless vacuum. Furthermore, the manifoldness of the world religions witness neither more nor less to the sinfulness of mankind in general than does denominational pluralism to the sinfulness of Christians in particular. Therefore, we must move beyond a strict dialectical recognition of a primal revelation to all men.[126] A primal notion of God to which nature, human existence, human history, and human intellect attest, does not adequately reflect the realities encountered in non-Christian religions. We have seen in our investigation of the "proofs" of the existence of God that it is a philosophical abstraction and already presupposes a religious commitment.

We must finally recognize that even outside the Christian faith doom can be experienced and the certitude of salvation can be encountered. A salvational egotism, confining salvation only to Christians, cannot be substantiated from either the Old or the New Testament. The early church already wrestled with the question of the ultimate destiny of those who had died before Christ ever appeared on earth and before he offered salvation to mankind. When it included the phrase into its creed that Christ had "descended to the dead," many of its theologians interpreted this to imply that he thereby offered at least the possibility of salvation to those who had died before him.[127] It would be utterly incongruous with what we know about God that he would permit those countless millions to live in eternity distant from him who never during their lifetime here on earth had an actual choice to accept him as he disclosed himself in Jesus Christ. Perhaps it was because the gospel was not proclaimed to them or that it was proclaimed to them in such a distorted way that they preferred to adhere to their native religions. How could we expect that they would have to bear the eternal consequences of the shortcomings of others? However, it borders on speculation to outline a definite way according to which those not confronted with the Christian gospel can or will be saved.

When we assert that salvation can be encountered outside the Christian faith, we do not open the doors to an everybody-may-believe-as-he-pleases attitude. For the Old and New Testament

there was never the slightest doubt that to members of its covenant, salvation would only be granted through exclusive allegiance
to God within the respective covenant relationship. For those outside the Judeo-Christian tradition, however, Wilfred Cantwell
Smith has expressed their situation very accurately when he said:
A Buddhist, a Hindu, or a Muslim "is saved only, because God is
the kind of God who Jesus Christ has revealed Him to be." [128]
As we will see more extensively later, without Jesus Christ we
would never have known, though we might perhaps have guessed,
that God is a God of love and compassion. We must agree here
with Luther that without Christ we really do not know for sure
what God is like. Thus the exclusivistically sounding statement:
"I am the way, and the truth, and the life; no one comes to the
Father, but by me" (John 14:6), ultimately points beyond the
Christian confines. It leads us to the recognition that anybody
who is saved, whether Christian or non-Christian, is saved by the
only thing that could possibly save him, the anguish and love of
God shown to us in Jesus Christ. Consequently, the New Testament command: "Go therefore, and make disciples of all nations,
baptizing them in the name of the Father and of the Son and of
the Holy Spirit" (Matt. 28:19), does not lose its urgency. But the
recognition of the salvability of non-Christians would prevent us
from the strange notion that their salvation depends on us and
our effectiveness. It would free us from the aweful responsibility
of having to win victories on the missionary battlefield to assure
the salvation of mankind. Instead, like Paul, we could state what
we share in common with the non-Christian religions and then
proceed to the joyful proclamation of God's self-disclosure in Jesus
Christ.

While we must admit that non-Christians can be saved we should
not embrace them in pseudo-brotherly love or confuse them and
us by calling them anonymous Christians. We have noticed that
even in primitive religions there is a notion of a high god. But
we also realized that only in monotheistic religions is the disclosure of God experienced in a definite personal I-thou encounter.
The culmination of this disclosive process, however, seems to come
in Jesus the Christ, the one God in human form. We have also
seen that the understanding that God calls and man responds is
present in the religious experience of non-Christians. Nevertheless,
they still put prime emphasis on man's ritual, legal, or devotional
obedience as being constitutive for God's activity.[129] Yet we will

see that the Judeo-Christian tradition emphasizes just the opposite, the total primacy of God's invitation to salvation out of which man's response follows.

Since our understanding of God always implies certain assertions concerning man, Christian proclamation will and must also include the practical and the anthropological level. An adequate elaboration of the common ground and the differences between Christian and non-Christian religions presupposed in any effective proclamation, will necessitate a dialog. But again a dialog dare not become a one-way street. It would not only mean learning more about someone else's faith. It would also make us more aware of our own religious peculiarities and thereby it would have a stimulating effect on our life attitude.[130] For instance, in a dialog with Buddhists we would become more aware of our unique understanding of God's solidarity with mankind through his suffering in Jesus Christ. But we might also wonder whether our aggressive attitude toward nature, which is missing in Buddhism, is really in accord with God's command to subdue the earth. The greatest contribution of any such dialog would probably be measured for us by the degree to which it challenges, clarifies and perhaps even modifies our Christian ideas and practices.[131] Needless to say, the presupposition of any such dialog cannot be that we cannot learn anything positive in our encounter with non-Christian religions.

While God's self-disclosure in Jesus Christ is illuminative for our understanding of the non-Christian religions they in turn form the larger horizon within which the Judeo-Christian tradition finds its appropriate place and testing ground. Thus Raimundo Pannikkar is right when he demands a truly dialogical approach which presupposes that nobody has sole access to the universal horizon of human experience.[132] Perhaps we should remind ourselves of Paul's own precept: "Not that I have already obtained this or am already perfect; but I press on to make it my own, because Jesus Christ has made me his own" (Phil. 3:12). Then we could have a chance to accomplish the task of the Christian Church, so eloquently described by J. Robert Nelson, "to make credible the historic claims which it preaches concerning its role in the ultimate reconciliation of mankind." [133]

Since religion is the foundation of culture and determines the forms of culture, the way we view family, state, economic order, art, and science,[134] Christian faith has a responsibility to non-Christian religions beyond strict dialog. We have noticed a secular move-

ment sweeping ever more rapidly around the globe, a movement
that results in pseudo-religious absolutisms, such as humanism, communism, socialism, scientism, and the like. It strives for a total
secularization of all facets of life. Contrary to the Judeo-Christian
attempt to desacralize the world while at the same time maintain-
ing its transparency for the sacred, the process of secularization
always tends to be strictly mono-dimensional. In its attempt to
cover the whole earth it threatens the very existence of non-Christian religions, disallowing for any deities and telling man that he
can reconcile his existential alienation on his own. Furthermore, it
disassociates its message concerning man and his history from its
Christian foundation in turning it into a strictly this-worldly phenomenon.

Modern secularity creates a spiritual uncertainty and vacuum
which will have dangerous results in the long run. We have seen
that man, being aware of his finite nature, always searches for
an ultimate foundation whether fictional or real, which he can trust
and from which he can obtain guidance for his basic life attitude.
However, if this ultimate foundation does not provide an adequate
understanding of man, it will mean that man will deliver himself
to dehumanizing forces. His secular pursuit of progress will end
in an increasing dehumanization instead of furthering his humanizing. Even Hinduism and Buddhism with their inherent mystical
attitudes do not stand a chance to survive the onrush of modern
secularization.[135] If they would open themselves to modern secular
civilization, it would not settle in their midst without destroying
their religious convictions. Hendrik Kraemer has recognized this
danger when he asserts that modern secularity "implies the atrophy
of the religious constituent in human nature." [136] Yet most nations
in which non-Christian religions are dominant actively seek the
influence of secularization and the process of Westernization, since
it promises them to attain a higher standard of living and to become modern nations. Arend Th. van Leeuwen captured these
temptations very well when he compares the affect of modern
technological revolution upon non-Western societies and religions
with that of a Trojan horse that eventually will dispense with religion.[137]

Van Leeuwen also recognizes that while the traditional domination of the West has come to an end, Western civilization it at
the point of achieving a conquest greater than any it has made
hitherto.[138] He is optimistic that the resultant process of trans-

culturalization among the Asian and African peoples will provide a new opportunity for the Christians to join with the non-Christians in getting down to work together.[139] This means that Christians can join non-Christians in rebuilding their respective civilization after the storm of modern industrialization has swept through and blown away the religious myths. Though we basically agree with van Leeuwen's analysis of our present situation, we wonder why we should wait at the graveside of Eastern and African religions until they are buried by the onslaught of modern secular civilization. Has he forgotten that by rejecting the religious sphere, modern secular civilization does not only reject God but man as a person too? Its increasing and more and more exclusive dominance could have a more devastating effect on the destiny of humanity than any religion, regardless of how "primitive" it might be. We should heed here Wolfhart Pannenberg's insight when he claims that "the world of religions and man's religious disposition documented in them are the actual battle-ground on which theology must stand in its discussion with atheism."[140] It was precisely in our review of man's religions that we have realized on a worldwide basis that the notion of God need not rest on a misunderstanding of man's potential and therefore should be discarded but that it is indicative of his actual nature as a finite and (God-) dependent creature.

Lest we evolve a world civilization without a heartbeat and without a sense of direction, Christian faith must assume a twofold task: It must continuously remind all Western pseudo-religious movements that their progressive drive, plagiarized from the Christian gospel, cannot retain its vitality in the long run, unless it is reintegrated into its original Christian understanding of man as a finite being endowed with infinite value. Moreover, it must not cease to offer to people everywhere, in America and Europe as well as in Asia or in Africa, a frame of reference within which they can understand, modify, and integrate the global onslaught of a secular civilization. To accomplish this task, however, we need an adequate notion of God's self-disclosure as encountered in the Judeo-Christian tradition, because this self-disclosure provides both a basis for understanding man and frame of reference for man's life and living.

PART III

GOD'S SELF-DISCLOSURE IN
THE JUDEO-CHRISTIAN TRADITION

So far we have only alluded to the peculiarity of the Judeo-Christian tradition, adducing it as the prime witness to salvation offered by God through a continuous invitation. We have also mentioned its intrinsic monotheistic character which produced a world-affirming mood and led to a thoroughgoing desacralization. Unlike modern secularity, engendered by the collaboration between Greco-Roman thought and Christian faith, the Judeo-Christian tradition perceived God's explicit command and not man's volition as the presupposition for man's conquest and administration of the world. Affirmation of the world was paired with a theocentric understanding of the whole world in all its details culminating in the ultimate hope for a new creation. In these final two chapters we now want to raise the question whether these claims made earlier can be substantiated by elucidating God's self-disclosure witnessed in the Judeo-Christian tradition.

The roughly 2000 years spanned by the biblical tradition witness to a variety of the ways in which God has disclosed himself and of the concepts with which this self-disclosure has been expressed. Yet amid all this diversity two themes keep recurring. The Judeo-Christian tradition concerning God's self-disclosure is unmistakably monotheistic and affirms a God who wants to save man not by having him obey certain laws or follow certain devotional activities, but on the sole basis of God's initiative, by his invitation. These two convictions can be traced from the beginning of Israel's understanding of God as a tribal God to the present Christian understanding of God as the savior of mankind.

157

6.

From a Tribal God
to the Savior of Mankind

1. The emerging God of Israelite faith.

God as we know him historically is inextricably connected with
the history of Israel. Yet browsing through the Old Testament we
notice that there are many "names" for God, such as Elohim, Yahweh, El Shaddai, El Elyon, Sabaoth, or simply El. However, the
main term for God in Hebrew is Elohim. It can denote either God
as a proper name, or a god, or gods, and even *the* gods. The various
functions of this term indicate that it is not reserved strictly for
the Israelite God. This is different with the term Yahweh.

Yahweh never denotes just a god, but only the God who is the
God of Israel (Ex. 5:1). Though the Old Testament make no attempt to hide the fact that Israel's ancestors have not always known
Yahweh, the Yahwist claims that the worship of Yahweh is the
primeval religion of mankind (Gen. 4:26).[1] But Israel did not
always know God by his proper name Yahweh. For instance, when
Moses was sent to Israel's rescue, he wondered how he should
introduce the God who had been with Israel's ancestors. The
answer is clear: It is Yahweh who was with Israel's ancestors and
who will now rescue Israel from the Egyptian oppression (Ex.
3:13f.).[2]

Further evidence of the later emergence of the name Yahweh is
strangely enough given by the youngest source of the Pentateuch,
the priestly writer. In both Genesis 17:1 and Exodus 6:2-3, the
writer affirms that God did not reveal himself to the patriarchs

158

with his proper name, Yahweh; for them he is still known as El Shaddai or God Almighty.[3] In the Israelite religion the proper name for God, Yahweh, is of later date and its appearance is closely connected with Moses. This coincides with the finding that only from the time of Moses onward do we find proper names that are compounds of the proper name Yahweh.[4] But who is then this anonymous God of Israel's forefathers?

a. *The God of the Fathers*

In our attempt to describe the early period of Israel's religion we are confronted with the dilemma that biblical sources are confessional documents. They neither provide nor intend to provide a strictly historical account of Israel's history. Above that, the extra-biblical sources covering the period of Israel's earliest history are rather fragmentary.[5] Yet since Albrecht Alt's epoch making work *The God of the Fathers* (1929), it has at least become clear that the patriarchal stories in the book of Genesis are not fairy tales but give us valuable information about the actual worship performed by historic persons, such as Abraham, Isaac, and Jacob.[6] In his study Alt assumed that there was an actual cult connected with the God of Abraham (Gen. 15:1), the Fear of Isaac (Gen. 31:42), and the Mighty One of Jacob. The three patriarchs venerated three distinct numina of a similar type.

In the course of the occupation of Palestine these numina were associated with different pre-Israelite sanctuaries and finally merged into the God of the Fathers under the "leadership" of God of Abraham.[7] Alt suggests that there certainly were other patriarchal gods, but only these three found their way into the Genesis narratives. According to Alt some of their characteristic features, such as their tie to certain groups of people, their care for the welfare of their worshippers, and their inclination toward social and historical functions, also are characteristics that are to a higher degree constituent of Yahweh's character. Consequently he suggests that these gods of the Fathers were eventually absorbed into Yahweh, the God of all Israel. Thus the transition was made from tribal and local gods to a national god and Alt rightly calls the gods of the Fathers, "the *paidagogoi* leading to the greater God, who later replaced them completely." [8]

Alt's conclusions bear great merit and most Old Testament scholars have accepted them with some modifications.[9] It is evident from his analysis that each patriarchal group had its own way of characterizing God. Perhaps these characterizations only denote the way these groups experienced and felt about God and are not proper names for the respective patriarchal gods as Alt had assumed.[10] Alt's own observation that these numina are of the same type seems to encourage this conclusion. Alt has also pointed out very interestingly that the leaders or founders of these tribal groups are not actual founders of the respective cults. The "founding process" was always initiated by the disclosure of the godhead to which the leader or founder was directed in one way or another. Only upon this first step of the godhead did the choice or decision of the leader then follow to select this godhead as his god. This decision naturally entailed the worship of the godhead. Because of this pattern of "challenge and response" the personal ties of the patriarchs to their gods are emphasized more than in most other religions. Thus we read of the God of Abraham, or of Isaac, or of Jacob. Alt has also shown that these patriarchal gods were neither sky gods nor gods of local sanctuaries, but gods who accompanied the early Israelite tribes on their nomadic journey protecting and guiding them amidst other and often hostile tribes. We have seen that these gods of the Fathers have neither proper names nor are their characteristics very distinct from those of the Yahweh. So we wonder whether it is necessary to refer to them with Alt as a plurality and not rather as we would suggest as preparatory manifestations of the one and same God who introduced himself later as Yahweh. Thereby, of course, it remains undenied that the forefathers of Israel initially worshipped other gods as the Old Testament documents candidly admit (Josh. 24:2;14f.).[11]

b. *The God of Sinai.*

Leaving the patriarchs we come to Moses, often called the founder of the Israelite religion. Though in the present state of the Old Testament texts Moses is intimately connected with both the Exodus and the Sinai events, research has questioned whether this has always been the case. For instance, Old Testament scholars noticed that the Sinai tradition has enjoyed an independent status longer than any other tradition.[12] Gerhard von Rad and others have assumed that only secondarily was it incorporated into the tradition of the migration in the desert. This conclusion should not surprise us, since we can easily detect from the present arrangement of the Old Testament that the Sinai tradition received preferred treatment as that tradition which provided the main legal code for the Yahweh-Israel relationship. The matter, however, comes under a different light when we consider the figure of Moses within the Exodus, Wilderness, Sinai complex. It would mean that the figure of Moses was secondarily added to some traditions and that we can no longer ascertain how things really took place.[13] However, we would overstate our difficulty with the question of historicity if we would resign ourselves with Martin Noth to a historical skepticism and state that the single most certain tradition is the one of the tomb of Moses and beyond that we cannot say much more concretely about him, especially not that he was involved in the Sinai events.[14]

We rather follow Albright's conclusion that "Moses was actually the founder of the Israelite commonwealth and the framer of Israel's religious system." [15] It would be wrong to assume that thereby Moses stands on the same level as Zoroaster, Buddha, or Confucius. The Yahwistic tradition in the Pentateuch, for instance, does not designate Moses as leader of Israel, but shows that the leadership of Israel is alone Yahweh's task. Moses is rather described as an inspired man whom Yahweh uses to make known his will.[16] Similarly, the Elohist tradition depicts Moses as an instrument of God, as his prophet who is actively involved in the events surrounding Yahweh's self-disclosure. Deuteronomy, to go one step further, portrays Moses as the example of a prophet through whose coming Yahweh guarantees the continuous connection between himself and his people. With its main interest in the Sinai events, the priestly tradition moves Moses beyond the traditional terms of miracle worker, prophet, or priest. Moses is seen as the mediator between God and his people, the only one through whom Yahweh talks to his people and the one who alone can talk to God. Though his reflection of God's glory terrifies his people (Ex. 34:29ff.), he is still totally man and not free from sin and rebellion against God. All these traditions talk about a real man, who, as far as we know, was a Hebrew, born in Egypt and reared under strong Egyptian influence.[17] However, not Moses but Yahweh is the center and starting point of these traditions.

It is Israel's primal confession that Yahweh once led Israel out of Egypt. For instance, the Creed in Deut. 26:5-9 says:

> A wandering Aramean was my father; and he went down into Egypt and sojourned there, few in number; and there he became a nation, great, mighty, and populous. And the Egyptians treated us harshly, and afflicted us, and laid upon us hard

bondage. Then we cried to the Lord the God of our fathers,
and the Lord heard our voice, and saw our affliction, our toil,
and our oppression; and the Lord brought us out of Egypt with
a mighty hand and an outstretched arm, with great terror, with
signs and wonders; and he brought us into this place and gave
us this land, a land flowing with milk and honey.

Yet it seems strange that not until the Sinai events does this
God actually disclose himself through Moses to all Israel. However,
in referring to his acts at the Exodus from Egypt he then decrees
his commandments and establishes a covenant with them at Mt.
Sinai (Ex. 20:2). While the Exodus and Sinai narratives undoubtedly form two distinct and different "themes," both traditions and
the events underlying them need not be attributed to different
groups of Israelites.[18] Moses' sojourn in Midian, the revelation at
Mount Sinai or the Mountain of God, the rescue promised there,
the appointment of Moses to announce or conduct this rescue, the
reference to the later Sinai events, the Exodus with rescue from
the persecutors, and the journey to Mount Sinai and the events
there, these are all items that cannot easily be divorced from each
other and attributed to different independent traditions. Very likely
they belong together from their very beginning.

But who is the God who stands behind these events? Though he
is assumed to be identical with the God of the Fathers (Ex. 3:6),
the Elohist feels it necessary to interpret the name of Yahweh as
"I am who I am" and "I am" (Ex. 3:14). The two questions that
result from this attempted explanation are: Why did the Israelites
not know the meaning of the name Yahweh? and What does this
name mean? Most scholars feel that the interpretation of the name
given by the Elohist is imprecise and it has in turn led to numerous
other explanations.[19] Contrary to our way of thinking, in Hebrew
"to be" is not understood as a static being, but as a dynamic, active existence. Therefore the Elohist's explanation of Yahweh's name
describes Yahweh not as eternal being but as an active, creative
God. Accordingly, Albright suggested that "I am who I am" should
be translated as "He Causes to Be What Comes into Existence."[20]
This notion of Yahweh, as the creator and life sustaining power of
everything that exists, is amply documented in the later Old Testament. This still leaves the question open why the Israelites did
not already know Yahweh's name. An answer to this question
may be found in the biblical references to the Midianites.

We hear that Moses spent some time in Midian where he married a daughter of the Midianite priest Jethro (cf. Ex. 2:15ff.). When Jethro visited his son-in-law (Ex. 18:12), without hesitation he offered sacrifice to Yahweh. The Midianites are also depicted as visiting the mountain of God in the wilderness (Ex. 18:5). Some of the Midianites seem to be related to the Kenites,[21] and we hear that the Kenites received special treatment by the Israelites since they "showed kindness to all the people of Israel when they came out of Egypt" (1 Sam. 15:6); according to Numbers 10:29-32 Moses' father-in-law also guided the Israelites through the wilderness after they had encamped near the mountain of God. Of course, it would be an oversimplification to conclude from these references that the Israelites simply adopted a Kenite or Midianite god.[22] Though Moses first encountered Yahweh in Midianite territory, it was the experience of their rescue from Egypt (provided by Yahweh) and the covenant (which he extended to them and upon which they agreed at Mount Sinai) that were constitutive for Israel's worship of Yahweh. Moses' function in this process can be paralleled with that of the patriarchs prior to him. He is the leader to whom God disclosed himself and he in turn inspired the groups led by him to accept the God he had encountered. But who is this God who was once accepted by the patriarchs, then by Moses, and eventually by all Israel?

Yahweh's features can be easily brought into analogy with some type of volcano or storm gods, with Egyptian gods, or with the godheads of Mesopotamia.[23] Though these analogies illuminate certain features of Yahweh, they are unable to explain him totally. The characteristics conferred upon Yahweh are not a product of syncretism, but result from the experience of a certain history which was understood as the effect of Yahweh's governance. This experience was facilitated through a basically anthropomorphic conception of Yahweh. While most near Eastern gods were thought of as appearing in astral, zoomorphic, or composite forms, Yahweh was always experienced in anthropomorphic form. This is true for the whole Israelite history starting with such harsh anthropomorphisms as God "walking in the garden in the cool of the day" (Gen. 3:8) and being continued in the New Testament with "Our father in heaven" which the Lord taught his disciples. Though his "mighty arm," his "loud voice," his love and hatred, his joy and sorrow, and his revenge and remorse intimate human form, Yahweh remains inaccessible and invisible because of his enveloping glory. The only exception in the Pentateuch is Exodus 33:23 where Moses is allowed to see Yahweh's back, but not his face.[24]

It would be easy here to claim that the anthropomorphic nature of Yahweh's appearance is patterned according to human needs and thus is a projection of the human mind. But we prefer rather to follow Albright's suggestion that those anthropomorphisms were sheer necessities (and still are) if Yahweh was to remain a God for the individual Israelite as well as for the people as a whole. For the Israelite it was

> very essential that his god be a divinity who can sympathize with his human feelings and emotions, a being whom he can love and fear alternately, and to whom he can transfer the holiest emotions connected with the memories of father and mother and friend. In other words, it was precisely the anthropomorphism of Yahweh which was essential to the initial success of Israel's religion.[25]

Even today when we advocate a much more spiritualized notion of God, it is still immensely difficult to have a meaningful relationship to "the ground of being" or to "the god who is love." Yet it was usually clear for Israel that these anthropomorphisms were not descriptions of Yahweh. Yahweh transcended all human characteristics that served as conceptualizations of his involvement with the individual and with Israel at large. It is noteworthy in this context that belief in Yahweh forbade any material representations of him. Whenever such representations are introduced, the Old Testament writers endeavor to show that these are trespasses against Yahweh's will which will not remain without consequences (Ex. 32).[26]

Another important feature of Yahweh is that, similar to the God of the Fathers, he was not conceived of as being restricted to a permanent residence or to a certain locale. He was not a territorial God, but a God who associated himself with a certain group of people and who came to their aid. Though he was the Lord of creation, controlling sun, moon, and the stars, he was not identified with any of them. Usually he was thought of as dwelling in heaven from where he came down either to a lofty mountain such as Sinai or Horeb, or to a shrine such as the tent of meeting, or to any spot he may choose. Occasionally he was also referred to as coming from Mount Seir or from Paran, or just from Edom. It almost appears as if the Israelites had no interest in localizing the exact spot of Yahweh's habitation. This does not mean that there were no sacred places, such as Mount Sinai, but that, since there was no special cult associated with them, their precise name and location were unimportant. It was much more crucial for the Israelites that Yahweh came from those places to be with his worshipers on their migrations, and to perform his mighty acts during the Exodus, in the wilderness, or in the cultivated land.

Yahweh's most important feature, however, was his relational character. Often this relational character was thought of in terms of a covenant which God makes with his people. Thus we speak of the old covenant or the Old Testament and the new covenant or the New Testament. But such terminology is easily misleading. The Hebrew term *berith* which is used in the Yahwist (Ex. 34:10; 27) and the Elohist traditions (Ex. 24:7f.) to denote the constitutive event which establishes the relationship between Yahweh and his people does not mean covenant or treaty.[27] It rather means that either Yahweh is undergoing an affirmative obligation or that he confers an obligation upon Israel. Thus we are not surprised to find the cultic (Ex. 34:10-26) and the ethical decalogs (Ex. 20:1-17) in the context of the "covenant." At Sinai a unique event had happened which was to establish a permanent relationship between Yahweh and those around Moses. Israel became Yahweh's people in the sense of being related to him as indicated in sharing the sacred meal (Ex. 24) and conforming to the same standards. Decisive in this "covenant" concept is that this relationship was founded on Yahweh's unconditioned will. God wanted to make himself known to Moses and he wanted to establish a lasting relationship with Israel. Thus this "covenant" was not a contractual relationship to secure certain services or to obtain certain privileges but it was Yahweh's offer to Israel mediated through their spokesman Moses.

Israel was always aware that the "covenant" with Yahweh was not the result of the unconditioned will of both partners, Yahweh and Israel. Also Israel was never so presumptuous as to think that it would make a "covenant" with Yahweh, since it was clearly understood as the result of Yahweh's own doing.[28] Though both partners are infinitely unequal, the relationship does not result in mere domination of one partner over the other. On the contrary, Yahweh obliges himself to a certain way of looking out for Israel and Israel responds with its willingness to fulfill certain obligations. Thus Yahweh's relational character implies always a definite promise on his side. Israel also knows that the covenant implies Yahweh's dominion over those who are related to him through it. This is, for instance, expressed in the conviction that Yahweh wants to be recognized as Israel's only God. As the Exodus events show, Yahweh's dominion has a very comforting aspect too, because it can even involve those nations who are linked with the well-being of his chosen people. This understanding of Yahweh's dominion was later expanded in two directions: that Yahweh is the Lord over all the world and that all mankind is included in his covenant. Yet the realization of the promises implied in the covenant was always contingent upon the way his chosen people act. Thus history seen in relationship to Yahweh became a decisional history, it was not simply a working out of Yahweh's promises, but was also seen as a consequence of Israel fulfilling or not fulfilling the obligations of its relationship to Yahweh.

c. *God and the gods.*

One of the astounding phenomena of Israelite faith was that the Israelites did not abandon their seemingly nomadic God once they settled in Palestine. The groups connected with the patriarchs did not leave behind their God of the Fathers once they moved into Canaanite territory. On the contrary, the Israelites kept allegiance to their God, though using pagan sanctuaries, and gradually even connected these with their own God. Some of the formerly Canaanite cult etiologies were reinterpreted and often used in such a way that the local gods were equated with the God of the Fathers. Especially the god El seems to have been identified with the God of the Fathers without even changing his name. Consequently, we still find narratives with El Olam (Gen. 21:14-19) or El Bethel (Gen. 28:10-22) or Penuel (Gen. 32:25-32) in the Old Testament.[29] Of course, this was not mere equation. It meant that specific elements of the God of the Fathers were introduced into these narratives, while at the same time allowing for considerable influx of Canaanite ideas into the Israelite understanding of God. But in the long run it proved to be an effective means for not only conquering Palestinian territory but for making any exclusive worship of Canaanite gods in the conquered territory impossible.

When those around Moses entered the promised land the identification of Yahweh with the God of the Fathers seemed to have posed no problems. The story was different with Yahweh and the gods of Canaan. There was no doubt that those other gods were actual powers that were the masters over other nations (cf. 1

Kings 11:7f.). Once the Israelites abandoned their nomadic existence and settled down in the cultured land these gods were a
great temptation for them. After all, customs and language of the
cultured land deeply reflected the intrinsic connection between
an agrarian way of life and the acceptance of those powers.[30] The
statement in Deuteronomy 32:17, dating from the 11th century B.C.:
"They sacrificed to demons which were no gods, to gods they had
never known, to new gods that had come in of late, whom your
fathers had never dreaded," [31] portrays the magnitude of the spiritual struggle taking place during the first centuries after Israel
had entered the promised land.

Gideon may serve as a prime example to document this inner
strife within the emerging Israelite community (Judges 6-8). He
himself was a strong supporter of Yahweh and destroyed an altar
of Baal in his native town of Ophrah and cut down the sacred
Asherah. But his name Jerubbaal betrays Canaanite influence, because it is a composite form of Baal, the name of a Canaanite
deity. The name of his father, Joash, was still a composite form
of Yahweh, the God of Israel. We also hear that Gideon's own
Israelite people were enraged about his destructive acts against
Canaanite deities. But then we are told that even Gideon himself
set up a golden ephod in Ophrah. As far as we know, an ephod
is a rich costume covered with gold or silver and studded with
stars and other cosmic symbols. The Israelites who still adhered to
the strict Mosaic tradition could easily interpret it as an idol in
analogy to Canaanite statutes of gods. But in the official Yahwist
cult of the day it could also be understood as the visible symbol
of the invisible deity.[32] The story of Gideon gives us some idea
of the kind of absorption, adaptation, and rejection that took place
in those first centuries after Israel settled down in the promised
land.

We have noticed that the Israelites sensed no difficulty identifying the Canaanite El first with the God of the Fathers and later
also with Yahweh. But the story was different as far as the Canaanite fertility god Baal is concerned. Initially, some Israelites may
have equated Baal with Yahweh or venerated him parallel to Yahweh. Even some of his characteristics may have been conferred
upon Yahweh. For instance, we find names that are composites
of the name Baal; such as Ishbaal, the son of Saul, and we see that,
in analogy to Aleyan Baal, the god of thunder, Yahweh was praised
as the one "who rides upon the clouds" (Ps. 68:4).[33] However, the

constant battle of the prophets against the worship under trees and in high places and sometimes even against the whole sacrificial cult (Amos 5:21-27) shows us in which direction prevailing thinking went.[34] Deuteronomy, reflecting upon the situation after Israel had entered Palestine, makes the point clear:

> When you come into the land which the Lord your God gives you, you shall not learn to follow the abominable practices of those nations. There shall not be found among you any one who burns his son or his daughter as an offering, any one who practices divination, a soothsayer, or an augur, or a sorcerer, or a charmer, or a medium, or a wizard, or a necromancer. For whoever does these things is an abomination to the Lord; and because of these abominable practices the Lord your God is driving them out before you. You shall be blameless before the Lord your God. For these nations, which you are about to dispossess, give heed to soothsayers and to diviners; but as for you, the Lord your God has not allowed you so to do.
>
> Deuteronomy 18:9-14

Of course, such a conviction does not advance a monotheistic stand in the modern sense of the word. The actuality of other powers besides Yahweh is still recognized. But there is no doubt that guidance and help can come alone from Yahweh who offered his assistance to Israel and who demanded their allegiance.

2. God's self-disclosure in Jesus Christ.

It is almost presumptuous to jump from the time of early Israel right into the New Testament time as if nothing substantially had happened since then. First we must recognize that there are great differences between the deliberately "crude" and picturesque anthropomorphisms of the Yahwist who depicts God walking in the garden in the cool of the day (Gen. 3), Isaiah's experience in the temple when he encountered the Lord sitting upon the throne (Isa. 6), Ezekiel's vision of the heavenly chariot by the river Chebar in Mesopotamia (Ezek. 1), and Jesus' reference to God as his Father who is in heaven. What is reflected here in these different parts of the Bible is a progressive and continuous reconceptualization of God. Especially Herbert Braun has pointed out that there is a movement traceable in the Bible from a more objectified understanding of God to a more spiritualized one.[35] Braun insists that this change is primarily a change according to the conceptual horizon of man. Starting with Israel's ancestors and ending with Jesus we start with polytheism, go through a stage of henotheism (veneration of just one god), and finally arrive at a monotheism, though often still in the gown of a "dramatic dualism" of the apocalyptic. But it is always the same God who stands at the center of man's experience.

Second, in apocalyptic, the transition period from the Old Testament to the New, some interesting changes occurred. During this period the national, ethnic God of Israel was more and more conceived of as the sole agent of all historic and finally of all cosmic processes. This understanding provided history with a basic unity. One supra-nationalistic and supra-worldly God, the God of Israel, was now seen as the sole agent of this historic process shaping and destining the world to his purpose.[36] At the same time when God was elevated beyond the ethnic history of Israel his name underwent a significant change. While in the Hebrew Old Testament the prevailing name for the God of Israel is his proper name Yahweh, the Greek translation of the Old Testament mostly uses Lord in place of Yahweh.[37] Outside the Bible the term Lord or Kyrios had been in use for a long time to refer to deities or to the emperor. In the New Testament, however, the terminology had changed again, because Kyrios or Lord is no longer the main term for God. Now it is usually superseded by the generic term *theos* or God. In other words, the growing awareness of God's universal domain goes hand in hand with changing his name from a proper name to the generic name for God. And we are not surprised to find that Luke and Paul, both being in close touch with the Hellenistic world, even resort to stoic-pantheistic conceptuality to proclaim God (Acts 17:27f.; Romans 11:36). Since God is the only God every (religious) person knows about him at least to some extent. Yet this knowledge is not sufficient, since without Christ, we do not know the full story of God's saving activity.

a. *God as the Father of Jesus Christ.*

The New Testament writers took great pains in demonstrating the continuity of the Christian community with the people of Israel. For instance, in the Gospel of Matthew the church founded by Jesus is through his authority the true Israel (Matt. 16:18).[38] The historic nation of Israel has neglected and lost its commission to be the light of the nations. Thus the church replaces it and steps into continuity with the Israel of promise. This continuity between Israel and the Christian community is seen as tied to the person of Jesus, since he is conceived of as fulfilling the Old Testament promises.[39] He did not come to abolish the law and the prophets, but to fulfill them (Matt. 5:17f.). He fulfilled the Immanuel promise (Isa. 7:14; Matt. 1:22f.), the Galilee promise (Isa. 9:1f; Matt. 4:12-16), the Bethlehem promise (Mic. 5:2; Matt. 2:5f.), the servant of the Lord promise (Isa. 53:4; Matt. 8:17), and many others. He also carries the multitude of Old Testament eschatological titles. He is the Messiah, the son of David, the king of Israel, the Son of God, and the Son of Man, to name just a few. These intended to show not so much that Jesus is the bringer of the eschaton, but more important that Jesus stands in true continuity with the Old Testament.

Paul in wrestling with the destiny of ethnic Israel came to the conclusion that bodily descent from the people of Israel does not guarantee one to be part of the true Israel (Rom. 9:6-8). In his sovereignty God has rejected those who did not accept Jesus Christ and has chosen those who accepted him. But Paul warned the Christian community not to pride itself in God's undeserved election as his chosen people (Rom. 11:20). Only through faith can this election and the succession in Israel's footsteps be maintained. While Israel can in some sense be regarded as the enabler of the succession, it serves at the same time as the warning sign for the Christians not to fall into the same pit of ethnic and religious security as Israel once did. Jesus Christ alone seems to make the difference between standing in true conformity with God or in his covenant and missing one's temporal, and eternal destiny. This conclusion seems to be attested to by the implications of Jesus' own proclamation.

Jesus' call to a decision, enunciated in his proclamation, implied the notion that God's revelation was taking place in his proclamation.[40] This means that those who rejected Jesus' proclamation rejected God's self-disclosure. The peculiarity of Jesus' proclamation was not that he decreed propositional sentences about God's will, but that he spoke as if he stood in God's place. No sane person had dared to do this before him. For instance, he claimed to forgive sins, he reinterpreted the law authoritatively (Mark 2:10; 28), and he drew the outcasts of society to himself and condemned those who were self-righteous (Matt. 11:16ff.). We also notice that Jesus applied to himself the Old Testament theophany concept.[41] The Jewish people understood the temple as the place of the presence of God. The great temple festivals were in the deepest sense theophany festivals in which the believers experienced the presence of God. According to Jewish thinking this self-disclosure of God occurred in the word. Thus the liturgical self-proclamation of God was decisive. For instance, the festival pericope of the Feast of the Tabernacles in the fall opened with the words: "I am the Lord your God, who brought you out of the land of Egypt, out of the house of bondage . . ." (Deut. 5:6). Or the Hallel psalms, which were sung at the Passover (Pss. 113-118), have the liturgical self-proclamation of Yahweh in many places. The theophany formula "I am" or "I am he" occurs also many times in Deutero-Isaiah and in post-exilic writings. The Greek translation of the term "I am" or the "I am he" is *ego eimi*.[42]

At a few decisive places in the gospels Jesus uses the term *ego eimi* in a way analogous to the Old Testament theophany formula. Jesus says in Mark 13:6: "Many will come in my name, saying, 'I am he!' and they will lead many astray." [43] In Matthew this theophanic self-predication is no longer understood and is replaced by "I am the Christ" (Matt. 24:5). Or in the trial when the High Priest asks Jesus: "Are you the Christ, the Son of the Blessed?" Jesus replies according to Mark 14:62: "I am; and you will see the Son of man sitting at the right hand of Power, and coming with the clouds of heaven." [44] He does not admit that he is the Messiah but he confronts the court with the Old Testament theophany formula. Small wonder that the trial is soon over, because in the eyes of the Sanhedrin Jesus has committed the worst crime possible. He has revealed himself as the self-disclosure of God and therefore as God himself. This was blasphemy and made any further investigation unnecessary. Jesus is also depicted in the gospels as allowing himself to be adored as in the case of the blind man who was healed (John 9:38), or by the mother of the sons of Zebedee when she asked him for a favor (Matt. 20:20). The term *proskynein*, used to describe this adoration, does not denote the homage and reverence accorded to a man, not even that given to a miracle worker, but paid to a divine figure.[45]

Jesus' understanding of his relation to God is best expressed with the term "son." According to the Old Testament, Israel understood itself as the firstborn of God, as elected among all nations (Deut. 14:1f.; Ex. 4:22; Jer. 31:9).[46] Though this election had been made historically manifest in the Exodus from Egypt, the Old Testament prophets constantly reminded Israel that this Father-

Son or Father-Child relationship was threatened by Israel's sinfulness (cf. Deut. 32:5f.; Jer. 3:19f.; Mal. 1:6; Isa. 64:7f., and many others). Joachim Jeremias has pointed out Jesus had taken up this Father-Son imagery in a unique way.[47] Jesus referred to God as his Father indicating that God had disclosed himself to Jesus in such a way as only a father can disclose himself to his son. This usage of the imagery, though foreshadowed in the Old Testament, does not find any correspondence in rabbinic literature. It is patterned according to the exclusive promise given to David to whom Yahweh spoke through his prophet Nathan: "I will be his father, and he shall be my son" (2 Sam. 7:14), and according to the royal announcements in Psalm 2:7 and 89:19f. Only later was this promise expanded to include all Israel. By using the Father-Son imagery in analogy to the relationship between Yahweh and David, the indication is made that we face in Jesus the true continuance of the promise to David.

Moreover, Jesus often connects the reference to the Father with the immediate disclosure of God's will (Matt. 11:25; 27). This means that he does not act as a prophet who announces the establishment of the Father-Son relation, but he acts as the Son who asserts his unique relationship with his Father. Bearing this in mind we are not surprised that Jesus always distinguishes between "my Father" and "your Father." In other words, the relationship between God and Jesus is exclusive and finds only its analogy and not its sameness in the relationship between God and Jesus' disciples. Even the opening words of the Lord's Prayer were originally "Father" or "Dear Father" and not "Our Father" (cf. Luke 11:2).[48] Nevertheless Jesus encouraged his disciples to trust God as their Father. Due to Jesus' own influence the first Christian community dared to call God their Father (Gal. 4:6; Rom. 8:15f.), and at the same time they called Jesus their Lord.[49] Both moves seem to be inextricably inter-related, if we consider the concept of a new covenant as the connecting piece. Since Jesus is God's self-disclosure and therefore identical with God, he can extend to his followers a new covenant in analogy to the old one. This new covenant opens for his followers as the new Israel the possibility to understand themselves as sons and God as their Father. Again this new sonship looks back at its historical manifestation, this time not in the Exodus, but in the life, death, (and resurrection), of Jesus the Christ. Since the former ethnic preference is no longer valid,

Jesus the Christ now becomes decisive for any cognizant relationship with God.

b. *Exclusiveness of God's revelation in Jesus Christ.*

The New Testament captured very well the understanding of the exclusiveness of God's revelation in Jesus Christ. For instance, in the Gospel of John we hear Jesus say to his disciples: "I am the way, and the truth, and the life; no one comes to the Father, but by me" (John 14:6).[50] Here the conviction is expressed that Jesus as the revealer provides the only access to God. This does not mean that Jesus mediates access to God and then becomes superfluous. Contrary to man's innermost yearning, there is no immediate access to God. God is only approachable in and through the historic Jesus of Nazareth. The encounter with Jesus, not the assent to certain esoteric rules or words of wisdom, is decisive for our knowledge of God or, to speak in Johannine terminology, for our "being in truth." He who rejects Jesus rejects God and his opportunity for being in conformity with God (John 3:18). In a similar way we hear Peter confess: "And there is salvation in no one else, for there is no other name under heaven given among men by which we must be saved" (Acts 4:12). The way this confession reads now there is no doubt that with the name which provides salvation the name of Jesus is meant. But considering the Jewish background of this statement we remember that once only the name of Yahweh could have been referred to in this manner.[51] This means that this quotation again attests to the exclusiveness of God's revelation in Christ by identifying Jesus the Christ with Yahweh.

Since the New Testament writers are convinced that God identified himself with Jesus of Nazareth and that Jesus of Nazareth identified himself with God their conclusion follows that this self-disclosure of God has unsurpassable character. We are confronted with an actual direct self-mediation of God in the best communicable form for man, in another man. God becomes man, he becomes communicable and understandable. Though such a self-disclosure of God in a thou, in a human being, is unsurpassable, the question is whether it is exclusive. God could identify himself totally with other men in the history of mankind too and thus the possibility of other redeemers could not be excluded. There could also be new covenants similar to the new covenant that the Christian community experienced. But the assumption of a plurality of ultimate self-disclosures of God will prove itself to be unwarranted.

Already the writer of the Letter to the Hebrews asserts in his opening sentence: "In many and various ways God spoke of old to our fathers by the prophets; but in these last days he has spoken to us by a Son, whom he appointed the heir of all things, through whom also he created the world." (Heb. 1:1f.)[52] The writer of this letter seems to remind his readers of the various ways through which God disclosed himself in Old Testament times, such as through dreams, visions, and auditions, through angels, and through animals. But now things are different, he says, because God has spoken in an eschatological time. And Jesus is the decisive factor, because he speaks in an eschatological time as an eschatological figure and preaches an eschatological message. Of course, in the apocalyptic situation prevalent at the time of Jesus, there were many others with whom eschatological expectations were connected, for instance, John the Baptist, the zealots Judas the Galilaean and Simon, son of Giora, and, above all, Bar Kochba[53] However, only in the life and destiny of Jesus can we recognize that the still outstanding eschaton has already started. For example, when Jesus claimed that through him "the blind receive their sight, the lame walk, lepers are cleansed, and the deaf hear, the dead are raised up, the poor have the good news preached to them" (Luke 7:22), then every alert Jew knew that Jesus applied to himself the Old Testament imageries that were associated with the time of salvation (Isa. 35:5f.). In other words, Jesus introduced himself as the one in whose actions salvation became manifest. The same is true for his proclamation. When he mentioned that new wine should not be poured into old wine skins (Matt. 9:17), he wanted to emphasize that the old time is past, and the time of salvation has been initiated. Once Jesus stated it even more clearly: "But if it is by the finger of God that I cast out demons, then the kingdom of God has come upon you" (Luke 11:20).

With Jesus the kingdom of God has already begun.[54] What had been expected for centuries, what had been projected into the future or into the present for many times has started now. The kingdom of God is in the midst of you, said Jesus. He did not call for an immediate decision because he was such an important preacher, or because he had such an important message. The kingdom of God had been realized with his appearance and thus it was time, decisive time. The coming of Jesus is the turning point of history.

But the emerging Christian community did not simply preserve

Jesus' message and the record of his actions. Under the impression of the Easter event the proclaimer suddenly became the proclaimed and therewith the focal point of the Christian gospel. In the context of apocalyptic expectations shared by Jesus, his disciples, and part of the Jewish community, this radical change becomes understandable. According to apocalyptic hopes the resurrection of the dead is an important part of the final eschatological drama. Sharing these hopes and expectations the disciples could now recognize that Jesus actually was what he said he was, the initiator of the eschaton which he had brought about in proleptic anticipation through his own resurrection.[55]

Yet Christ's resurrection was not understood as a mere confirmation of prevalent apocalyptic ideas. When Paul, for instance, refers to Christ's resurrection he does not simply refer to him as the validation of the apocalyptic hope for a resurrection, but he understands Christ's resurrection as the presupposition of our own resurrection.[56] In other words, through the resurrection of Jesus Christ the apocalyptic *idea* of a common resurrection is modified to the Christian *hope* in the resurrection, because of Christ and because of his resurrection. Thus Christ is not only the turning point or focal point of history, he is at the same time the goal of history, a goal which he proleptically anticipated in his own resurrection. Each Christian can and will participate in this anticipation, because, as Paul said, "If any one is in Christ, he is a new creation; the old has passed away, behold, the new has come" (2 Cor. 5:17). This does not mean that Christians are not subject to the conditions and limitations of this phenomenal world. However, insofar as they identify themselves with Christ, their ultimate destiny is not identical with that of this world, but with that of Christ.

Thus the idea of an on-going revelation apart from Jesus Christ and his destiny, or even beyond it, would contradict his anticipatory character.[57] A revelation of the God who provided this world with its foundation, its present course, and its ultimate destiny cannot be thought of apart from Jesus Christ. Of course, the question must be posed here whether the emphasis on the exclusiveness of God's self-disclosure would contradict the status we have attributed earlier to non-Christian religions. We have observed that the revelatory history of God starting with the founding fathers of Israel and culminating in the life and destiny of Jesus the Christ, is basically a history of God's initiative, or in other words the history of the great invitation. The religious history of mankind apart from this invitation is neither just an expression of man's sinfulness nor a history simply leading up to Christ. It is the history of man as creature who is moved by the existential separation from his creator. While some religious manifestations express more the misconception that finite man can heal his existential separation from God, others convey the notion that only God can reconcile the world with himself.

The emphasis on the exclusiveness of God's self-disclosure in Jesus Christ, however, is not directed against non-Christian religions *per se*. Rather, it is pronounced to those who are confronted with the Christian gospel. Those who are encountered by the gospel and its call for a decision cannot but respond, and, as far as we know, their response will have eternal significance. Concerning the non-Christian religions our conclusions must be of much more modest character. Since God disclosed himself in an unsurpassable way in Jesus Christ, we know what kind of God he is. Knowing that he is not just a God of holiness but also of compassion, we can affirm hope for those never properly confronted with the Christian gospel. This means that the God-disclosive history of the Judeo-Christian tradition becomes a source of clarity and hope in our understanding of all religious history. Of course, one could now object and ask why God's self-disclosure in Jesus Christ must be exclusive and unsurpassable. Such objection can only be adequately dealt with in referring to God's own primacy in the whole revelatory process. The recognition of "it pleased God" is the deepest reason for the exclusiveness of his self-disclosure in Jesus Christ.

c. *Ambiguity of God's revelation in Jesus Christ.*

We have seen that ultimately the exclusiveness of God's self-disclosure in Jesus Christ is as little demonstrable as the fact that such self-disclosure occurred at all. This basic insight in the structural ambiguity of God's self-disclosure in Jesus Christ is nothing new.

At first the emerging Christian church thought it could define on strictly logical grounds how God was present in the man Jesus. Yet after several generations of intensive spiritual and political struggle it became more and more evident that the issue how the man Jesus of Nazareth was related to his God-disclosive or divine nature could not be so easily settled. The church understood him to be identical with God and still a true human being, or in other words that he was true God and true man.[58] But when the church assembled for its ecumenical council at Chalcedon (A.D. 451) it finally recognized the limits of human reason and instead of defining the relationship between the divine and the human nature in Jesus Christ it restricted itself to only a negative solution. Both natures, it said, were present in Jesus in such a way that they were neither mixed together nor changed to a "higher" entity, neither torn apart nor even separable. This restraint from defining how both natures are related to each other in Jesus the Christ while at the same time insisting on their actual presence and inextricable togetherness saved God's ultimate self-disclosure from being distorted to a timeless philosophical truth.

The church stated first of all that what happened to Jesus occurred to someone within space and time. At the same time it affirmed that that which happened is not something available or accessible in the space-time continuum. If the opposite were true, there would be no reasons why the church could not rationally define how God's self-disclosure in Jesus is related to another phenomenon of space and time, namely Jesus' human nature. Consequently, empirical research can never come up with a statement like, "Jesus was God's self-disclosure." Even exegesis can only unearth bits about a truly human being called Jesus of Nazareth. If it arrived at assertions about Jesus' divine nature, it would leave its empirical ground and enter either the realm of faith or of speculation. Naturally, such conclusions must affect our understanding of Jesus Christ as the God-disclosive event.

We have seen before that the significance of Jesus can only be appropriately understood in the context of Israel's history of promise and expectation. Thus only in the contextual history of Israel and not as an isolated event does the Christ event reveal the Godhead of Yahweh.[59] But the history of Israel is not a special case of history whose course, culminating in the Christ event, would make God's self-disclosure unmistakably evident. On the other hand through these historical events both Israel and the Christian community gained insight that transcends empirical verification. In other words, the history of Israel and the Christ event seem to have God-disclosive power. How can God then be disclosed in such events if, as the Chalcedonian confession recognized, he is neither an additional component of the historic process nor separable from it? The only solution is to consider this process as an obvious paradox.

Though every cause and component of the Judeo-Christian salvation history *(Heilsgeschichte)* can be explained within a strictly empirical reference system, it must at the same time be understood as a totally God-wrought process. Observing this paradox, Jesus' proclamation, action, and destiny are not the result of a religious fanatic, but a disclosure of God's demand and promise. This paradox will not allow us to forget that it is the man Jesus of Nazareth through whom God becomes transparent. Since we always perceive God's ultimate pronouncement and action through an anthropomorphic veil, we do not perceive God in himself, but in his approximative anthropomorphic form. Therefore this ultimate self-disclosure of God is still disclosure in approximation, God becoming communicable in human form.

The necessary approximation through which God descends to our phenomenal level together with the paradox of Jesus being true God and true man result in the decision-demanding character of God's self-disclosure in Jesus Christ. Since the Judeo-Christian *Heilsgeschichte* confronts the listener with the claim that it is the God-disclosive history, he cannot escape from making a choice. Yet a positive decision does not simply result from an option between two possibilities. Since the Judeo-Christian history of salvation has the power to convince the skeptic as well as to withhold its God-wrought nature from the seeker, the believer recognizes that God himself is involved in the decision making process. Once the decision of accepting the basic paradox has been reached, the approximation character of this self-disclosure allows for increasingly deeper investigation of this disclosive process. The result will be an ever deeper understanding of God's self-disclosure contained in the human form of Jesus of Nazareth. But what is God like in this self-disclosure?

7.

The Likeness of God

How can man talk about God? If we want to talk about what God is like, at once a host of problems emerges. Kierkegaard noticed that there is an infinitive qualitative difference between God and man. Karl Barth, pursuing a similar line, stated the resulting difficulty very precisely: *"As ministers we ought to speak of God. We are human, however, and so cannot speak of God. We ought therefore to recognize both,* our obligation and our inability *and by that very recognition give God the glory.* This is our perplexity. The rest of our task fades into insignificance in comparison." [1] In their attempt to talk about God many philosophers and theologians have followed the path outlined by Pseudo-Dionysius (ca. A.D. 500). Though he was actually a disciple of the neo-platonic philosopher Plotinus, he wrote under the pseudonym Dionysius the Areopagite, a convert of St. Paul in Athens, and consequently gained almost apostolic authority. In his treatise *The Divine Names* he outlines his methodology saying:

> Furthermore, we must ask how it is that we know God when He cannot be perceived by the mind or the senses and is not a particular Being. Perhaps 'tis true to say that we know not God by His Nature (for this is unknowable and beyond the reach of all Reason and Intuition), yet by means of that ordering of all things which (being as it were projected out of Him) possesses certain images and semblances of His Divine Exemplars, we mount upwards (so far as our feet can tread that ordered path), advancing through the Negation and Transcendence of all things and through a conception of a Universal Cause, towards That Which is beyond all things.[2]

Pseudo-Dionysius advocates here a three-fold way to arrive at a notion of the likeness of God, the *via negativa,* or the negative way, the *via eminentia,* or the superlative way, and the *via causalitatis,* or the way of causal inference. Thus we attribute to God adjectives such as infinite, immortal, incomprehensible according to the negative way by trying to negate attributes that are usually consigned to human beings, such as finite, mortal and comprehensible. Or we confer upon God adjectives such as omnipotent, omniscient, or omnipresent according to the superlative way by attempting to surpass attributes that are usually associated with human beings, such as potency, knowledge, or presence. Finally God is referred to as the first uncaused cause or the creator of all things according to the way of causal inference. Even statements such as God as the moral order of the world (Kant) or the holy (Otto) or the pure act (scholasticism) are ultimately related to one of the three ways that Pseudo-Dionysius lined out.

Of course, hardly any of these descriptions of God were ever taken literally. They were usually immediately qualified by the admission that they are not intended to be literal.[3] Paul Tillich, for instance, has pointed out in volume 1 of his *Systematic Theology* that all statements about God are of symbolic nature. Only "the statement that God is being-itself is a non-symbolic statement. It does not point beyond itself. It means what it says directly and properly."[4] In volume 2 he is still more cautious, saying: "Thus it follows that everything religion has to say about God, including his qualities, actions, manifestations, has a symbolic character and that the meaning of 'God' is completely missed if one takes the symbolic language literally." Asking himself whether there is a non-symbolic statement about God possible he concludes: ". . . There is a point at which a non-symbolic assertion about God must be made . . . , namely, the statement that everything we say about God is symbolic."[5] With this concession Tillich has recognized that regardless of what we say about God all our assertions have at best symbolic character. However, for Tillich this does not mean they are of no value.

Tillich distinguishes between sign and symbol saying "while the sign bears no necessary relation to that to which it points, the symbol participates in the reality of that for which it stands."[6] Therefore, a religious symbol not only points to the divine, but if it is a true symbol it even participates in the power of the divine. Reviewing the abundant literature concerning the God issue, however, one wonders whether the symbols advocated there actually disclosed much about God, since there seems to be hardly any consensus about them. Wolfgang Trillhaas characterized the situation very aptly when he said:

> Each dogmatician, especially among the modern ones, decrees the attributes (of God) differently than another, so that one cannot refute the impression that this process is governed by a certain arbitrary speculation which is nourished by the richness of biblical and at the same time philosophical tradition.[7]

Already Friedrich Schleiermacher sensed this subjective and speculative tendency when he mentioned that after the age of scholasticism metaphysics was treated separately and apart from Christian doctrine in the philosophical discipline called natural theology. Yet he asserted that one should not forget that the representations of the divine attributes are of religious and not of philosophical origin. Therefore, *"all attributes which we ascribe to God are to be taken as denoting not something special in God, but only something special in the manner in which the feeling of absolute dependence is to be related to Him."* [8] In other words, the adjectives we attribute to God are neither descriptive of him nor do they originate from human fantasy. They are an attempt to express how we experience God's relationship to us. Thus to talk about God and his likeness is different from speaking in a raised voice about man.[9] If these concepts truly express how we experience God's relationship to us they do disclose some modality of God to us. Or to use Tillich's terminology, they are true symbols and participate in the power of the divine to which they point.

But it should also become clear that these concepts do not disclose how God is in his divine "essence," this means apart from his self-disclosure. Luther stated this restriction very appropriately when he said in his drastic and picturesque manner:

> It is therefore insane to argue about God and the divine nature without the word or any covering. . . . If someone wants to be safe and not in danger while dealing with such great matters, let him simply cling to the forms, the signs, and the coverings of the Godhead, such as his word and his works. For in his word and in the works God shows himself to us.[10]

At another occasion he also warned:

Through their speculations some ascend into heaven and speculate about God the creator, etc. Do not get mixed up with this God. Whoever wishes to be saved should move away from God in his majesty, for He and the human creature are enemies. Rather grasp that God whom David also grasps. He is the God who is clothed in his promises. . . . Such a God one must have. . . . We know no other God than the one who is clothed in his promises. If he would talk to me in his majesty I would run away like the Jews did. But when he is clothed in the voice of man and accommodates himself to our capacity to understand, I can approach him.[11]

It would certainly be interesting to speculate about the omnipotence or the aseity of God. Yet the only directive we can get in our desire to talk theologically about God is to use as our sole criterion the God-disclosive history which culminated in Jesus Christ. This does not mean that philosophic concepts concerning God's likeness are without any validity. The reflection on God's self-disclosure as recorded in the Bible is not written in original "Bible language." It shows on almost every page that its conceptuality is borrowed from many different sources. But all conceptual tools must be judged, transformed, or verified by the degree in which they support the coming into language of the one who disclosed himself in this history. Since the whole disclosive history culminated in God's final self-disclosure in Jesus Christ, we might also say that the meaning and truth attributed to all such (philosophic and religious) experiences and concepts must be determined with the reference to Jesus the Christ.[12]

Willy-nilly we are directed to Luther's reformation principle that whatever communicates Christ is true and acceptable. Therefore, Luther said in his picturesque way: "Whatever does not teach Christ is certainly not apostolic even though St. Peter or St. Paul teach it. Again whatever preaches Christ is apostolic even though Judas, Annas, Pilate, or Herod might say it." [13] It would be naive to assume that in talking about God we could ever arrive at a pure distillate form of revelation, uncontaminated by human, especially "pagan" or "non-biblical" experience and thought. After all Jesus himself was a real human being. Our talk about God should not be concerned about avoiding all anthropomorphic, transcendental, ontological, or whatever reference systems, but it should make sure that regardless of what conceptual tools we use they illuminate the God who disclosed himself in Jesus Christ.

1. God as immensely personal.

In an age in which God is sometimes equated with love or depicted as the cosmic force of the evolutionary process the essential personal nature of God has not remained unquestioned. Yet it is exactly his immensely personal character that stands at the center of his self-disclosure. We have noticed that we can express God only in his relation to man. Since his relation to man as documented in the God-disclosive Judeo-Christian history is essentially a relation that entails not a set of principles but a great and continuous invitation, it would be misleading to talk about God in non-personal terms.

a. *God and person.*

God as immensely personal denotes man's experience that God is an addressing as well as an addressable God, a God who is active. The imagery of a personal God is implied in his ultimate self-disclosure in the person of Jesus as well as in his constant encounters with people or a whole nation in the God-disclosive Israelite history. Martin Buber rightly claims:

> The description of God as a Person is indispensable for everyone who like myself means by God not a principle (although mystics like Eckhart sometimes identify him with 'Being') and like myself means by 'God' not an idea (although philosophers like Plato at times could hold that he was this): but who rather means by 'God,' as I do, him who—whatever else he may be —enters into direct relation with us men in creative, revealing and redeeming acts, and thus makes it possible for us to enter into a direct relation with him.[14]

Such a statement does, of course, not suggest that by using the concept of God as a personal being we determine God's essential being. The experience of the God-disclosive history points in the opposite direction. Since God encounters us as a Thou, we are determined as beings that are enabled and encouraged to respond to him as an I. The history of this great invitation shows at innumerable occasions that, without being compelled to do so, God seeks and offers our relation to him.[15]

Illuminating passages to determine the appropriateness of the concept of a personal God are Genesis 1:27 where the priestly writer states: "So God created man in his own image, in the image of God he created him." While usually the question is put how God

can be conceived of as personal, here the question is turned
around: How can one speak of man as a person apart from God? [16]
The assertion that man is created in the image of God does not
refer just to the dignity of man, or to his personality, or to his
ability for moral decision.[17] Yet it does not mean either that man
is a replica of God though this thought might be inferred. Just
before our quoted passage we hear God say: "Let us make man
in our image." The plural form suggests that perhaps even the
priestly writer felt uncomfortable with the daring statement that
God created man in his own image. Thus the plural form implies
that man is created in the image of both God and all the heavenly
beings associated with God. This sentiment coincides with the
statement in one of the creation psalms that God has made man
"little less than God" (Ps. 8:5). Again with reference to God and
his heavenly court Elohim, the plural form for God, is used here.[18]
But what does this being made in the image of God entail?

Passages such as Genesis 3:22; 2 Samuel 14:17; 20; 1 Samuel
29:9 indicate that God and his heavenly court are considered
blameless and knowing the difference between good and evil. Yet
the priestly writer is not much interested in defining what the
image of God entails. He rather emphasizes the purpose for which
it is given, namely to subdue the earth and to have dominion over
it. In other words man was created in the image of God to secure
and to maintain God's dominion over the earth. To accomplish
this purpose he was created knowing the difference between good
and evil and therefore blameless. But we know that this is not the
end of the story.

Man has used and continues to use his faculty of discrimination
between good and evil to choose the evil and therefore has lost
his blameless state. Instead of caring about God's dominion over
the earth he seeks to establish his own dominion. Since he cares
only about his own self, mankind is no longer striving for a common goal; everyone is striving for his own goal. The result can
either be that one succeeds in impressing upon others his own goal
so that in fascist like fashion they have to submit their own goals
to his, or that in the fashion of Thomas Hobbes' *Leviathan* everyone pursues his own goal at the expense of everyone else's and
attempts to become a self-made man. Both extreme positions are
repeated in the history of mankind in many different ways and
show that the loss of man's awareness of his being created in the
image of God also results in a loss of personhood. This is espe-

cially true for modern secular man, who in his alienation from God is without any guidance beyond his own self. Yet while in the whole history of mankind man has never been so independent, at the same time he has never been exposed to so many hidden and overt pressures by institutions, society, and business enterprises.

It is utterly wrong to assume that we would infringe upon our personhood and upon our relationship to other persons once we acknowledge a personal God. It is rather through our awareness of God as the person and through our relationship to him that we become persons in a true sense and are able to recognize other individuals as persons.[19] When this awareness sets in, the above mentioned pressures do not suddenly subside. They still influence decisively our individual existence, but they no longer determine our personal existence. While a Christian still lives in this world and while his life continues to be a historical existence in which he is governed by the powers who control this world, his ultimate goal and responsibility is no longer confined to the power play of often hostile forces.[20] In recognizing God as the Lord at whose name "every knee should bow, in heaven and on earth and under the earth, and every tongue confess that Jesus Christ is Lord" (Phil. 2:10) his ultimate destiny is taken up into the larger whole of history. Through God's self-disclosure in Jesus Christ he is able to recognize that the God whom he acknowledges as his Lord has not only provided the beginning of human history but will also provide its fulfillment as foreshadowed in the Christ event.

It is becoming increasingly clear that modern secular spirit in its attempt to divorce itself from its Christian roots must ultimately turn against man himself. Christian faith, however, without abandoning the dynamic drive that modern secularity exhibits, would lead to true humanizing of man. Therefore, we must pursue a reintegration of this dynamic drive into Christianity without sacrificing Christian spirituality. In this reintegration lies the great promise of the Christian faith not only for the "Christian West" but for mankind as a whole.

We could now also discuss at length such questions as to whether the notion of God as a person implies that he is understood to be male or where he resides. Though these questions are certainly interesting they are clearly secondary and are answered somewhat differently by each generation according to the then available conceptual tools. While Israel did not deny certain man-like features to Yahweh, the idea of Yahweh's sexual differentiation was beyond interest. Yahweh is no fertility God. Similarly, as long as the temple in Jerusalem was the central sanctuary, Yahweh was understood to be present in his temple. Yet at the same time we hear a Solomon say: "But will God indeed dwell on the earth? Behold, heaven and the highest heaven cannot contain thee; how much less this house which I have built!" (1 Kings 8:27). In other words, God is not limited to a physical abode.

The decisive point concerning God being a personal God is not where he is or what he looks like, but that man can only be a true person in being related to a personal God. This is, of course, substantiated by our earlier observation that man is basically a religious being. While man can to some extent attain his personhood in being related to the God who comes into language in the multitude of man's religions, he can only be a person in the full sense if he is related to God as he came to man through his ultimate and final self-disclosure in Jesus Christ. Only there man's primordially intended wholeness becomes an actual proleptic possibility for him, because only there, in the redemptive Christ event, does he encounter God's ultimate compassion and holiness.

b. *Compassion and holiness.*

The whole invitational history is an illustration of God's compassion with man.[21] There is no indication in the Bible that God needed man as his companion. God created man out of his free will. Even hereditary research implicitly attests to this when it states that man is not a necessary but an accidental product of evolution. There is also no indication that God needed another chosen people after the first had turned away from him. The frequently used imagery that we are like clay in the potter's hand (Jer. 18:6; Isa. 64:8, etc.) reinforces this point.

While there is absolutely no necessity for God's compassion we nevertheless read: "Behold, to the Lord your God belong heaven and the heaven of heavens, the earth with all that is in it; yet the Lord set his heart in love upon your fathers and chose their descendants after them, you above all peoples, as at this day" (Deut. 10:14f.). God has once shown unconditional compassion to Israel's forefathers and now he shows it to Israel itself. This compassion is expressed in the unconditioned love to his people despite their shortcomings. Since love in the Old Testament's understanding is the attitude of a superior toward an inferior it does not describe the relationship between man and God, but between

God and man. Yet only in a few cases are we told that God loves individuals (cf. 2 Sam. 12:24 and Neh. 13:26), and they are of royal blood. In the vast majority of the cases love denotes God's relationship to his people. Due to God's love for his people, they are then in turn enabled and encouraged to love him.

Often God's relationship to his people is expressed with the image of a marriage.[22] Underlying marriage is a spontaneous feeling (love) which leads to the making of a choice. But this feeling is exercised according to rule and is subject to certain laws. A covenant is established by means of faithfulness. Herewith we have encountered three constitutive terms for God's compassion: love, faithfulness and covenant.[23] Each of them is different, yet all three are interrelated. In the book of Jeremiah, for instance, the relation between love and faithfulness is expressed in God's saying: "I have loved you with an everlasting love; therefore I have continued my faithfulness to you" (Jer. 31:3). In other words, God's compassion implies that he does not revoke his initial choice. He continues his faithfulness towards Israel. This faithfulness is the power which guarantees his covenant with Israel and which makes it strong and durable.[24] "Know therefore that the Lord your God is God, the faithful God who keeps covenant and steadfast love with those who love him and keep his commandments, to a thousand generations," we read in Deuteronomy 7:9. Again the triad, love, faithfulness and covenant, is mentioned in the intimate relation of its components.

By making a covenant with Israel God has shown his faithfulness. The likeness of God is described here not in terms of God's being, but in the way God relates himself to his people. From passages such as Micah 6:8 "He (Yahweh) has shown you, O man, what is good; and what does the Lord require of you but to do justice, and steadfast love, and to walk humbly with your God?" we gather that faithfulness and love are not conceived of as having originated in man's own sphere.[25] They are derived from the way God relates himself to man and only then do they become human possibilities. Yet love, faithfulness, and covenant do not only characterize God's present relation to Israel. Israel can recognize from its history of broken covenants, broken by Israel yet renewed by God, that God's compassion emerged out of the past and extends itself into the future. God will even make an "everlasting covenant" with Israel (Isa. 55:3) whose fulfillment the people await. God's steadfast love is also expanded beyond the confines of Israel. History as well as the whole creative and life-sustaining activity of God is interpreted as an expression of his steadfast love (Ps. 136).[26]

Since the Christian community understood itself in succession of God's chosen people, we need not wonder that God's compassion assumes a prominent place in the New Testament. The compassion of God finds its central expression in a new covenant. Already in the book of Jeremiah we hear the promise of a new covenant which will be radically different from the old one.

> Behold, the days are coming, says the Lord, when I will make a new covenant with the house of Israel and the house of Judah, not like the covenant which I made with their fathers when I took them by the hand to bring them out of the land of Egypt, my covenant which they broke, though I was their husband, says the Lord. But this is the covenant which I will make with the house of Israel after those days, says the Lord: I will put my law within them, and I will write it upon their hearts; and I will be their God, and they shall be my people.
>
> Jer. 31:31ff.

But not until Jesus the Christ did this new covenant become a reality. Through the power of Jesus' sacrificial death a new covenant was instituted (1 Cor. 11:25). While the Old Testament understanding of the covenant concept is continued, it is no longer the same covenant. There is now an old covenant (2 Cor. 3:14) and a new one.[27] But it is still the sameness of God's compassionate will that finally prevails over man's sinfulness. The term covenant denotes "from first to last the 'disposition' of God, the mighty declaration of the sovereign will of God in history, by which He orders the relation between Himself and men according to His own saving purpose, and which carries with it the authoritative divine ordering, the one order of things which is in accordance with it."[28] Thus compassion cannot be equated with senile stubbornness. It is the sovereign will of God that comes to expression here in his concern for mankind, a concern so radical that God does not hesitate to dissolve one covenant to further the advance of his salvational interest in mankind.

In analogy to Old Testament thinking, God's compassion for mankind is again expressed through the term love. For instance, in the Gospel of John we read the conviction that "God so loved the world that he gave his only Son, that whoever believes in him should not perish but have eternal life" (John 3:16). Through his love God calls his people into communion with him and with each other (Rom. 1:7). Of course, love is also the sign of those whom God loves. Yet God and man do not gather around the common concern to love, but because God loved those whom he called they in turn love each other and their fellowmen (1 John 4:19). Though God is the "object" of human love too, the love toward God is only tangentially mentioned in the New Testament.[29] God's love is primarily intended to enable human love to extend itself to other people. The ethical demands of the New Testament concerning our fellowmen are understood to be fulfillable only because of the primacy of God's love.

We can see from the life and destiny of Jesus Christ, the prime example of God's love, that love is neither sentimentality nor sexually oriented. As the extension of God's love Jesus Christ shows compassion and solidarity even to the point of suffering and self-annihilation. Therefore the faithfulness of Jesus Christ and the love of God are at times mentioned in one breath (2 Cor. 13:14). The love of God expresses itself in the faithfulness of Jesus Christ, in his sacrificial death and in his continued presence with the Christian community. God's faithfulness in the New Testament is enunciated with terms such as *eleos* and *charis*. Though in the New Testament *eleos* is often used "for the divinely required attitude of man to man," Paul in Titus 3:5 makes it clear that such "requirement" is not determinative for God's *eleos,* for his eschatological act of salvation in Jesus Christ.[30] Man's "required" *eleos* to his fellowman is rather seen as in response to God's grace.

Charis is used in a way very similar to *eleos.*[31] For instance, Paul uses *charis* as the central term to express God's saving event in Jesus Christ. The whole structure of the saving event is seen under the aspect of God's faithfulness or God's grace. It is an undeserved gift of God (Rom. 3:24f.) which culminates in Jesus' sacrificial death. Its undeserved character excludes any cooperative disposition of man. Grace as God's compassion for man is not only the presupposition for making man acceptable to God, but it constitutes itself in the gifts of grace (1 Cor. 13) and it institutes the apostolate to communicate grace to others (cf. Rom. 1:5). In other words, man's Christian existence is an existence through grace and in grace. To avoid the impression that the compassion of God would be misunderstood as his indulgence of man's alienation we now must turn to the other basic trait in God's self-disclosure, his holiness.

We remember that holiness is a basic concept of religion, closely related to mana and tabu. The understanding of holiness as a supernatural and mysterious force which confers a special quality upon particular persons and things is not foreign to the Old Testament.[32] For instance, when Uzzah touched the ark, the place of God's presence, he had to die, because he had come in contact with the holy (2 Sam. 6:6f.). Holiness is always a manifestation of power. According to the Old Testament all power is concentrated in the person of Yahweh, apart from whom no life is possible in nature or mankind. Holiness is not a divine quality besides others, it is the characteristic of Yahweh. Israelites and non-Israelites alike experienced that God is a holy God before whom nobody can stand (1 Sam. 6:20). He is a holy God who makes man realize the infinite qualitative difference between God and man and who causes fear and dread (Isa. 8:13).[33] The places of God's presence are holy too and, because of him, are treated with special respect (Ps. 93:5; Ex. 3:5).

While the essential aspect of holiness is that of power, it is power in the service of the God who uses all things to make his kingdom triumph.[34] Thus no longer the prohibitive aspect of holiness is decisive, but the aspect of communion which bestows life. Holiness is always and particularly connected with the God of the covenant. The prophet Isaiah expresses this with the thought that Yahweh is the holy one of Israel (Isa. 5:24). "Yahweh is the holy one of Israel not because he is consecrated to Israel but because he has consecrated Israel to himself, and Israel itself is holy only because of this consecration to Yahweh." [35] "Consecrate yourselves therefore, and be holy, for I am holy" says the Lord (Lev. 11:44). Since the holy one of Israel is experienced as a God who is always near to help (Isa. 31:1), his mighty acts in history through which Israel was delivered from its enemies are seen as manifestations of his holiness. Even the gathering of Israel after the exile and the reestablishment of its own nation is understood as a demonstration of his holiness (Ezek. 20:41). Hosea already interprets God's presence among his people as a sign of God's holiness (Hos. 11:9). Through God's holiness Israel is gathered and preserved in the face of all other nations and inspired to become a holy or God-dedicated nation.

Closely connected with his holiness is God's righteousness. Righteousness is understood as conformity to a norm and not primarily punitive, distributive, or justificatory. It expresses itself in a certain way of acting and manifests itself in God's relation to man which is experienced in his action in history. God is a righteous God and delights in righteousness (Ps. 11:7). Neither the wickedness is left unpunished nor the good unrecognized. Therefore the righteous and upright shall dwell in the presence of the Lord (Ps. 140:13). Righteousness can sometimes almost become identical with God's faithfulness, since God recognizes the pleading of his people (Ps. 143:1). This means that though righteousness implies justice and judgment it is exercised in conformity with God's covenantal compassion with his people. This is summed up best in the book of Jeremiah where we read: "Let him who glories glory in this, that he understands and knows me, that I am the Lord who practices steadfast love, justice, and righteousness in the earth; for in these things I delight, says the Lord" (Jer. 9:24). God is not the primordial tyrant who uncompassionately distributes good and evil to those who deserve it. Norman Snaith appropriately reminds us that in the Israelite understanding there is "no *Ananke* (Necessity) and no *Dike* (Justice) to which both gods and men must conform. God is His own necessity"[36] and his will shows a persistent tendency to ensue in benevolent action. God's salvational activity, though shy of any sentimental leniency, always looks out for the benefit of man and for the ultimate victory of his kingship. This is also true when we now consider another facet of God's holiness, his wrath.

Naturally, the thought emerges that wrath reflects a human characteristic that in turn was projected into God. Yet the overwhelming number of passages that talk about wrath in the Old Testament do not talk about a human disposition, but about God. "Wrath is so much part of the figure of God in the Old Testament that the ancient Israelites saw no problem in it, but they accepted this reality as being a normal part of the irrational and mysterious in God."[37] It is the prerogative of God to show his power and wrath even if nothing has provoked it (cf. the classic example of Job, or 2 Sam. 24:1).[38] Israel, however, realized that the wrath of God is not just a demonstration of God's power and sovereignty. The Pentateuch, especially in its exhortations in Deuteronomy, as well as the prophets, relate the outburst of God's wrath to Israel's transgression of the covenant (Deut. 6:15; Ezek. 5:13). God is a jealous God, we hear, and his anger will be kindled against them if they neglect his laws. Other nations too are under God's wrath for their pride and their contempt of the elementary rules of humanity. We also hear of a day of wrath when definite sins are judged (cf. Amos 1 and 2).

Israel's whole history can be understood as a history of God's wrath, since it is a history of Israel's aversion from God. Though the day of the Lord as a day of wrath looms high over Israel, we surprisingly hear from God: "I will not execute my fierce anger, I will not again destroy Ephraim; for I am God and not man, the Holy One in your midst, and I will not come to destroy" (Hos. 11:9).[39] Was the Psalmist right, when he said of God: "For his anger is but for a moment, and his favor is for a lifetime?" (Ps. 30:5). God's self-disclosive history, we have noticed, is the history of a great invitation. It seems that even God's wrath has as its ultimate goal the accomplishment of this invitation. This is at least the conviction as far as the New Testament is concerned.

The trends present in the Old Testament concerning the understanding of God's holiness are in part continued and in part modified in the New. In analogy to the Old Testament, God is still regarded as the Holy One (Rev. 4:8; 1 Peter 1:15f.), but this attribute is now also conferred upon Jesus the Christ (cf. Mark 1:24), and upon the Spirit. Similarly to Noah's dove indicating a new age after the flood (Gen. 8:8ff.), so the Spirit of God descending upon Jesus in the form of a dove signifies the dawn of a new age initiated through Jesus' baptism (1 Peter 3:19ff.). The Holy Spirit of God, first exclusively connected with the figure of Jesus, is set free through Christ's resurrection (John 20:22) and communicated to his disciples. Especially Luke emphasizes the activity of the Holy Spirit who since Pentecost works creatively and directingly in the Christian community. The Holy Spirit of God who at the time of Moses and even in the post-exilic period had lived in Israel (Isa. 63:10f.; Hag. 2:5), dwells now in the Christian community (1 Thess. 4:8).[40] The signs of this new community are the baptism by the Holy Spirit of God, made possible through the death of Jesus the Christ, and the Lord's Supper (1 Cor. 12:13). Therefore Christians can be called the holy ones (Col. 3:12) who are sanctified through the sacrificial death of Christ. The intention of God's holiness to create a community of those who are again one with God has been accomplished by God's coming to man in Jesus the Christ and by the creative and guiding function of his Spirit. The salvational fulfillment aspect of God's holiness is even more emphasized in the understanding of his righteousness.

Already in the Septuagint, the Greek translation of the Hebrew

Old Testament, we notice that righteousness *(dikaiosyne)* is not only used to translate the Hebrew word righteousness *(tsedaka)*, but also to render the Hebrew faithfulness or compassion *(chesed)* into Greek (cf. Gen. 19:19).[41] This gives us some indication that already in the Septuagint God's righteousness is being interpreted with greater emphasis on his dispensing of salvation. In a few New Testament instances righteousness is still understood as God's righteous judgment at the parousia of Christ (Acts 17:31) or as God's righteousness which guides the activity of the Christian community (2 Peter 1:1). Yet outside the Pauline writings the term righteousness describes in most cases a condition of man. It is the term "for the right conduct of man which follows the will of God and is pleasing to Him, for rectitude of life before God, for uprightness before his judgment."[42] The clue to the change of the term righteousness from describing primarily an attitude of God to denoting almost exclusively a condition of man may be found in Paul's view of the term righteousness of God.

Paul understands the righteousness of God as God's alone while man is taken up into it and set in it. Righteousness is a conjunction of judgment and grace which God enjoys and demonstrates. Ultimately, it is a pardoning sentence by which he draws man into a new life in his kingdom and which will be fully manifested in the last judgment (cf. Rom. 1:16f.). Paul's interpretation of God's righteousness must be seen against the background of the Old Testament. There God was conceived of as the judge who demands obedience and who rewards and punishes. Through the encounter with Christ, however, Paul has deeply realized—far more than the Judaism out of which he came—that to accomplish obedience to God through exact fulfillment of the Law is an optimistic utopia. Yet Paul maintains that only the righteous can enjoy fellowship with a holy and righteous God. Paul is convinced, however, that righteousness that enables fellowship with God can no longer be —if it ever has been—established by man; it is solely God's doing. This righteousness has been brought about through God's sovereign, gracious, and decisive intervention in Jesus the Christ (Rom. 3:25f.).

Therefore, righteousness of God becomes a power that leads to new life. Since God's activity is always tending toward fulfillment of his kingship, his righteousness concerns itself not just with the present but equally important with the eschatological fulfillment in life eternal (Rom. 5:21). Now we understand why in the New

Testament righteousness of God is so frequently used to denote
an anthropological phenomenon. The righteousness of God, demonstrated in the Christ event, enables man to be righteous again
and to attain communion with the one who is righteous (cf. Matt.
6:33 and Luke 1:75). This also implies a shift in understanding
God's wrath.

It would be a gross misunderstanding to assume that the New
Testament gospel suddenly enlightens man about the real nature
of God, and that God who has until now been understood as
angry would now suddenly become gracious.[43] God is and remains a God of wrath even for the Christian. Both Jesus and John
the Baptist are portrayed in the New Testament proclaiming a
gospel that includes the pronouncement of God's wrath (cf. Matt.
3:7; Luke 21:23). The wrath of God is intrinsic to understanding
God even in the New Testament, since "it is a fearful thing to fall
into the hands of the living God" (Heb. 10:31). Biblical thought
can hardly substantiate Schleiermacher's claim that apart from
Christ man need not be "the object of divine displeasure and
wrath, for there is no such object." [44] We must rather agree with
Paul Althaus that one cannot disclaim the reality of God's wrath by
referring to God's unconditional love.[45] Both the magnitude of
God's wrath and the magnitude of his compassion have to be taken
with utmost seriousness. Of course, passages such as Romans 1:17f.
and 3:23f. might intimate that the disclosure of God's wrath is
rather the necessary background over against which the disclosure
of his grace gains its brightness. This would mean that even the
sinfulness of man and the resulting wrath of God in the last analysis only magnify the triumph of God's compassionate righteousness.

Yet we are confronted here with a paradoxical mystery: On the
one hand everything is founded in and contributes to the salvational
plan of God. On the other hand the guilt of all anti-Godly moves
cannot be made undone and deserves the unlimited wrath of God.
This wrath, indicated in the wrath of Jesus over all anti-Godly
resistance (cf. Matt. 12:34; Mark 1:25, etc.), will find its culmination in his wrath as the eschatological judge (cf. Matt. 22:13). He
who claims him on his side, however, who is both the judge and
was also judged for man's sake, need no longer be afraid of the
still outstanding finalization of God's wrath.[46] For him the time
of the wrath has passed away and something new has come, because through Christ God reconciled the world to himself (2 Cor.
5:17f.).

In attempting to outline the biblical understanding of God's compassion and holiness we have seen that the main terms which describe these characteristics, such as love, faithfulness, covenant, righteousness, and wrath are not conceived of as originating from the observation of human conditions which then are projected unto God. They are regarded as originating from the experience of God relating himself to man, an experience which in turn enables man to display characteristics such as love, faithfulness, covenant, and righteousness.[47] Furthermore, compassion and holiness were not understood as telling us something about God's essence, but about the way he encounters man.[48] This would mean that these "attributes" of God tell the story how the Judeo-Christian community was encountered by God and they invite us to be encountered likewise so that our existence is characterized too by such actions as love, faithfulness, righteousness, and holiness. Since these terms describe a history they also tell us about a movement of this history, a movement that culminates in the full realization of God's compassion and holiness for all mankind. In being confronted with Christ as the focal point and goal of this history we are invited to anticipate it already now proleptically in the Christian community.

2. God as a history-making God.

In talking about the likeness of God we are constantly referred to his self-disclosure in history. Yet in our considerations of history we have dealt almost exclusively with the God-disclosive history as presented in Judeo-Christian reflection. The question must be asked here whether such preoccupation with Judeo-Christian history does not ultimately result in a very narrow and distorted view of history. Thus we are confronted with the question how the Judeo-Christian history of revelation and salvation is related to history in general.

a. History and salvation history (Heilsgeschichte).

The question how to relate salvation history or *Heilsgeschichte* to history in general already becomes urgent for the Israelite history itself as it is reflected in the Old Testament. Old Testament research has shown that the factual history covering the time of the Old Testament is not identical with the history recorded in the Old Testament documents. In his monumental *Theology of the Old*

Testament Gerhard von Rad has demonstrated that the Old Testament reflections on Israel's history are of basically confessional nature and are handed down to us in a variety of witnesses and understanding which the compilers of the historical traditions and schools of thought in Israel had of this tradition. While von Rad's own endeavor to delineate the origin and transformation of such traditions presupposes a fairly solid reconstruction of Israel's history, he comes close to advancing the idea that in the Old Testament we have only a kerygmatic history, i.e. a history of proclamation.[49] Yet he admits that "even the earliest avowals of Jahweh were historically determined, that is, they connect the name of this God with some statement about an action in history." [50] One of these confessions is that Yahweh brought Israel out of Egypt, while others designate Yahweh as the one who called the patriarchs and who promised them the land, etc.

One of the most prominent and extensive confessions is the creed in Deuteronomy 26:5-9 which recapitulates the main events in the salvation history from the time of the patriarchs down to the conquest of the promised land: [51]

> A wandering Aramean was my father; and he went down into Egypt and sojourned there, few in number; and there he became a nation, great, mighty, and populous. And the Egyptians treated us harshly, and afflicted us, and laid upon us hard bondage. Then we cried to the Lord the God of our fathers, and the Lord heard our voice, and saw our affliction, our toil, and our oppression; and the Lord brought us out of Egypt with a mighty hand and an outstretched arm, with great terror, with signs and wonders; and he brought us into this place and gave us this land, a land flowing with milk and honey.

Though the passage cited does not just contain objective facts, we nevertheless notice a close concentration on objective facts. The general outline of Israel's history which is reported is seen in the light of God's actions. In other words, the biblical events in this creed and in most other parts of the Old Testament are a concentration and sometimes even distillation of historical events, events that are at the same time interpreted as God's action.[52]

Thus the Old Testament presents the course of history as a kind of salvation history which was shaped and led to fulfillment by a word of judgment and salvation continually injected into it. The continual and progressive reinterpretation of the traditions of Israel are necessitated through the factual course of history and make this course part of the tradition. This means that the older promises are never abandoned or superseded by the actual progression of history but are incorporated into it in a fulfilled, modified, and expanded way. The tension between promise and fulfillment was not replaced by the simple advance of Israel's history, but was strongly creative of Israel's historic progress.[53]

Israel's understanding of salvation history was not only expanded towards the future, it was also expanded into trans-national and trans-human terms. We have seen that already the prophets understood that other nations were included in God's plan for Israel and vice versa (cf. Isa. 2:2-4; Amos 1:6-8, etc.). But it was especially in the period of apocalyptic that not just the world of men and nations but the whole cosmos was understood to be involved in God's salvation history. This historifying of the whole cosmos in terms of a universal salvation history is of tremendous importance for theology. Without apocalyptic the Israelite salvation history would have been "bogged down in the ethnic history of men or the existential history of the individual."[54] Having started with the patriarchs, God's salvation history eventually included all Israel, all nations, and all the world. This means that at the beginning of the New Testament, history was understood as the working out of God's purposes or simply as salvation history.[55]

New Testament scholars, however, are divided on the issue whether this perspective is continued in the New Testament. In 1806 the German idealistic philosopher Johann Gottlieb Fichte wrote: "Only the metaphysical but not the historical contributes to our salvation; the latter one only contributes to our knowledge."[56] Before Fichte, Gotthold Ephraim Lessing had pointed out that it is difficult to bridge "the ugly, broad ditch" between the accidental facts of history and the necessary facts of reason.[57] These examples which could easily be multiplied, show us that it has been felt for a long time that history does not provide a trustworthy enough foundation for faith and for salvation. Rudolf Bultmann centered in on this evident dilemma when he admitted that all knowledge of the historical Jesus is very uncertain. "Here research ends with a large question mark." Contrary to others, however, he did not give up in despair, but he concluded his observation with the assertion: "And here it *ought* to end."[58] For Bultmann Jesus Christ is only an accidental historical event of history too. But nevertheless he insisted that this event encounters us with the claim that it is God's revelation. Consequently Bultmann did not divorce Jesus Christ completely from history.

Bultmann recognized that though the emerging church did not consider the content of Jesus' message as decisive, it made the decision that Jesus demanded during his lifetime, namely to accept the person of Jesus as the bearer of God's word.[59] The result of its positive response was that for the church the proclaimer of God's word became the proclaimed, or, in short, it acknowledged "God's revelation in Jesus." The emerging church

> understood Jesus as the one whom God by the resurrection has made Messiah, and that they awaited him as the coming Son of Man. For it is apparent that in that very fact they understood his sending as God's decisive act. In expecting him as the Coming One they understood themselves as the Congregation of the end of days called by him. For them factually— no matter to what degree it may have been clearly conscious —the old had passed away and the world had become new.[60]

Since God sent his son "when the time had fully come" (Gal. 4:4), the Christ event means the end of history and the end of salvation history. History and salvation history have reached their goal and thereby "history is swallowed up in eschatology." [61]

Bultmann claimed that the first Christian community understood itself as an eschatological and not as a historical phenomenon. It knows that it no longer belongs to the present world but to the new aeon which is at the door. On the other hand Bultmann asserted that the eschatological drama never took place as the New Testament expected. "History did not come to an end, and, as every schoolboy knows, it will continue to run its course." [62] However, Bultmann suggested that already Paul and the Gospel of John did not expect the eschatological event as a dramatic cosmic catastrophe but as happening within history, "beginning with the appearance of Jesus Christ and in continuity with this occurring again and again in history, but not as the kind of historical development which can be confirmed by any historian." [63] Consequently, the meaning and future development of history becomes secondary for a Christian. Decisive is only the confrontation with the eschatological event, with Jesus Christ, in the proclamation of the church. This proclamation demands a decision from us and enables us to understand us to be free from the world and its historical process yet still part of this process. While we remain historical beings, we receive God's forgiving grace. Therefore, we are not just the resultant of our past but are allowed to have a genuinely new beginning.

Many of Bultmann's students share his strictly dialectic view of history.[64] Other theologians, however, are more reluctant in divorcing God's saving event from history. Karl Barth, for instance, claims in his *Church Dogmatic* that "the history of salvation is *the* history" which encloses all other history and to which in some way all other history belongs as its illustration and reflection.[65] But he warns us not to confuse salvation history with the history of religion or the history of the religious spirit, because in so doing we would downgrade it to be only one history among many. Barth understands salvation history as "the nexus of the particular speech and action of God for the reconciliation of the world with Himself which at its center and climax is the history of Jesus Christ." [66]

Especially Oscar Cullmann, largely in dialog with Bultmann and his followers, emphasized the importance of salvation history for our understanding of history in general. According to Cullmann the coming of Jesus signifies the mid-point of history. Thus the whole New Testament holds the view that the mid-point of time does no longer lie in the future but in the past.[67] The reason for this notion is not just found in the fact that the New Testament was written from the perspective of Christ's resurrection. Jesus himself emphasized that the kingdom of God is already in the midst of the people when they saw him expelling demons by the finger of God, healing the sick, checking the power of death, and forgiving sins. Yet at the same time Jesus maintains the future character of the kingdom. In the light of the Christ event as the mid-point of history the whole Old Testament history is seen as a preparatory history moving towards this mid-point.[68] This view is especially dominant in the Gospel according to Matthew in which Jesus is depicted fulfilling a multitude of Old Testament promises and carrying a large number of Old Testament messianic titles. However, the history of salvation after this mid-point is described in the New Testament as an unfolding of the Christ event. The first Christian community regarded the Christ event together with its New Testament interpretation as the revelation of the divine plan according to which salvation history will continue to develop up to the end.[69] Of course, the question that interests us at this point is how one can distinguish between salvation history and history in general.

Cullmann is aware that a secular historian would not describe the history of Israel, including the emergence of Christianity, as salvation history but as connected with the histories of other peoples.[70] However, Cullmann claims that salvation history rests on "the *divine selection* of events within the whole of history." It forms a very narrow line which continues on "for the salvation of all mankind, leading ultimately to the funnelling of all history into this line, in other words, a merging of secular history with salvation history." [71] Since all history finally merges into salvation history, Cullmann would find it exciting to show the hidden ways in which, in the light of the biblical revelation, the preparation for salvation was made in the history of the Gentiles and their religions.[72] But Cullmann refrains from attempting a historical proof of the factuality of salvation history, knowing that the events of salvation history are experienced as divine revelation in such a way that God's actions as well as the meaning of his actions can only be grasped through faith.[73] With this concession, Cullmann admits that salvation history does not consist of pure historical facts but of an understanding of these facts which together with their occurrence is attributed to God's self-disclosure.

Wolfhart Pannenberg seems dissatisfied with a view that, in connection with God's saving activity, emphasizes the historical occurrences, while ultimately leaving it up to God's faith-empowering action to make us aware of God's self-disclosure contained in them. Pannenberg does not want to distinguish between a special salvation history and the rest of history because "God's redemptive deed took place within the universal correlative connections of human history and not in a ghetto of redemptive history." [74] Consequently Pannenberg postulates: "In contradistinction to special appearances of the Godhead, revelation in history is open to everyone. It has universal character." [75] The Holy Spirit or faith are not necessary to recognize God's self-disclosure in the events attested to in the Bible.[76] These events have convincing power if they are perceived in their historical context, because then they speak the language of facts and God has disclosed himself in that language.

In making these statements Pannenberg does not want to dispose of faith. Pannenberg suggests that faith is engendered through the unbiased perception of these events. Faith trusts in the realization of the future which is foreshadowed in the Christ event and conducts itself accordingly. But the question must be asked here whether faith is only trust in the future or also trust in the trustworthiness of God's self-disclosure as reflected in the biblical docu-

ments.[77] Pannenberg, however, counters our question with the affirmation that faith needs a rational knowledge of its basis lest it be
converted to credulity.[78] Thus he maintains that there is only a
"natural" knowledge of history possible, but not also a special
knowledge of faith. Yet he is aware that the mere acknowledge-
ment of history is not enough.

History, and this means especially the history of Jesus, must be
grasped as an event that has bearing on one's existence. "*Mere*
historical faith, which is satisfied with the establishment that the
event happened and does not allow itself to be grasped by this
event, thus has precisely not understood aright the inherent meaning of this history, but has diminished it." [79] Pannenberg realizes
too that not everybody accepts the Christ event as something that
touches his own existence. Thus he cannot but admit that an illumination is necessary for a man psychologically to apprehend the
significance of the Christ event. Nevertheless Pannenberg wants to
reserve the term faith for the trust that that which has occurred in
proleptic anticipation in the life, destiny, and resurrection of Jesus
Christ, namely the end of history and the fulfillment of revelation,
will be brought to its final completion. In other words, for Pannenberg faith lies in the trustworthiness of that which Christ stands
for, namely in God and his future.

Pannenberg has convincingly elaborated the dynamic thrust of
the Christ event. He also pointed out that to recover the meaning
of the Christ event one has to perceive it in its historical context,
i.e. of Jewish apocalyptic. Yet to recognize that this part of history
which started with ancient Israel and culminated in the Christ
event is not just a piece of near Eastern history but the history
from which all other history receives its illumination, direction, and
judgment, this insight does not result from a rational proof. Not-
withstanding his immense effort to show the intelligibility of this
history, Pannenberg has to concede that man needs illumination to
accept its decisiveness for his own future. Ultimately it is God's
own doing that opens our eyes to perceive the significance of this
little piece of history, called salvation history, for the understanding
of all other history, including our own.

b. *The causation and determination of history.*

When we mentioned that the salvation history, culminating in the
Christ event, illuminates, directs, and judges all other history we
did not want to convey the impression that only salvation history

is God's history. All history is God's history, while salvation history is like a red thread which guides us in our way through history.

"The primeval religious phenomenon of Israel's religion is the experience of being saved by Yahweh," namely through the deliverance from Egypt and the miraculous preservation during the years in the desert.[80] In the same manner the primeval religious phenomenon of the Christian religion is the experience of being saved by God, namely through the life, death and resurrection of Jesus the Christ (cf. 1 Cor. 15:14). This means the phenomena constitutive of the Judeo-Christian tradition are, at least in part, of historical nature. They express the conviction that God is at work in the world for the penultimate and ultimate benefit of man. God is not only one agent among many who are responsible for the present course of history; he is the agent. However, the sole-activity of God within the historical process is never conceived of in an absolute sense.

Whenever God is introduced as the one for whom nothing is impossible and who determines the course of history, it is to express the conviction that God will bring his saving plan to completion (Gen: 18:14 and Luke 1:37), but not to rule out the actuality of destructive and adverse forces within this process. Furthermore, both Old and New Testament are convinced that the God who ordains the present course of history is also the one who brought the world and with it history into being. But we already find in the Old Testament that the doctrine of the creation of the world does not stand on its own, forming the main theme of a passage in its own right. "It has always been related to something else, and subordinated to the interests and content of the doctrine of redemption." [81] It is only in the wisdom literature of Israel that we encounter unequivocal, self-justified statements of belief concerning creation.

In most cases the doctrine of creation either remained a cosmic foil against which soteriological pronouncements stood out the more effectively, or it was wholly incorporated into the complex of soteriological thought.[82] These tendencies are even more dominant in the New Testament. For instance, the Gospel of John introduces the saving figure of Jesus as the one through whom all things were made (John 1:3). Paul too, is clear analogy to the first creation, mentions that if anyone is in Christ he is a new creation in whom the old has passed away and the new has come (2 Cor. 5:17). These soteriological references to the creation in the beginning not only emphasize the fact that the God who created the world also saves it. They also want to convey the idea that there are actually no other divine powers at work in the world. Though the New Testament does not overlook the threatening reality of other forces within the world, it is convinced that they are already "judged" through Jesus' coming into the world. Their power can in no way influence the ultimate outcome of history (cf. John 12:31; 16:11). Bultmann is right when he asserts: "No future in this world's history can bring anything new." [83] In and through the Christ event the goal of this world has not only been decided upon, it has already been proleptically anticipated. That which has been expected as the goal of history, namely the new creation, has already been anticipated in a proleptic way in Christ's resurrection.

One might be tempted to conclude that such predetermination of history's ultimate goal deprives man of any significant involvement in the process of history. But the opposite is true. In the Greco-Roman world, for instance, history was conceived of as a history of man's deeds, purposes, successes, and failures. The gods had no plan of their own for the development of human affairs. They only granted success or decreed failure for the plans of men.[84] Christian faith rejected such an optimistic understanding of man's potential for the advance of history and asserted at the same time that the goal of man's destiny had already been provided for. The historical process was now conceived of as the working out of God's purposes and not of man's. However, in Christ each human being is invited to participate in Christ's proleptic anticipation of this eternal purpose. Imitating Jesus and envisioning the new creation foreshadowed in the Christ event, man is able to contribute to a better world.

The roots of attributing significance to man's actions lie in the Old Testament understanding that man is created in God's image and entrusted with dominion over the world. Man's involvement, however, gained significance only through Christ, because Christ's saving power prevents us from thinking that the eternal outcome of man's destiny is still contingent upon man's own achievements. The Christ event as God's resolution of the over-all outcome of history has relieved man of the worries about what end the world will come to. Man is now elevated to a free and acceptable partner who, in response to God's salvific action, is invited to work out the details of history within the larger framework of salvation. He is called to assume this position with responsibility and in responsiveness to God. Thus God's salvific causation and determination of history as shown in the Judeo-Christian tradition invites man as the free agent to tackle the problems of today.

We have arrived at the end of our investigation. Confronted with the process of secularization which embraces more and more facets of our life we have attempted to uncover the roots of this process. We have found that similar to Christianity's own progressive spirit it is rooted in Judeo-Christian faith. But contrary to this progressive spirit its immediate cause must be attributed to outside forces stemming from Greek and Roman antiquity. Then we have investigated the attempts to prove God's existence and realized in each instance that at best we can arrive at an either-or, God is or is not. We face the same ambiguity in logically asserting other ultimate foundations for our life-style, such as relativism, existentialism, and the like. At the same time we have noticed man's intrinsic yearning to be free from his finitude, a yearning primarily documented in his religious endeavors.

While acknowledging religion as a basic human phenomenon, we were unable to delineate an actual religious progression. Nonetheless we had to conclude that monotheism, perhaps because of its affinity to the Judeo-Christian tradition, allows best for man's active mastery of the world. Monotheism, however, is advanced in predominantly three ways: It is either a religion in which man works out his salvation through adherence to certain laws, or he pursues salvation through (mystic) devotion, or he responds to God's continual and great invitation issued alone through God's initiative. Of course, none of these monotheistic strands ever existed for any length of time in its pure form. The predominance of these first two forms in a religion always proves to be somewhat restrictive for man's active involvement in the world, as we have seen in the cases of Islam and of Buddhism. Yet the third type of monotheism, historically evolved in the Judeo-Christian tradition, and culminating in the Christ event as the salvific goal of all creation, endows man's activity in the world with an incentive, a direction, and a limitation. The imitation of Jesus, the proleptic anticipation of the new creation foreshadowed in Christ's resurrection, and the expectation of Christ provide a framework for building a better world though knowing that it will not be the perfect world.

Secular man, however, has eliminated the Christian faith in God the creator and determinator of history while still pursuing the progressive, linear view of history which such faith enabled. In so doing he has lost sight of the origin and destiny of history and advocates perpetual progress (of history) without knowing whence it comes and whither it will finally go. Thus the pursuit of the future will eventually become a goal in itself while being more and more emptied of any deeper meaning. In an age in which modern technology, conceived by a progressive spirit, is carried to the remotest spots of the earth, an age in which the impact of modern civilization hopelessly emasculates most world religions, Christian faith is challenged too. Yet this challenge is not one of threatening extinction. It is the challenge and the obligation to engage secular man in an ongoing dialog about man and his future, rediscovering together with him the ambiguity and depth of human history which he is about to forget. Remembering that true humanity always implies the God question, the search for true humanity also calls for the unashamed witness to God who disclosed himself in Jesus Christ as the origin and the goal of history, a history that without him is dark and ultimately without meaning. Yet in a secular and pluralistic world, apologetics and proclamation dare not be the only expression of Christian faith.[85] The most important contact is often first made through action. People will rightly lose curiosity in the presence of the Christian witness if the believing community shows no regard for the world as it is and if it does not move in the world in a way congruent with its profession. Our profession as a Christian community, however, is to respond to God's great and continuous invitation in a faith made active in love. Such response will not remain unheard.

NOTES

Chapter 1: Is God Alive?

1. Cf. Antoinette Mann Paterson, *The Infinite Worlds of Giordano Bruno* (Springfield, Ill.: Charles C. Thomas, 1970), esp. pp. 19ff.; cf. also Giordano Bruno, "Zwiegespräche vom unendlichen All und den Welten," in *Gesammelte Werke*, ed. and trans. by L. Kuhlenbeck, Vol. 3 (Jena: Eugen Dietrichs, 1904), p. 40, where he asserts that the infinity of the worlds and mankinds results a priori from common principles.

2. Friedrich Nietzsche, *The Gay Science* (125), in *The Portable Nietzsche*, ed. and trans. by Walter Kaufmann (New York: Viking, 1960), p. 95.

3. Antony Flew, *News Essays in Philosophical Theology*, ed. by Antony Flew and Alasdair MacIntyre (New York: Macmillan, 1955), p. 96. In a slightly different way this parable was first told by John Wisdom, "Gods" (1944), in *Philosophy and Psycho-Analysis* (Berkley: University of California: 1969), pp. 154ff. Though the more traditional form of posing the God question, in probing theoretically the possibility for God's existence, still needs to be carried on, more recently the practical question concerning God's activity has been advanced with much rigor. We agree with Gregory Baum, "Cultural Causes for the Change of the God Question," in *New Questions on God*, ed. by Johannes B. Metz, *Concilium* Vol. 76 (New York: Herder and Herder, 1972), p. 56, that the "question about God has become a question about God's presence in human life as creator and redeemer, i.e., the question about the meaning and destiny of history, personal and social." Cf. also the instructive essay by Philip Hefner, "The Relocation of the

207

God-Question," *Zygon,* V (March, 1970), p. 10, who goes along
similar lines asserting that "the trustworthiness of the processes
of evolution upon which man depends" is foremost on people's
mind when they ask about God.

4. Roger Garaudy, *From Anathema to Dialogue. A Marxist Challenge
to the Christian Churches,* trans. by L. O'Neill (New York: Herder
and Herder, 1966), p. 32.

5. Plato, *Laws* (X, 909f.), in *The Collected Dialogues of Plato Including the Letters,* ed. by Edith Hamilton and Huntington Cairns
(New York: Bollingen Foundation, 1961), pp. 1464f.

6. H. Richard Niebuhr, *Radical Monotheism and Western Culture.
With Supplementary Essays* (New York: Harper, 1960), esp. pp.
88f., has given us an excellent description of the impact of this
"radical monotheism" on the spheres of religion, politics, and science. He affirms that radical monotheism, as the gift of confidence
in the principle of being itself, protests against the religions and
ethics of closed societies, centering in little gods or in little ideas
of God.

7. Louis Monden, *Signs and Wonders. A Study of the Miraculous
Event in Religion,* (New York: Desclee, 1966), esp. pp. 46-50,
who mentions that Thomas Aquinas saw a miracle primarily under
the aspect of God's power, whereas Monden suggests that the sign
aspect is decisive.

8. Cf. Niccolo Machiavelli in *Renaissance Thought: Dante and Machiavelli,* ed. by Norman F. Cantor and Peter L. Klein (Waltham,
Mass.: Ginn-Blaisdell, 1969), p. 179, where he says in chap. 18:
"Therefore it is unnecessary for a prince to have all the good qualities I have enumerated, but it is very necessary to appear to have
them. And I shall dare to say this also, that to have them and
always to observe them is injurious, and that to appear to have
them is useful; to appear merciful, faithful, humane, religious,
upright, and to be so, but with a mind so framed that should
you require not to be so, you may be able and know how to
change to the opposite."

9. For a good analysis of Nathan the Wise cf. Henry E. Allison, *Lessing and the Enlightenment. His Philosophy of Religion and Its Relation to Eighteenth-Century Thought* (Ann Arbor: University of
Michigan, 1966), pp. 139ff.

10. Giovanni Boccaccio, *The Decameron,* trans. by J. Payne, intr. by
Sir Walter Raleigh (New York: Liverlight, 1943), pp. 43ff.

11. Cf. for the following Karl Heim, "Zur Geschichte des Satzes von
der doppelten Wahrheit," in *Glaube und Leben. Gesammelte Aufsätze und Vorträge* (Berlin: Furche, 1926), esp. pp. 82f.; cf. also
R. Arnaldez, "Ibn Rushd," in *The Encyclopedia of Islam. New
Edition,* Vol. 3, pp. 911f., in his interpretation of Averroes' "Au-

thoritative treatise and exposition of the convergence which exists between the religious law and philosophy."

12. Marsilio Ficino in the preface to his *Theologia Platonica*, as quoted in Paul Oskar Kristeller, *The Philosophy of Marsilio Ficino* trans. by V. Conant (Gloucester, Mass.: Peter Smith, 1964), p. 24.

13. Charles Trinkhaus in his impressive work *In Our Image and Likeness. Humanity and Divinity in Italian Humanist Thought*, Vol. 2 (Chicago: University of Chicago, 1970), pp. 734f., has demonstrated that with his insistence on the close kinship between wisdom and religion Ficino does not imply that both are identical. Nevertheless he indicates a strong interdependence between will and intellect, when he says that according to Ficino "the wise and holy men of all nations were philosophers and priests."

14. Paul Oskar Kristeller, *The Philosophy of Marsilio Ficino*, p. 19.

15. Cf. Hans Schwarz, "Theistic or Non-Theistic Talk about God?" *Theologische Zeitschrift (Basel)*, Vol. XXVI (May-June, 1970), pp. 199f.

16. Herbert of Cherbury, *De Veritate*, as quoted in Cornelio Fabro, *God in Exile. Modern Atheism. A Study of the Internal Dynamic of Modern Atheism, from Its Roots in the Cartesian Cogito to the Present Day*, trans. and ed. by A. Gibson (Westminster, Md.: Newman, 1968), pp. 227f.

17. Anthony Collins, *A Discourse of Freethinking*, p. 105, as quoted in Cornelio Fabro, *op. cit.*, p. 343.

18. Emanuel Hirsch, *Geschichte der neuern evangelischen Theologie im Zusammenhang mit den allgemeinen Bewegungen des europäischen Denkens*, Vol. 1 (Gütersloh: C. Bertelsmann, 1949), pp. 312f.

19. For the following cf. Emanuel Hirsch, *op. cit.*, pp. 64-75.

20. For the following cf. Cornelio Fabro, *op. cit.*, pp. 376-383.

21. Cf. Paul Baron d' Holbach, *Système de la Nature; ou des Loix du Monde Physique et du Monde Moral* (A Londres: Par Mirabaud, 1780), Vol. 1, p. 262.

22. Ludwig Feuerbach, *The Essence of Christianity*, trans. by G. Eliot, intr. by Karl Barth, and foreword by H. Richard Niebuhr (New York: Harper Torchbook, 1957), pp. 1f.

23. *Ibid.*, p. 13.

24. *Ibid.*, p. 17.

25. *Ibid.*, p. 281.

26. Karl Marx, "Theses on Feuerbach" (1845), in Karl Marx and Friedrich Engels, *On Religion*, intr. by Reinhold Niebuhr (New York: Schocken, 1964), p. 70.

27. *Ibid.*, p. 71.

28. Karl Marx, "Contribution to the Critique of Hegel's Philosophy of Right" (1844), in Karl Marx and Friedrich Engels, *op. cit.*, p. 41.

29. *Ibid.*, p. 42.
30. *Ibid.*, p. 50.
31. Cf. Karl Marx's last thesis on Feuerbach in Karl Marx und Friedrich Engels, *op. cit.*, p. 72.
32. Cf. George L. Kline, in his instructive book *Religious and Antireligious Thought in Russia* (Chicago: University of Chicago, 1968), p. 141.
33. Vladimir Il'ich Lenin, "Socialism and Religion," in *Collected Works*, Vol. 10 (Moscow: Foreign Languages Publishing House, 1962), p. 83.
34. *Ibid.*, p. 87.
35. *Ibid.*, pp. 84 and 87.
36. George L. Kline, *op. cit.*, pp. 143f.
37. Vladimir Il'ich Lenin, *loc. cit.*, p. 86. Jan Milic Lochman, *Church in a Marxist Society. A Czechoslovak View* (New York: Harper, 1970), pp. 54f., also underlines this sentiment when he points out that classic Marxist tradition does not consider religion to be simply the root of all social evil. Religion is rather "an expression of that really radical evil which is the unjust social order." Thus in authentic Marxism there is always kept open a space of practical tolerance for religious communities in a socialist society. Yet history shows that the width of this area, or *der Lebensraum*, is often narrowed down or temporarily widened at will.
38. Cf. Patrick Masterson, *Atheism and Alienation. A Study of the Philosophical Sources of Contemporary Atheism* (Notre Dame: University of Notre Dame, 1971), p. 7.
39. Cf. Karl Heim, *The World: Its Creation and Consummation* (Philadelphia: Muhlenberg, 1962), pp. 85ff., who points out the ideological implications that can be drawn from Mayer's law of the conservation of energy.
40. Ernst Haeckel, *The Riddle of the Universe at the Close of the Nineteenth Century*, trans. by J. McCabe (New York: Harper, 1900), esp. pp. 287f.
41. Friedrich Nietzsche, *The Gay Science* (125), in *The Portable Nietzsche*, p. 95.
42. Roger Garaudy, *Marxism in the Twentieth Century*, trans. by R. Hague (New York: Charles Scribner's 1970), p. 107.
43. *Ibid.*, pp. 208f.
44. Ernst Bloch, *Thomas Müntzer als Theologe der Revolution* (1921) (Frankfurt am Main: Suhrkamp, 1969), p. 229.
45. Ernst Bloch, *Das Prinzip Hoffnung*, Vol. 3 (Frankfurt am Main: Suhrkamp, 1969), p. 1628.
46. Ernst Bloch, *Atheism in Christianity, The Religion of the Exodus and the Kingdom*, trans. by J. T. Swann (New York: Herder and Herder, 1972), p. 266. If one compares the German original,

Atheismus im Christentum (Frankfurt am Main: Suhrkamp, 1968), with the English translation one discovers that the translation is considerably condensed. Also the conclusive German motif of the book, "Only an atheist can be a good Christian; only a Christian can be a good atheist," has been omitted from the title page.

47. Ernst Bloch, *Atheism in Christianity*, p. 265.

48. *Ibid.*, p. 272. We should at least parenthetically refer here to Vitezslav Gardavsky. In his important book, *Gott ist nicht ganz tot. Ein Marxist über Religion und Atheismus,* intr. by Jürgen Molt-mann (Munich: Chr. Kaiser, 1969), esp. pp. 229f., he seems to combine very impressively the Marxist concern for society with that for the individual in portraying a strictly immanent hope. While he affirms that there is no hope for the individual beyond death, he claims that the individual gives hope to others who survive him. Even when he dies the end result of his life con-tributes to hope for others. Thus each life gains importance from the community to the sustenance of which the individual con-tributes.

49. Karl Barth, "The Word of God and the Task of the Ministry" (1922), in *The Word of God and the Word of Man,* trans. by D. Horton (New York: Harper Torchbook, 1957), p. 186. As a good introduction to the present discussion of the "God question" cf. Frederick Herzog, *Understanding God. The Key Issue in Present-Day Protestant Thought* (New York: Charles Scribner's, 1966).

50. Karl Barth, *loc. cit.,* p. 196. Barth's accusation that Schleiermacher does not speak of God but speaks only in a loud voice of man is an exaggeration. Surely, Schleiermacher is no dialectic theologian. Nevertheless he went beyond Kant who had confined religion to ethics and rediscovered religion's proper sphere. Cf. Friedrich Schleiermacher, *On Religion: Speeches to Its Cultured Despisers,* trans. by J. Oman (London: Kegan Paul, Trench, Trübner, 1893), p. 277, where he says that the essence of religion is "neither think-ing nor acting, but intuition and feeling."

51. Karl Barth, *The Epistle to the Romans,* trans. from the 6th edition by E. C. Hoskyns (London: Oxford University, 1933), p. 28.

52. Karl Barth, *Church Dogmatics,* Vol. 1/II: *The Doctrine of the Word of God,* trans. by G. T. Thomson and H. Knight (New York: Charles Scribner's, 1956), pp. 299f.

53. *Ibid.*, pp. 302f.

54. *Ibid.*, pp. 307ff.

55. *Ibid.*, p. 326.

56. *Ibid.*, p. 347.

57. *Ibid.*, p. 349.

58. *Ibid.*, p. 343.

59. Otto Weber, *Karl Barth's Church Dogmatics,* trans. by A. C. Cochrane (Philadelphia: Westminster, 1953), p. 54.

60. Cf. Karl Barth, *Church Dogmatics,* Vol. 1/II, pp. 318-323.

61. Cf. Ernst Bloch, *Das Prinzip Hoffnung,* Vol. 3, pp. 1625ff.

62. Rainer Mayer, *Christuswirklichkeit, Grundlagen, Entwicklung und Konsequenzen der Theologie Dietrich Bonhoeffers* (Stuttgart: Calwer Verlag, 1969), p. 229.

63. Dietrich Bonhoeffer, *Letters and Papers from Prison,* ed. by Eberhard Bethge (Rev. ed.: New York: Macmillan, 1967), p. 123.

64. *Ibid.,* p. 152.

65. *Ibid.,* pp. 154f.

66. *Ibid.,* pp. 179ff.

67. *Ibid.,* pp. 196f.

68. Dietrich Bonhoeffer, *Christ the Center,* trans. by J. Bowden, intr. by E. H. Robertson (New York: Harper, 1966), p. 117. He states that only at the point of the parousia Christ will have ceased to be the lowly one. Then he will have broken through his incognito. Of course, it is true that the resurrection is no proof of the divinity of Christ. Yet it is not just a this-worldly phenomenon either. Luther's insistence in his theology of the cross on the paradoxical nature of Christ seems to be underemphasized here in favor of the hiddenness of God.

69. John A. T. Robinson, *Honest to God* (Philadelphia: Westminster, 1963), p. 29.

70. *Ibid.,* pp. 33f.

71. *Ibid.,* pp. 37ff.

72. Cf. with the following John A. T. Robinson, *op. cit.,* pp. 48-53.

73. William Hamilton, *The New Essence of Christianity* (New York: Association, 1966), pp. 54ff.

74. *Ibid.,* p. 65.

75. *Ibid.,* p. 95.

76. *Ibid.,* pp. 115f. n. 34.

77. *Ibid.,* pp. 42f.

78. *Ibid.,* p. 64.

79. William Hamilton, "Thursday's Child," in Thomas J. J. Altizer-William Hamilton, *Radical Theology and the Death of God* (Indianapolis: Bobbs-Merrill, 1966), p. 92.

80. Cf. the prefatory remarks of John A. T. Robinson in William Hamilton's book *The New Essence of Christianity,* pp. 5f.

81. Paul M. van Buren, *The Secular Meaning of the Gospel Based on an Analysis of Its Language* (New York: Macmillan, 1963), p. 2.

82. Paul M. van Buren, *op. cit.,* p. 102. Of course, one should also listen to E. L. Mascall's careful argumentation, *The Secularization of Christianity. An Analysis and a Critique* (New York: Holt, Rinehart and Winston, 1966), p. 102, who states that, unless adopted

onesidedly and uncritically, modern science and historical study "in no way demand the radical secularization of the Christian faith and its traditional beliefs and notions which van Buren so enthusiastically undertakes."

83. Paul M. van Buren, *op. cit.*, p. 83.
84. *Ibid.*, p. 100.
85. *Ibid.*, p. 89.
86. *Ibid.*, p. 91. In a more recent publication, *Theological Explorations* (New York: Macmillan, 1968), p. 180, van Buren again suggests a duality of "seeing as," especially the duality of seeing the ordinary as extra-ordinary. Yet according to van Buren, such dualities of human experience do not lead us to a doctrine of God. For van Buren God seems to be too close to us and at the same time too ineffable to be talked about in a meaningful way.
87. Paul M. van Buren, *The Secular Meaning of the Gospel*, pp. 98f.
88. *Ibid.*, p. 106.
89. *Ibid.*, p. 186.
90. *Ibid.*, p. 198. Don Cupitt, "What Is the Gospel?" *Theology*, LXVII (August, 1964), pp. 343-347, is right when he objects that van Buren's approach might easily lead to a transformation of theology into anthropology à la Feuerbach. However, when Cupitt claims that the proclamation of the gospel must presuppose a natural theology, van Buren might rightly answer that while such notion was once justified, today a natural theology can no longer be presupposed. In a more recent book, *The Edges of Language. An Essay in the Logic of a Religion* (New York: Macmillan, 1972), van Buren again works within the strict limits of Wittgenstein's linguistic analysis. Though he admits now the logic of religious discourse, the word "God" still remains the limit of language (p. 132f.) and Christian existence is telling the story "which Israel told of its own history and which some first-century Jews told about the Jew Jesus" (p. 168). Thus Jesus Christ still remains reduced to Jesus as an exclusively human phenomenon.
91. Thomas J. J. Altizer, *The Gospel of Christian Atheism* (Philadelphia: Westminster, 1966), p. 11.
92. *Ibid.*, p. 43.
93. Thomas J. J. Altizer, "America and the Future of Theology," in Thomas J. J. Altizer-William Hamilton, *Radical Theology and the Death of God*, pp. 11f.
94. Thomas J. J. Altizer, *The Gospel of Christian Atheism*, p. 103.
95. *Ibid.*, p. 111. Altizer seems to allude here to Paul's statement that the Christian dies (and rises) with Christ. Since Christ was God, this seems to indicate for Altizer that in the death on the cross God himself died and thereby merged completely with humanity. This historic occurrence is re-enacted in each Christian by taking

over Christ. Yet Altizer does not seem to be clear at this point. Cf. also the provocative response to Altizer, Hamilton, and van Buren by J. Robert Nelson, "Deicide, Theothanasia, or What Do You Mean?" *The Christian Century*, LXXXII (November 17, 1965), pp. 1414-1417.

96. Thomas J. J. Altizer, *The Gospel of Christian Atheism*, p. 110.
97. Thomas J. J. Altizer, "America and the Future of Theology," p. 12.
98. Thomas J. J. Altizer, *The New Apocalypse: The Radical Christian Vision of William Blake* (Michigan State University, 1967), p. XI.
99. Thomas J. J. Altizer, *The Gospel of Christian Atheism*, p. 83.
100. *Ibid.*, pp. 36ff.; and Thomas J. J. Altizer, *Oriental Mysticism and Biblical Eschatology* (Philadelphia: Westminster, 1961), pp. 111f.
101. Thomas J. J. Altizer, *Oriental Mysticism and Biblical Eschatology*, p. 198.
102. Altizer explains the historical process of secularization as the "necessary and inevitable expression" of Christianity's universality (Thomas J. J. Altizer, "Response," in *The Theology of Altizer: Critique and Response*, ed. by John B. Cobb, Jr. [Philadelphia: Westminster, 1970], p. 68). Of course, it is easy for Altizer to be optimistic about secularization, because in Hegelian dialectic fashion the radical negation of God then leads for him to a new resurgence of God beyond the death of God in the rediscovery of the sacred.
103. Friedrich Gogarten, *Was ist Christentum?* (Göttingen: Vandenhoeck & Ruprecht, 1959), p. 73.
104. Friedrich Gogarten, *Despair and Hope for Our Time*, trans. by Th. Wieser (Philadelphia: Pilgrim, 1970), p. 76.
105. For the following cf. Friedrich Gogarten, *op. cit.*, pp. 27ff.
106. Friedrich Gogarten, *Was ist Christentum?*, p. 68.
107. Friedrich Gogarten, *The Reality of Faith. The Problem of Subjectivism in Theology*, trans. by C. Michalson *et al.* (Philadelphia: Westminster, 1959), p. 168.
108. *Ibid.*, pp. 156ff.
109. For the following cf. Friedrich Gogarten, *Despair and Hope for Our Time*, pp. 108f.
110. Cf. Friedrich Gogarten, *The Reality of Faith*, pp. 97 and 156ff.
111. *Ibid.*, p. 187; cf. also the whole enlightening passage, pp. 181-189, of Gogarten's book. For a good assessment of Gogarten's contribution to the theological interpretation of secularization cf. Larry Shiner, *The Secularization of History. An Introduction to the Theology of Friedrich Gogarten* (Nashville: Abingdon, 1966), esp. pp. 174-190. We agree with Shiner that Gogarten "is far from disparaging the sacred, nor does he think that modern man's loss of a sense for the mystery of nature is an unalloyed benefit" (p. 177). Yet we wonder whether Gogarten has clearly enough spelled

out the blind alley in which modern secular mood finds itself. We also wonder whether he has emphasized enough the necessity for secular man to rediscover the Judeo-Christian tradition as his lost point of orientation. Gogarten's dialectic of law and gospel (or freedom) is too static to convince modern man of his need for "conversion."

112. Harvey Cox, "Afterward," in *The Secular City Debate,* ed. by Daniel Callahan (New York: Macmillan, 1966), p. 190.

113. Harvey Cox, *The Secular City. Secularization and Urbanization in Theological Perspective* (New York: Macmillan, 1966), pp. 4f.

114. *Ibid.,* p. 21.

115. *Ibid.,* p. 23.

116. *Ibid.,* p. 26.

117. *Ibid.,* p. 32.

118. Harvey Cox, *On Not Leaving It to the Snake* (New York: Macmillan, 1967), p. 51.

119. *Ibid.,* p. 19.

120. Harvey Cox, *The Secular City,* p. 58, where he argues that mobile man will be less tempted to demote Yahweh into a baal, since he will usually not idolatrize any town or nation. Idolatry of one particular city or nation, however, is not restricted to those who live there. Moreover, modern "faithfulness" to certain sports teams is as irrational as any traditional "bigotry" might have been.

121. For the following cf. Harvey Cox, *The Secular City,* pp. 258-261.

122. Cf. Ernst Troeltsch, *Protestantism and Progress. A Historical Study of the Relation of Protestantism to the Modern World,* trans. by W. Montgomery (Boston: Beacon, 1958), esp. pp. 85-88. Cf. also Helmut Thielicke, *Der Evangelische Glaube. Grundzüge der Dogmatik,* Vol. 1: *Prolegomena. Die Beziehung der Theologie zu den Denkformen der Neuzeit* (Tübingen: J. C. B. Mohr, 1968), p. 471, who with reference to Troeltsch asserts too that though there are certain presuppositions contained in Christian faith that make secularization possible, Christian faith did not cause it. *"Christian theology 'contracted' secularization."* Peter L. Berger, in his inspiring book, *The Sacred Canopy. Elements of a Social Theory of Religion* (Garden City, N.J.: Doubleday, 1967), p. 206 n. 16, claims to follow closely Weber's and Troeltsch's interpretation of the origin and process of secularization. Yet contrary to Troeltsch, Berger sees a close historical nexus between Protestantism and secularization (p. 113). When he finds the roots of secularization already in the Old Testament, especially in the Exodus and in the creation accounts, he reminds us somewhat of Harvey Cox, though being much less far-reaching in his conclusions (pp. 113ff.). Unfortunately Peter Berger does not pursue the important question "to what an extent the historical coincidence of the impact of

Protestantism with that of the Renaissance, with its resurgence of
the quite different secularizing forces of classical antiquity, was
simply an accident or rather a mutually dependent phenomenon"
(p. 124).

We must also mention here the important essay by Wilfred
Cantwell Smith, "Secularity and the History of Religion," in *The
Spirit and Power of Christian Secularity*, ed. by Albert L. Schlitzer
(Notre Dame: Notre Dame University, 1969), p. 48, in which he
mentions a controversy between two types of faith, "a faith in
reason and a faith in God; or a faith through the Greek tradition
and a faith through the Judaeo-Christian tradition." Acknowledging the generally progressive spirit of modern secularity, Smith sees
its roots in the Renaissance, its "trunk and branches" in the Enlightenment, and its flowering in the 19th century. While we can
easily identify its progressive, dynamic drive as intrinsically Christian, its inclination toward a mono-dimensional world view seems
to stem from elements of classical antiquity.

We would also like to note at least Smith's attempt to distinguish three stages in the development of modern secularity, starting with the correlative stage, in which the secular and the religious co-existed, progressing to the exclusivist stage, in which
the secular attempted to rid itself from the religious, and ending
with the inclusivist stage, in which the secular is understood as
the religious. Of course, Smith does not want to leave the impression that these stages are exclusive, they only indicate the
dominance of one type of secularity over the other two.

The godlessness exhibited by secularity as a method, and by
secularism as a principle, necessitates that man becomes the penultimate or ultimate reference point. In the Christian understanding of the world, however, the origin of all being is through God,
toward whom it also moves as its goal. Thus it seems to be a
contradiction in terms to talk about a Christian secularity in identifying the progressive, dynamic drive exhibited in Christian faith.
Rather we should talk about the power, intrinsic in Christian faith,
to desacralize the world, a power which paved the way for our
modern age but which did not intend to render it secular.

123. So also Helmut Thielicke, *op. cit.*, p. 470.

Chapter 2: Can God's Existence Be Demonstrated?

1. Cf. Jaroslav Pelikan, *The Christian Tradition. A History of the
Development of Doctrine*. Vol. 1: *The Emergence of the Catholic
Tradition (100-600)* (Chicago: University of Chicago, 1971), pp.
31f., who shows the importance of the concept of the seminal *logos*

for the confrontation of the Christian Apologists with the defenders of paganism.

2. Anselm of Canterbury, *Proslogion* (preface), in *St. Anselm's Proslogion with a Reply on Behalf of the Fool by Gaunilo and The Author's Reply to Gaunilo,* trans., intr. and philosophical commentary by M. J. Charlesworth (Oxford: Clarendon Press, 1965), p. 103.

3. Anselm of Canterbury, *op. cit.* (II), p. 117.

4. Cf. Charles Hartshorne, "What Did Anselm Discover?" in *The Many-Faced Argument. Recent Studies on the Ontological Argument for the Existence of God,* ed. by John Hick and Arthur C. McGill (New York: Macmillan, 1967), pp. 321-333, for a good treatment of the problems involved in Anselm's argument.

5. Gaunilo, *A Reply on Behalf of the Fool* (6), in *St. Anselm's Proslogion,* pp. 163ff.

6. Immanuel Kant, *Critique of Pure Reason* (A599, B627), abridged ed., trans. with an intr. by N. K. Smith (New York: Random House, Modern Library, 1958), p. 282.

7. Cf. Charles Hartshorne, *loc. cit.,* p. 322; and Charles Hartshorne, *Anselm's Discovery: A Re-examination of the Ontological Proof for God's Existence* (Lasalle, Ill.: Open Court, 1965), p. 302, where he emphasizes the necessity to re-examine Kant's rejection of the theistic proofs of the existence of God. However, Hartshorne seems to go beyond Anselm in attempting to arrive at the ontological argument without Anselm's unquestioned premise of faith in God's existence.

8. Anselm *op. cit.* (III), p. 119.

9. *Ibid.* (IV), p. 121.

10. This was vigorously advanced for the first time by Karl Barth, *Anselm: Fides Quaerens Intellectum. Anselm's Proof of the Existence of God in the Context of his Theological Scheme,* trans. by I. W. Robertson (London: SCM, 1960), p. 77.

11. *Ibid.,* p. 78.

12. *Ibid.,* p. 171.

13. Charles Hartshorne, for instance, in his introduction to *St. Anselm. Basic Writings,* trans. by S. W. Deane (2nd ed.: Lasalle, Ill.: Open Court, 1962), p. 19, intimates that Anselm's theory of the contingency and necessity of God, if carefully reflected upon could carry us "well beyond his type of philosophy and theology."

14. René Descartes, *Meditations on First Philosophy,* in *Descartes. Philosophical Writings,* selected and trans. by N. K. Smith (New York: Random House, Modern Library, 1958), pp. 204f.

15. *Ibid.,* pp. 225f.

16. Norman Kemp Smith, *New Studies in the Philosophy of Descartes. Descartes as Pioneer* (London: Macmillan, 1952), p. 306, has pointed out very convincingly that according to Descartes only in

the case of God, God and existence are inseparable in thought, while for all other contents of thought existence is not a necessary attribute. Thus it is not us who impose upon God the necessity of existence, but God himself exists by the very necessity of being God.

17. René Descartes, *op. cit.*, p. 229.
18. Werner Heisenberg, *Physics and Philosophy. The Revolution in Modern Physics* (New York: Harper, World Perspectives, 1958), pp. 80f., demonstrates that though the mechanics of Newton was based on certain principles of Descartes' philosophy it "started from the assumption that one can describe the world without speaking about God or ourselves. This possibility soon seemed almost a necessary condition for natural science in general." Cf. also Werner Heisenberg, *Physics and Beyond. Encounters and Conversations,* trans. by A. J. Pomerans (New York: Harper Torchbook, 1972), pp. 82ff.
19. So Plato, *Laws* (X, 894e) in *The Collected Dialogues of Plato Including the Letters,* p. 1450. A good sourcebook containing excerpts from the most prominent advocators of both the cosmological and the teleological arguments is *The Cosmological Arguments. A Spectrum of Opinion,* ed. by Donald R. Burrill (Garden City, N.J.: Doubleday, Anchor Book, 1967).
20. Aristotle, *Metaphysics* (XII, 6f.; 1071a, 38-1072a, 25), in *The Basic Works of Aristotle* ed. by Richard McKeon (New York: Random House, 1941), pp. 878f.
21. Aristotle, *Metaphysics* (XII, 3; 1069b, 36f.), in *op. cit.*, p. 873.
22. Thomas Aquinas, *Summa Theologiae* (1a, 2, 3), Latin text and English trans., intr., notes, appendices, and glossaries, Vol. 2 (London: Blackfriars, 1964), pp. 13-17.
23. *Ibid.*, p. 15.
24. *Ibid.*, p. 17.
25. Bertrand Russell, *Why I Am Not a Christian and Other Essays on Religion and Related Subjects* (New York: Simon and Schuster, 1963), pp. 6f.
26. Immanuel Kant, *Critique of Pure Reason* (A604, B632), p. 285.
27. *Ibid.* (A452ff., B480ff.), pp. 224ff.
28. *Ibid.* (A609f., B637f.), pp. 288f.
29. Felix M. Cleve, *The Giants of Pre-Sophistic Greek Philosophy. An Attempt to Reconstruct Their Thoughts,* Vol. 1 (The Hague: Martinus Nijhoff, 1969), p. 198, already indicates a danger inherent in the teleological argument when he states: "The world of Anaxagoras is certainly no blind mechanism; it is a seeing mechanism; but—a mechanism."
30. Marcus Tullius Cicero, *De Natura Deorum* (III/IX, 23), in *Cicero, De Natura Deorum. Academica,* with an English trans. by H. Rackham (London: William Heinemann, 1933), p. 308. Of course, this

statement does not imply for Cicero that there must be a God or gods who have everything superbly organized.

31. Cf. Hans Driesch, "The Breakdown of Materialism," in *The Great Design. Order and Intelligence in Nature*, ed. by Francis Mason, intr. by Sir J. Arthur Thomson (New York: Macmillan, 1935), p. 288, who says: "Matter *and something else* are at work, and this 'something else' acts in a teleological, a *whole-making* way." Cf. also his Gifford Lectures, published as *The Science and Philosophy of the Organism*, 2 Vols. (London: A. and C. Black, 1907/8).

32. Charles Darwin in a letter to Asa Gray, November 26, 1860, published in *The Life and Letters of Charles Darwin Including an Autobiographical Chapter*, ed. by Francis Darwin, Vol. 2 (New York: D. Appleton, 1898), p. 146.

33. Immanuel Kant, *Critique of Pure Reason* (A623, B651), p. 293.

34. *Ibid.* (A627, B655), p. 296.

35. *Ibid.* (A630, B658), p. 298.

36. Thomas Aquinas, *Summa Theologiae* (1a, 2, 3), p. 17.

37. Gottfried Wilhelm Leibniz, *New System* (10), in *Leibniz. The Monadology and Other Philosophical Writings*, trans. with intr. and notes by Robert Latta (London: Oxford University, 1951), p. 309.

38. Gottfried Wilhelm Leibniz, *Principles of Nature and Grace, Founded on Reason* (12), *ibid.*, p. 418.

39. Gottfried Wilhelm Leibniz, *New System* (16), *ibid.*, p. 316.

40. William Paley, *Natural Theology* (I/8), reprinted in *The Cosmological Arguments. A Spectrum of Opinion*, ed. by Donald R. Burrill, p. 170.

41. Raymundus de Sabunde, *Theologia Naturalis; Sive Liber Creaturarum* (Martin Flach, 1501).

42. Immanuel Kant, *Critique of Practical Reason* (V, 161), in *Critique of Practical Reason and Other Writings in Moral Philosophy*, trans. and ed. with an intr. by Lewis White Beck (Chicago: University of Chicago, 1950), p. 258.

43. *Ibid.*, (V, 121f.), pp. 225f.

44. *Ibid.*, (V, 125f.), pp. 228f.

45. Immanuel Kant, *Critique of Judgment* (par. 86), trans. with an intr. by J. H. Bernhard (New York: Hafner, 1951), p. 293.

46. Johann Gottlieb Fichte, *Die Bestimmung des Menschen* (III), ed. with an intr. by Eduard Spranger (Hamburg: Felix Meiner, 1954), esp. pp. 134-139.

47. Friedrich Schiller in his poem "Resignation" (1786), in Friedrich Schiller, *Gesammelte Werke in fünf Bänden*, ed. by Reinhold Netolitzky (Gütersloh: C. Bertelsmann Lesering, 1959), Vol. 3, p. 394. As we can see from his inaugural lecture in Jena of 1789, "Was heisst und zu welchem Ende studiert man Universalgeschichte?" in

Gesammelte Werke, Vol. 4, esp. pp. 95f., Schiller was actually rather pessimistic about discerning a teleological principle according to which world history does proceed.

48. John A. O'Brien, *Truths Men Live By. A Philosophy of Religion and Life* (New York: Macmillan, 1950), pp. 141f., reaffirms the argument of common consent stating that the belief in God has existed among all the races of mankind from the earliest times down to the present. Then he continues to demonstrate that though the advance of modern science is fatal to all polytheistic forms of religion, Christian monotheism "is necessary to supplement and complete the fragmentary interpretation of nature afforded by science." Of course, such "demonstration" of the necessity of Christian faith does not take into account that science itself can become a religion.

49. Heinrich Denzinger, *The Sources of Catholic Dogma* (2305), trans. by R. J. Deferrari (St. Louis, Mo.: B. Herder, 1957), p. 635. It should be added here that with this statement no "naive" proof is advanced, because in the same breath the encyclical admits that "not a few obstacles prevent man's reason from efficaciously and fruitfully using this natural faculty which it possesses."

50. Heinrich Denzinger, *op. cit.* (1785), p. 443, which is more affirmative than the statement quoted above.

51. Cf. Johann Georg Hamann in a letter of February 18, 1786, in which he says: "For if it is fools who say in their heart, There is no God, those who try to prove his existence seem to me to be even more foolish" (reprinted in Ronald Gregor Smith, *J. G. Hamann. 1730-1788. A Study in Christian Existence. With Selections from His Writings* [New York: Harper, 1960], p. 253). Cf. also Johann Georg Hamann in a letter of May 4, 1788, to Johann Gottlieb Stendel, in *Hamann's Schriften,* ed. by Friedrich Roth, Vol. 7 (Leipzig: G. Reimer, 1825), pp. 418f.: and Walter Leibrecht, *God and Man in the Thought of Hamann,* trans. by J. H. Stam and M. H. Bertram (Philadelphia: Fortress, 1966), esp. pp. 33f., where he refers to the hiddenness of God according to Hamann.

52. Heinrich Denzinger, *op. cit.* (1785), p. 443.

53. Søren Kierkegaard, *Concluding Unscientific Postscripts,* trans. by D. F. Swenson and W. Lowrie (Princeton: Princeton University, 1941), p. 485; cf. also his penetrating criticism of the ontological argument *ibid.,* p. 298. For further treatment of the issue cf. Walter Lowrie, *Kierkegaard,* Vol. 2 (New York: Harper Torchbook, 1962), pp. 335f.

54. Gustave Weigel–Arthur G. Madden, *Religion and the Knowledge of God* (Englewood Cliffs, N.J.: Prentice-Hall, 1961), p. 157, rightly reminds us that for men like Anselm natural theology contained in these "proofs" is not used as a defense for anything, nor as a

means for quieting doubts. It is rather an enthusiastic act of faith trying to illuminate the discovery of God already made by faith.

55. Alfred North Whitehead, *Process and Reality. An Essay in Cosmology* (New York: Macmillan, 1960), p. 519.

56. Alfred North Whitehead, *Religion in the Making* (New York: Macmillan, 1926), p. 76. The notion of a "primordial tyrant" against which most process thinkers are fighting is certainly a distortion of the compassionate and loving God portrayed in the Bible and it was never advanced by any serious theologian except when clearly marked as caricature.

57. Alfred North Whitehead, *Process and Reality*, pp. 520f.

58. *Ibid.*, p. 521.

59. Cf. Alfred North Whitehead, *Religion in the Making*, p. 157.

60. Alfred North Whitehead, *Process and Reality*, p. 523.

61. Alfred North Whitehead, *Religion in the Making*, p. 158.

62. Alfred North Whitehead, *Process and Reality*, p. 532. With this last statement Whitehead does by no means consider God as a projection of a father image. God is rather for him the ground of all reality including that of our finite being. This is substantiated when he says at another occasion: God can be conceived "as the supreme ground for limitation, it stands in His very nature to divide the Good from the Evil, and to establish Reason 'within her dominions supreme'" (*Science and the Modern World* [1925] [New York: Macmillan, 1960], p. 258).

63. Daniel D. Williams, "Reality, Monarchy, and Metaphysics: Whitehead's Critique of the Theological Tradition," in *The Relevance of Whitehead. Philosophical Essays in Commemoration of the Centenary of the Birth of Alfred North Whitehead*, ed. by Ivor Leclerc (London: George Allen & Unwin, 1961), p. 372, is right when he states that it is a great gain for Christian theology to be able to conceive of God in a coherent, intelligible metaphysical structure as a fellow-sufferer who understands instead of depicting him as the unfeeling and unmoved monarch.

64. Norman Pittenger emphasizes this point in his concise and illuminative introduction, *Alfred North Whitehead* (Richmond, Va.: John Knox, 1969), p. XIV.

65. Whitehead's Platonism, especially in *Process and Reality*, is very well analyzed by Edward Pols, *Whitehead's Metaphysics. A Critical Examination of Process and Reality* (Carbondale: Southern Illinois University, 1967), esp. pp. 159ff.

66. Charles Hartshorne, *A Natural Theology for Our Time* (Lasalle, Ill.: Open Court, 1967), p. 137.

67. Charles Hartshorne, *Man's Vision of God and the Logic of Theism* (Chicago: Willett, Clark & Co., 1941), pp. 11f.

68. Charles Hartshorne, *The Logic of Perfection and Other Essays in*

Neo-classical Metaphysics (Lasalle, Ill.: Open Court, 1962), p. 4. While Hartshorne wants to push the possibilities of human reason as far as possible, he is still aware that God cannot be defined, i.e. limited by human concepts.

69. Charles Hartshorne, *A Natural Theology for Our Time*, p. 128.
70. Ralph E. James, *The Concrete God. A New Beginning for Theology —The Thought of Charles Hartshorne* (Indianapolis: Bobbs-Merrill, 1967), p. 125.
71. Charles Hartshorne, *Man's Vision of God and the Logic of Theism*, p. 72.
72. Ralph E. James, *op. cit.*, p. 126. James is right when he emphasizes that Hartshorne strives for and is convinced of an ultimate theological-ontological harmony (*ibid.*, pp. 175f.).
73. Charles Hartshorne, *Beyond Humanism. Essays in the Philosophy of Nature* (1937) (Lincoln: University of Nebraska, Bison Book, 1968), p. 7.
74. *Ibid.*, pp. 315f.
75. Cf. Charles Hartshorne's dedication of his book *A Natural Theology for Our Time*, in which he mentions in one breath among others Fausto Sozzini, Gustav Fechner, Nikolai Berdyaev, and Alfred North Whitehead. When Howard L. Parsons, "Religious Naturalism and the Philosophy of Charles Hartshorne," in *Process and Divinity. Philosophical Essays Presented to Charles Hartshorne*, ed. by William L. Reese and Eugene Freeman (Lasalle, Ill.: Open Court, 1964), pp. 533-560, classifies Hartshorne's philosophy of religion as a new naturalism, he seems to have captured Hartshorne's intentions very precisely.
76. John B. Cobb, Jr., *Living Options in Protestant Theology. A Survey of Methods* (Philadelphia: Westminster, 1962), pp. 320f.
77. Cf. for the following John B. Cobb, Jr., *A Christian Natural Theology. Based on the Thought of Alfred North Whitehead* (Philadelphia: Westminster, 1965), pp. 11-15.
78. *Ibid.*, p. 260.
79. *Ibid.*, p. 268.
80. *Ibid.*, p. 266.
81. Cf. also for the following *ibid.*, pp. 277ff.
82. *Ibid.*, p. 282.
83. *Ibid.*, p. 284.
84. John B. Cobb, Jr., *The Structure of Christian Existence* (Philadelphia: Westminster, 1967), p. 137.
85. *Ibid.*, p. 149.
86. Schubert M. Ogden, *Christ without Myth. A Study Based on the Theology of Rudolf Bultmann* (New York: Harper, 1961), p. 144.
87. So Schubert M. Ogden, *op. cit.*, pp. 153-156, esp. p. 156.
88. *Ibid.*, p. 163.

89. Cf. for the following Schubert M. Ogden, *The Reality of God and Other Essays* (New York: Harper, 1966), pp. 37-45.
90. *Ibid.*, pp. 48ff.
91. *Ibid.*, pp. 56f.
92. Cf. for the following *ibid.*, pp. 62-67.
93. *Ibid.*, p. 177.
94. For the following cf. *ibid.*, pp. 203ff.
95. Wolfhart Pannenberg has especially pursued this issue in the opening chapter of *What Is Man? Contemporary Anthropology in Theological Perspective*, trans. by D. A. Priebe (Philadelphia: Fortress, 1970), pp. 1-13.
96. Arnold Gehlen, *Der Mensch. Seine Natur und seine Stellung in der Welt* (Bonn: Athenäum, 1958), pp. 349ff., to whom Pannenberg refers, talks here about an "indefinite obligation" which makes man restless and which to some extent is a root of all religious life.
97. Augustine, *The Confessions* (I/1), in *The Library of Christian Classics*, Vol. 7: *Augustine: Confessions and Enchiridion*, trans. and ed. by Albert C. Outler (Philadelphia: Westminster, 1955), p. 31.
98. For the following cf. Wolfhart Pannenberg, "The Question of God," in *Basic Questions in Theology. Collected Essays*, Vol. 2, trans. by G. H. Kehm (Philadelphia: Fortress, 1971), pp. 223f., where Pannenberg relates the search beyond the available to the proofs of the existence of God. He states that the "so-called proofs for the existence of God show only that man must inquire beyond the world and himself if he is to find a ground capable of supporting the being and meaning of his existence."

Chapter 3: Questionableness of the Human Situation

1. Cf. Antoinette Mann Paterson, *The Infinite Worlds of Giordano Bruno*, pp. 19ff., who supports this notion with many quotations from Bruno and who also mentions the impact that his idea of many other mankinds made on the self-esteem of Western man.
2. Wilhelm Pauck, *Harnack and Troeltsch. Two Historical Theologians* (New York: Oxford University, 1968), p. 90, rightly cautions that in relativizing truth Troeltsch did not speak as a skeptic.
3. Ernst Troeltsch, *The Absoluteness of Christianity and the History of Religions*, intr. by James Luther Adams, trans. by D. Reid (Richmond, Va.: John Knox, 1971), pp. 86-90.
4. Cf. for the following, Ernst Troeltsch, *op. cit.*, pp. 91f.
5. Ernst Troeltsch, *Christian Thought. Its History and Application*, ed. with an intr. by Baron F. von Hügel (New York: Meridian, Living Age Book, 1957), p. 61, and Wilhelm Pauck, *op. cit.*, p. 91, who indicates that though Troeltsch still upheld this vision he was clearly filled with a certain pessimism at the end of his life.

6. Cf. Arnold J. Toynbee, *Civilization on Trial* (New York: Oxford University, 1948), pp. 15 and 38f., where he emphasizes that the important question is not whether our own civilization survives, but whether the rise and decline of subsequent civilizations does not indicate that some purposeful enterprise, higher than theirs, may all the time be making headway. Toynbee himself advocates the reality of such a "divine plan."

7. John Locke, *An Essay Concerning Human Understanding*, ed. by Alexander C. Fraser, Vol. 1 (New York: Dover, 1959), pp. 37-118.

8. Cf. *Locke on Politics, Religion, and Education*, ed. with an intr. by Maurice Cranston (New York: Collier, 1965), p. 12.

9. For the following cf. David Hume, *An Inquiry Concerning Human Understanding*, in *Hume: On Human Nature and the Understanding*, ed. by Antony Flew (New York: Collier, 1962), pp. 38f.

10. *Ibid.*, p. 47.

11. *Ibid.*, p. 74.

12. *Ibid.*, p. 163. Though Hume may sound very negative on religion, he was too consistent in his relativism to consider himself an atheist. He rejected any attempt to go beyond life, as it appears, and explain it through some ultimate principle. Cf. Richard Wollheim, ed., in his intr. to *Hume on Religion*, (Cleveland: World, Meridian Book, 1964), pp. 28f.

13. Werner Heisenberg, *Physics and Philosophy. The Revolution in Modern Science*, pp. 114f.

14. Cf. for the following Werner Heisenberg, *op. cit.*, pp. 144f; and William Cecil Dampier, *A History of Science and Its Relation with Philosophy and Religion* (Cambridge: Cambridge University, 1961), pp. 397 and 480f.

15. Albert Rosenfeld, *The Second Genesis. The Coming Control of Life* (Englewood Cliffs, N.J.: Prentice-Hall, 1969), esp. pp. 187-277, provides a popularized but nevertheless correct picture of the possible impact of psychopharmaca on the human psyche.

16. Dale Carnegie, *How to Win Friends and Influence People* (New York: Simon and Schuster, 1937).

17. Cf. for the following Auguste Comte, *Introduction to Positive Philosophy*, ed. with an intr. and a rev. trans. by Frederick Ferré (Indianapolis: Bobbs-Merrill, 1970), pp. 1f. For a good and thorough introduction to positivism cf. Walter M. Simon, *European Positivism in the Nineteenth Century. An Essay in Intellectual History* (Port Washington, N.Y.: Kennikat, 1972).

18. Ludwig Wittgenstein in the preface to his *Tractatus Logico-Philosphicus*, with a new trans. by D. F. Pears and B. F. McGuinness, intr. by Bertrand Russell (London: Routledge & Kegan Paul, 1961), p. 3.

19. Cf. Ludwig Wittgenstein, *op. cit.* (2.01), p. 7.

20. *Ibid.* (6.432 and 6.52), p. 149.

21. *Ibid.* (6.522), p. 151.

22. Especially Wittgenstein's *Notebooks* indicate that he was far from being an atheist. Cf. Ludwig Wittgenstein, *Notebooks. 1914-1916,* ed. by G. H. von Wright and G. E. M. Anscombe, trans. by G. E. M. Anscombe (New York: Harper, 1961), especially p. 74e (8.7.16). We wonder if Eddy Zemach, "Wittgenstein's Philosophy of the Mystical," in *Essays on Wittgenstein's Tractatus* ed. by Irving M. Copi and Robert W. Beard (New York: Macmillan, 1966), pp. 366f., is not too optimistic when he interprets Wittgenstein's notion of God as the limit of the world. We are rather inclined to agree with Newton Garver, "Wittgenstein's Pantheism: A New Light on the Ontology of the *Tractatus*," in *Essays on Wittgenstein,* ed. by E. D. Klemke (Urbana: University of Illinois, 1971), p. 128, who sees Wittgenstein's pantheism in close affinity to Spinoza's *deus-sive-natura* concept. However, we must agree with both of them when they suggest that for Wittgenstein the world of facts is self-sufficient. Yet we must also remember that contemporary science has threatened such materialistic notion in pointing to the necessary (subjective) participation of the observer in the cognitive process.

23. Hans Reichenbach, *Experience and Prediction. An Analysis of the Foundation and the Structure of Knowledge* (Chicago: University of Chicago, 1966), p. 104, emphatically insists that "there is a surplus meaning in the statement about the existence of external things." Therefore the transition from external things to impressions is not one of a reduction, but one of a projection. This means there is a primacy of the external things.

24. Martin Heidegger, *Being and Time,* trans. by J. Macquarrie and E. Robinson (London: SCM, 1962), p. 234.

25. *Ibid.,* pp. 304f.

26. *Ibid.,* p. 307.

27. Laszlo Versényi, *Heidegger, Being, and Truth* (New Haven: Yale University, 1965), p. 184, rightly objects that Heidegger provides neither a practical process nor usable criteria for distinguishing between authentic and unauthentic possibilities of being.

28. Jean-Paul Sartre, *Being and Nothingness. An Essay on Phenomenological Ontology,* trans. with an intr. by Hazel E. Barnes (New York: Philosophical Library, 1956), p. 485. Sartre's claim of support from Heidegger seems to be unwarranted at this point.

29. Jean-Paul Sartre, *No Exit,* in *No Exit and Three Other Plays,* trans. by L. Abel (New York: Alfred A. Knopf, Vintage Book, 1949), p. 47.

30. Jean-Paul Sartre, *Being and Nothingness,* pp. 555f.

31. *Ibid.,* p. 70.

32. For an excellent comparison between the "dramatic obsession with

crisis" in Jean-Paul Sartre's writings and Camus' sober limitation to concrete experience cf. Germaine Brée, *Camus and Sartre. Crisis and Commitment* (New York: Delacorte, 1972).

33. Albert Camus, *The Myth of Sisyphus and Other Essays*, trans. by J. O'Brien (New York: Alfred A. Knopf, 1967).

34. Albert Camus, *The Rebel. An Essay on Man in Revolt*, foreword by Sir Herbert Read, trans. by A. Bower (New York: Alfred A. Knopf, 1961). Yet already at' the conclusion of this book Camus mentions that "rebellion cannot exist without a strange form of love" (p. 304), however, without his elaborating any further on the meaning of love.

35. Albert Camus, *The Fall*, trans. by J. O'Brien (New York: Alfred A. Knopf, 1960).

36. Albert Camus, "The Growing Stone," in *Exile and the Kingdom*, trans. by J. O'Brien (New York: Alfred A. Knopf, 1958).

37. Of course, a Buddhist would not talk about an innermost "yearning," since he attempts to abstain from any kind of attachment. But such "strife" itself is a principle seen worthy of pursuing.

38. Cf. Albert Schweitzer, *Reverence for Life*, trans. by R. H. Fuller (New York: Harper, 1969), p. 116, where he says: "Reverence concerning all life is the greatest commandment in its most elementary form."

39. Arthur Schopenhauer, *The World as Will and Idea*, Vol. 1, trans. by R. B. Haldane and J. Kemp (London: Routledge & Kegan Paul, 1957), pp. 490f. In his insistence on the denial of the will to live, Schopenhauer does not advocate suicide, because he rightly sees suicide as the rejection of life in only one particular individual manifestation, but not as the total renunciation of the will to live (pp. 514f.).

40. Immanuel Kant, *Foundations of the Metaphysics of Morals* (IV, 421), in *Critique of Practical Reason and Other Writings in Moral Philosophy*, p. 80.

41. So Ludwig Feuerbach is his preface to Jacob Moleschott, *Lehre der Nahrungsmittel. Für das Volk* (Erlangen: F. Enke, 1858).

42. Roger Garaudy, *Marxism in the Twentieth Century*, pp. 53ff.

43. Karl Heim, *Christian Faith and Natural Science*, trans. by N. H. Smith (London: SCM, 1953), pp. 180ff., has emphasized more than anyone else the inescapable and bewildering nature of these why-questions.

44. Karl Barth, *Church Dogmatics*, Vol. 3/I: *The Doctrine of Creation*, trans. by J. W. Edwards *et al.* (Edinburgh: T. & T. Clark, 1958), p. 186. Even in his discussion with Emil Brunner, Barth concedes the possibility of a point of contact, though he asserts that the point of contact is not "real outside faith but only in faith" (Karl Barth,

Church Dogmatics, Vol. 1/I: *The Doctrine of the Word of God*, trans. by G. T. Thomson [Edinburgh: T. & T. Clark, 1936], p. 273).

45. Emil Brunner, *Dogmatics*, Vol. 1: *The Christian Doctrine of God*, trans. by O. Wyon (Philadelphia: Westminster, 1950), pp. 134f.; Brunner rightly refers here to Rom. 1:19ff. But when Brunner talks in this context about "revelation in Creation," or, as in his book *Revelation and Reason*, about "general revelation," we are not surprised that Karl Barth was unhappy about this indiscriminate use of these terms and the contents they involve.

46. Emil Brunner, *Revelation and Reason. The Christian Doctrine of Faith and Knowledge* (Philadelphia: Westminster, 1946), p. 76.

47. Cf. Paul Tillich, *Systematic Theology*, Vol. 1 (Chicago: University of Chicago, 1951), esp. pp. 63ff.

48. Karl Jaspers, *Reason and Existenz. Five Lectures*, trans. with an intr. by W. Earle (New York: Noonday, 1955), p. 67. At least parenthetically we must mention here the important work by Wilhelm Weischedel, *Der Gott der Philosophen. Grundlegung einer philosophischen Theologie im Zeitalter des Nihilismus*, 2 Vols. (Darmstadt: Wissenschaftliche Buchgesellschaft, 1971/72). After a penetrating review of philosophical theology from the pre-Socratics to the present, Weischedel attempts to found his own point of departure. Respecting his "neutrality" as philosopher, he arrives at a philosophical-theological attitude of openness *(Offenheit)* to the questionableness of all reality and of farewell *(Abschied)* to all securities in approaching the uncertain and the unknown. Of course, this attitude of "philosophical modesty" would provide an excellent point of contact for a theologian.

49. Langdon Gilkey, *Religion and the Scientific Future. Reflections on Myth, Science, and Theology* (New York: Harper, 1970), p. 124.

50. *Ibid.*, p. 85.

51. Cf. Langdon Gilkey, *Naming the Whirlwind. The Renewal of God-Language* (Indianapolis: Bobbs-Merrill, 1969), esp. pp. 305-364.

52. Peter L. Berger, *A Rumor of Angels. Modern Society and the Rediscovery of the Supernatural* (Garden City, N.Y.: Doubleday, 1969), p. 65.

53. *Ibid.*, pp. 61-94.

54. Michael Novak, *Ascent of the Mountain, Flight of the Dove. An Initiation to Religious Studies* (New York: Harper, 1971).

55. Bernard J. F. Lonergan, *Insight. A Study of Human Understanding* (New York: Philosophical Library, 1970), pp. 636f.

56. Cf. David B. Burrell, "The Possibility of a Natural Theology," *Encounter* XXIX (Spring, 1968), p. 162. There seems to be an evident affinity between Lonergan and Pannenberg concerning their understanding of man's "transcending spirit." Cf. also Lonergan's more recent book, *Method in Theology* (New York: Herder and Herder,

1972), esp. pp. 101-112, where he wonders whether "the universe could be intelligible without having an intelligent ground," and where he again affirms that "the question of God is implicit in all our questioning." Pannenberg, however, considers himself more "objective" than Lonergan. He detects that Lonergan's model of theology "rests on a personal decision" and he charges that his approach "seems to turn out a well known combination of subjectivism and authority which is characteristic of so much of modern protestant theology." Cf. Wolfhart Pannenberg, "History and Meaning in Bernard Lonergan's Approach to Theological Method," *The Irish Theological Quarterly*, Vol. XL (April, 1973), p. 113. We will later take a closer look at Pannenberg's more "rationalistic" approach (cf. chapter 7).

57. Cf. Leslie Dewart, *Religion, Language and Truth* (New York: Herder and Herder, 1970), pp. 146-169, esp. pp. 158f.

58. Leslie Dewart, *The Foundations of Belief* (New York: Herder and Herder, 1969), pp. 365ff. and 382ff.

59. *Ibid.*, p. 479.

60. Cf. Wolfhart Pannenberg in his important essay, "Anthropologie und Gottesgedanke," in *Gottesgedanke und menschliche Freiheit* (Göttingen: Vandenhoeck & Ruprecht, 1972), p. 24, who comments that one cannot expect that theological anthropology proves the reality of God. However, he adds, it can elaborate the religious dimension of man and show that the theme of religious experience is as constitutive for being man as upright posture or the ability to use fire and tools. (The essays contained in this volume are now translated as Wolfhart Pannenberg, *The Idea of God and Human Freedom* [Philadelphia: Westminster, 1973]).

61. For the following cf. Karl Heim, *Christian Faith and Natural Science*, pp. 139-150, esp. pp. 144ff.; cf. also Gordon D. Kaufman in his valuable collection of essays, *God the Problem* (Cambridge, Mass.: Harvard University, 1972), p. 150, where he states very correctly: "The fact of human finitude implies that if there is to be knowledge of a transcendent God at all, it can only be on the basis of his self-revelation."

Chapter 4: The Mystery of Man's Religions I

1. Marcus Tullius Cicero, *De Natura Deorum* (II/XXVIII, 72), in *De Natura Deorum. Academica,* with an English trans. by R. Hackham (London: William Heinemann, n.d.), p. 192, where he also mentions that there is always "censure and approval" involved in religion.

2. Lactantius, *The Divine Institutes* (IV, 28), trans. by M. F. Mc-
Donald, *The Fathers of the Church. A New Translation*, Vol. 49
(Washington, D.C.: Catholic University of America, 1964), p. 318.
3. Augustine, *Of True Religion* (X, 19 and LV, 111f.), in *Augustine:
Earlier Writings*, trans. with an intr. by J. H. S. Burleigh, *The Library of Christian Classics*, Vol. 6 (Philadelphia: Westminster,
1953), pp. 234f. and 281f.
4. Cf. Friedrich Schleiermacher, *The Christian Faith* (par. 4, 4) ed. by
H. R. Mackintosh and J. S. Stewart (Edinburgh: T. & T. Clark,
1960), pp. 17f. Though Schleiermacher does not use the term "religion" there, it is evident that he means religion with this definition.
5. Georg Wilhelm Friedrich Hegel, "Vorrede zu Hinrich's Religionsphilosophie," in *Berliner Schriften. 1818-1831*, ed. by Johannes Hoff-
meister (Hamburg: Felix Meiner, 1956), p. 74. Hegel continues
that a dog even has feelings of salvation when he has satisfied his
hunger with a big meaty bone. Hegel in turn advocates freedom
and liberation as constitutive elements of religion, "since only the
free spirit has religion and can have religion."
6. Friedrich Schleiermacher, *On Religion. Speeches to Its Cultured
Despisers*, trans. by J. Oman (New York: Frederick Ungar, 1955),
p. 20.
7. Sir James George Frazer, *The Golden Bough. A Study in Magic and
Religion*, abridged edition (New York: Macmillan, 1958), pp. 57f.
8. Sir Edward Burnett Tylor, *Religion in Primitive Culture* (Part II of
"Primitive Culture"), intr. by Paul Radin (New York: Harper Torchbook, 1958), pp. 9f.
9. *Ibid.*, pp. 10f.
10. *Ibid.*, pp. 194f.
11. *Ibid.*, pp. 333f.
12. Rudolf Otto, *The Idea of the Holy. An Inquiry into the Non-rational Factor in the Idea of the Divine and Its Relation to the Rational*, trans. by J. W. Harvey (London: Oxford University, 1957),
p. 119, denies the possibility of even this development. He objects:
"Even in itself this entire theory of an ostensible attribution of 'soul'
or the principle of animation to everything is a mere fabrication of
the study."
13. So in retrospect R. R. Marett in the preface to his book, *The Threshold of Religion* (London: Methuen, 1929), p. VIII.
14. *Ibid.*, p. XXVIII.
15. *Ibid.*, p. XXXI.
16. This objection is rightly raised by Hans-Joachim Schoeps, *The Religions of Mankind*, trans. by R. and C. Winston (Garden City, N.Y.:
Doubleday, 1966), p. 8.
17. R. R. Marett, *op. cit.*, p. 73.

18. So Geo Widengren, *Religionsphänomenologie* (Berlin: Walter de Gruyter, 1969), p. 8.

19. Gustav Mensching, *Die Religion. Erscheinungsformen, Strukturtypen und Lebensgesetze* (Stuttgart: Curt E. Schwab, 1959), p. 134, rightly emphasizes the close interdependence of magic and religion in primitive religion that makes it impossible to assert priority for one or the other.

20. R. R. Marett, *op. cit.*, p. VIII.

21. Andrew Lang, *The Making of Religion* (London: Longmans, Green, and Co., 1898).

22. Wilhelm Schmidt, *Der Ursprung der Gottesidee*, 12 vols. (Münster i.W: Aschendorffsche Verlagsbuchhandlung, 1912-1955). An abridged English trans. of the first volumes is available as Wilhelm Schmidt, *The Origin and Growth of Religion. Facts and Theories*, trans. by H. J. Rose (New York: Lincoln Macveagh, 1931).

23. Rudolf Otto, *The Idea of the Holy*, p. 129, might be right when he calls this theory an "offspring of missionary apologetic, which, eager to save the second chapter of Genesis, yet feels the shame of a modern at the walking of Yahweh 'in the garden in the cool of the day.'" Nevertheless, Otto feels that it points to facts "which remain downright riddles, if we start from any naturalistic foundation of religion—whether animism, pantheism, or another."

24. Cf. Gerhardus van der Leeuw, *Religion in Essence & Manifestation. A Study in Phenomenology* (18, 1), trans. by J. E. Turner (London: George Allen & Unwin, 1938), p. 161. The remark of Schoeps in his otherwise excellent study, *The Religions of Mankind*, p. 9, that "the Dutch scholar van der Leeuw and others have argued that the concept of a single God is a latecomer in the history of religions," is somewhat misleading. Van der Leeuw certainly agrees with the existence of a primitive worship of a supreme being, while rejecting at the same time the idea of an original monotheism.

25. John M. Allegro, *The End of a Road* (London: Macgibbon & Kee, 1970), p. 9.

26. See his "proof" in John M. Allegro, *The Sacred Mushroom and the Cross. A Study of the Nature and Origins of Christianity within the Fertility Cults of the Ancient Near East* (London: Hodder and Stoughton, 1970), pp. 215f., n. 1.

27. John M. Allegro, *The End of a Road*, pp. 22f.

28. *Ibid.*, p. 32.

29. *Ibid.*, p. 9.

30. *Ibid.*, pp. 38f.

31. *Ibid.*, p. 178.

32. *Ibid.*, p. 184.

33. So rightly John C. King, *A Christian View of the Mushroom Myth* (London: Hodder and Stoughton, 1970), p. 11.

34. Weston La Barre, *The Ghost Dance. Origins of Religion* (Garden City, N.Y.: Doubleday, 1970), pp. 609f.

35. Gerhardus van der Leeuw in his monumental study, *Religion in Essence & Manifestation*, confronts us with an almost bewildering diversity of "means and objects," showing persuasively that nothing pertaining to man and his environment is excluded from having potentially religious significance. It is obvious that we cannot cover here the whole spectrum of religious phenomenology, since we are primarily concerned with those phenomena that are especially transparent for the God question.

36. Cf. for this distinction and for the following Mircea Eliade, *The Sacred and the Profane. The Nature of Religion*, trans. by W. R. Trask (New York: Harcourt, Brace and Co., 1959), p. 12.

37. Bronislaw Malinowski, *Magic, Science and Religion; and Other Essays*, intr. by Robert Redfield (Garden City, N.Y.: Doubleday Anchor Book, 1954), p. 24.

38. Martin Luther, *Kirchenpostille* (1522), in his exposition of Luke 2:37, reprinted in *D. Martin Luthers Werke, Kritische Gesamtausgabe* (Weimar: Hermann Böhlaus, 1883-), Vol. 10, I, 1, p. 413, 7-9. This edition is hereafter referred to as WA, followed by the volume number in Arabic numerals, the subvolume, if any, in Roman numerals, the parts thereof, if any, in Arabic numerals, and the page(s) and line(s) in Arabic numerals; cf. WA (volume) 10, (subvolume) I, (part) 1, (page) 413, (lines) 7-9.

39. At this point we want to confine ourselves simply to pointing out the diversity of the means and objects in religion. For further information cf. the helpful book of W. Richard Comstock, *The Study of Religion and Primitive Religions* (New York: Harper, 1972), esp. pp. 28-72. Comstock distinguishes in religion between myth and ritual, both of them being highly symbolic, and then defines religion as symbolic expression. Of course, this leaves the question open of what or who is symbolically expressed?

40. Andrew Lang, *Magic and Religion* (London: Longmans, Green, and Co., 1901), esp. pp. 15-45, vehemently disclaims this possibility in citing considerable evidence that excludes the influence of missionaries. Cf. also Nathan Söderblom, *The Living God. Basal Forms of Personal Religion*, with a biographical intr. by Yngve Brilioth (Boston: Beacon, 1962), pp. 21f.; and Bronislaw Malinowski, *op. cit.*, p. 23.

41. Geo Widengren, *Religionsphänomenologie*, p. 53.

42. Nathan Söderblom, *The Living God*, p. 22.

43. Raffaele Pettazzoni, "The Supreme Being: Phenomenological Structure and Historical Development," in *The History of Religions. Essays in Methodology*, ed. by Mircea Eliade and Joseph M. Kitagawa,

preface by Jerald C. Brauer (Chicago: University of Chicago, 1959), p. 60.

44. *Ibid.*, p. 63.

45. *Ibid.*, pp. 64ff.

46. Geo Widengren, *Religionsphänomenologie*, p. 129.

47. *Ibid.*, pp. 47ff.

48. *Ibid.*, pp. 52f.

49. Cf. for the following Geo Widengren, *op. cit.*, pp. 123ff.

50. Cf. Hans-Joachim Schoeps, *The Religions of Mankind*, p. 123.

51. Cf. for the following Geo Widengren, *op. cit.*, pp. 125ff.

52. Cf. Geo Widengren, *op. cit.*, pp. 89-92.

53. Cf. for the following Rudolf Otto, *The Idea of the Holy*, pp. 10f.

54. *Ibid.*, p. 17.

55. *Ibid.*, p. 23.

56. *Ibid.*, p. 31.

57. Nathan Söderblom, *The Living God*, p. 21.

58. Hans Schaer, *Religion and the Cure of Souls in Jung's Psychology*, trans. by R. F. C. Hull, Vol. 21 of Bollingen Series (New York: Pantheon Book, 1950), pp. 62f.

59. Carl Gustav Jung, *Psychology and Religion* (New Haven: Yale University, 1940), p. 4.

60. William James, *The Varieties of Religious Experience. A Study in Human Nature*, enlarged edition with appendices and intr. by Joseph Ratner (New Hyde Park, N.Y.: University Books, 1963), p 512.

61. *Ibid.*, pp. 485ff.

62. Sigmund Freud, *Psychopathology of Everyday Life* (XII), in *The Basic Writings of Sigmund Freud*, trans., ed., and intr. by A. A. Brill (New York: Random House, Modern Library, 1938), p. 164.

63. Cf. Sigmund Freud, *Totem and Taboo* (III/1), in *The Basic Writings of Sigmund Freud*, pp. 866f.

64. Sigmund Freud, *The Poet and Day-Dreaming* (1908), in *On Creativity and the Unconscious. Papers on the Psychology of Art, Literature, Love, Religion*, sel. with an intr. by Benjamin Nelson (New York: Harper Torchbook, 1958), p. 53.

65. Sigmund Freud, "The Theme of the Three Caskets" (I), in *Collected Papers*, Vol. 4, trans. by J. Riviere (London: Hogarth, 1956), p. 245.

66. Sigmund Freud, "Obsessive Acts and Religious Practices" (1907), *ibid.*, Vol. 2, trans. by J. Riviere, pp. 34f.; cf. also Sigmund Freud, *Das Unbehagen in der Kultur* (III), in *Gesammelte Werke*, Vol. 14: *Werke aus den Jahren 1925-1931* (London: Imago, 1947), pp. 450f.

67. Cf. Sigmund Freud, *Eine Kindheitserinnerung des Leonardo da Vinci* (V), *ibid.*, Vol. 8: *Werke aus den Jahren 1909-1913*, p. 195. Of course, Freud is right when he claims that for children God is

often a projection of the parental image. But does this disqualify the notion of a personal God as mere projection? Cf. also Sigmund Freud, *Totem and Taboo* (IV/6), in *op cit.*, p. 920, and Sigmund Freud, *The Future of an Illusion* (VI), trans. by W. D. Robson-Scott (Garden City, N.Y.: Doubleday, Anchor Book, n.d.), p. 52.

68. For the following cf. Sigmund Freud, *Totem and Taboo* (IV/5), in *op. cit.*, pp. 914-917.

69. Sigmund Freud, *New Introductory Lectures on Psychoanalysis* (XXXV) (1938), in *The Complete Introductory Lectures on Psychoanalysis*, trans. and ed. by James Strachey (New York: W. W. Norton, 1966), pp. 627f.

70. Sigmund Freud, *Totem and Taboo* (IV/6), in *op. cit.*, p. 921.

71. Sigmund Freud, *New Introductory Lectures on Psychoanalysis* (XXXV), p. 632 (own trans.). Though Freud himself recognized that by classifying religion as illusion, it can neither be proved nor refuted *(The Future of an Illusion*, p. 54), he clearly attempts its "scientific" refutation.

72. Cf., for instance, for the Roman Catholic discussion in Germany the excellent survey by Kasimir Birk, *Sigmund Freud und die Religion* (Münsterschwarzach: Vier-Türme-Verlag, 1970), esp. pp. 77-118.

73. According to Kasimir Birk, *op. cit.*, pp. 88ff.

74. Benjamin G. Sanders, *Christianity after Freud. An Interpretation of the Christian Experience in the Light of Psycho-Analytic Theory* (London: Geoffrey Bles, 1949), pp. 155ff., concludes his study with the fitting remark that the application of the psycho-analytic method itself proves nothing concerning the nature of belief in God.

75. Cf. Paul Ricoeur, *Freud and Philosophy. An Essay on Interpretation*, trans. by D. Savage (New Haven: Yale University, 1970), p. 533, where he affirms that psychoanalysis has no way to prove whether religious phenomena simply result from obsession and whether faith is merely consolation on the childhood pattern.

76. So Paul Ricoeur, *op. cit.*, p. 543.

77. Arthur Guirdham, *Christ and Freud. A Study of Religious Experience and Observance*, preface by L. Durrell (London: George Allen & Unwin, 1959), p. 57, rightly cautions us in connection with Freud against intellectual systems that explain all things too neatly. "The human mind is not a computating machine and mathematics is, after all, not a form of truth but the ultimate abstraction."

78. Hans-Joachim Schoeps, *The Religions of Mankind*, pp. 13f.

79. Bronislaw Malinowski, *Magic, Science and Religion*, p. 78.

80. *Ibid.*, p. 90.

81. Gustav Mensching, *Die Religion*, pp. 134f., introduces a very helpful nomenclature when he distinguishes between two kinds of magic, a religious and a profane. According to Mensching the profane magic, to which secular man adheres, has nothing to do with re-

ligion but rather with superstition. Cf. also Carl Heinz Ratschow, *Magie und Religion* (Gütersloh: C. Bertelsmann, 1955), esp. pp. 148ff., who points out that in magic there exists a feeling of union which is widely lost today *(unio magica)*, whereas religion betrays a historical consciousness and strives to regain this union which it feels is lost for man. It makes us wonder, however, why modern man is often tempted to return to a non-historical state, either in deliberately renouncing history and by living in a kind of counter-culture, or implicitly through total neglect of historical realities. Should this indicate that he is not as far removed from a magical state than he assumes he is?

82. Sigmund Mowinckel, *Psalmstudien,* Vol. 2: *Das Thronbesteigungs-fest Jahwäs und der Ursprung der Eschatologie* (Amsterdam: P. Schippers, 1961; reprint of Oslo, 1921), and Ivan Engnell, especially in his doctoral dissertation, *Studies in Divine Kingship in the Ancient Near East* (Oxford: Basil Blackwell [1943], 1967). For further discussion cf. Hans Schwarz, *On the Way to the Future. A Christian View of Eschatology in the Light of Current Trends in Religion, Philosophy, and Science* (Minneapolis, Minn.: Augsburg, 1972), p. 33, n. 1.

83. Georg Fohrer, *History of Israelite Religion,* trans. by D. E. Green (Nashville: Abingdon, 1972), pp. 143ff. and 204f.

84. Mishnah Sanhedrin 2:5, in Herbert Danby, *The Mishnah,* trans. from the Hebrew with intr. and brief explanatory notes (London: Oxford University, 1933), p. 385. Cf. also to this passage Hans-Joachim Schoeps, *The Religions of Mankind,* p. 17.

85. For the following cf. Hans-Joachim Schoeps, *op. cit.,* pp. 17f.; and Geo Widengren, *Religionsphänomenologie,* pp. 369ff.

86. Friedrich Heiler, *Erscheinungsformen und Wesen der Religion* (Stuttgart: W. Kohlhammer, 1961), p. 368.

Chapter 5: The Mystery of Man's Religions II

1. Cf. for the following the enlightening comments of Gustav Mensching, *Die Religion,* pp. 300ff.

2. Cf. Paul Radin, *Primitive Religion. Its Nature and Origin* (New York: Dover, 1957), p. 192.

3. Cf. Kurt Goldammer, "Die Religion der schriftlosen Völker der Neuzeit," in Friedrich Heiler, *Die Religionen der Menschheit in Vergangenheit und Gegenwart* (Stuttgart: Reclam, 1959), p. 73.

4. *Ibid.,* p. 57.

5. Bronislaw Malinowski, *Magic, Science and Religion,* pp. 88f.

6. It is unclear to us why Radin, *op. cit.,* p. 75, asserts on the one hand that magic very definitely preceded religion, while rejecting on the other hand the idea that "religion grew specifically out of

magic." Both are so closely connected on a primitive level that it is next to impossible to prove either a genetic or a historical priority.

7. Kurt Goldammer, *loc. cit.*, p. 89.

8. So Paul Radin, *op. cit.*, p. 266. We agree with Radin that religion cannot be understood apart from life and from the vicissitudes of the economic order in which it is so intimately embedded. Yet we wonder whether Radin's approach does justice to the religions of the primitives. Radin is still tempted to relegate primitive religion to an archaic phenomenon of the past. The question here is of eminent importance whether certain cultures and societies allow only for certain religious phenomena or whether religious phenomena might in part be responsible for a specific development of cultures and societies. If the latter is true as, for instance, Max Weber on a sociological level and, to some extent, E. E. Evans-Pritchard, *Theories of Primitive Religion* (Oxford: Clarendon Press, 1965), on a religious anthropological level assert, then religious phenomena may also in part "transcend" the cultures and societies in which they appear. Therefore Mircea Eliade is right when he mentions that, whatever their contribution to the advance of science and technology might have been, the real genius of the primitives was not expressed on this level, measured according to our scales. "Their creativity was expressed almost exclusively on the religious plane" (Mircea Eliade, "On Understanding Primitive Religions," in *Glaube, Geist, Geschichte. Festschrift für Ernst Benz zum 60. Geburtstage am 17. November 1967*, ed. by Gerhard Müller and Winfried Zeller [Leiden: E. J. Brill, 1967], p. 504).

9. For a good survey of the African scene cf. Marie-Louise Martin, *The Biblical Concept of Messianism and Messianism in Southern Africa* (Morija, Basutoland: Morija Sesuto Book Depot, 1964), esp. pp. 158ff.

10. Xenophanes of Colophon (21:10, 11, and 16) says: "Aethiopians have gods with snub noses and black hair, Thracians have gods with grey eyes and red hair" . . . "But Homer and Hesiod have attributed to the gods all things that are shameful and a reproach to mankind: theft, adultery, and mutual deception. They have narrated every possible wicked story of the gods: theft, adultery, and mutual deception." Cf. Kathleen Freeman, *Ancilla to the Pre-Socratic Philosophers. A Complete Translation of the Fragments in Diels, "Fragmente der Vorsokratiker."* (Oxford: Basil Blackwell, 1952), p. 22.

11. Kurt Goldammer, "Die Religion der Römer," in Friedrich Heiler, *Die Religionen der Menschheit in Vergangenheit und Gegenwart*, p. 493.

12. Here we must disagree with S. Radhakrishnan, *East and West in Religion* (New York: Barnes & Noble, 1958), p. 58, where he says:

"The emphasis on definite creeds and absolutist dogmatism, with its consequences of intolerance, exclusiveness and confusion of piety with patriotism, are the striking features of Western Christianity." Intolerance, exclusiveness, and nationalism, though undoubtedly often exhibited by Christianity, are not specifically Christian. These traits were already existent in the polytheistic religions of Greece and Rome, and are still alive in both polytheistic and monotheistic religions of today, even in "civilized" countries. While we cannot condone their occasionally arrogant attitude, they contain to some extent a necessary feature of any religion, because a believer is always convinced of the validity of that in which he believes.

13. Cf. Hans Schwarz, *On the Way to the Future*, p. 18; and Xenophanes (21:13), in Kathleen Freeman, *Ancilla to the Pre-Socratic Philosophers*, p. 22. Xenophanes (22:23 and 24) himself suggests to abandon the idea of gods and believe in just one God, who sets everything in motion and who is "not at all like mortals in body or in mind." However, his notion does not yet imply monotheism. Cf. Kathleen Freeman, *The Pre-Socratic Philosophers. A Companion to Diels, "Fragmente der Vorsokratiker"* (Oxford: Basil Blackwell, 1953), pp. 97f.

14. So Annemarie Schimmel, "Der Islam," in Friedrich Heiler, *Die Religionen der Menschheit in Vergangenheit und Gegenwart*, p. 819.

15. John Alden Williams, *Islam* (New York: George Braziller, 1961), p. 92.

16. Cf. for the following Annemarie Schimmel, *loc. cit.*, p. 820.

17. Cf. for the following Mahmud Shaltout, "Islamic Beliefs and Code of Laws," in *Islam—The Straight Path. Islam Interpreted by Muslims*, ed. by Kenneth W. Morgan (New York: Roland Press, 1958), p. 88.

18. *Ibid.*, p. 134.

19. So John Alden Williams, *Islam*, p. 88.

20. Mahmud Shaltout, *loc. cit.*, p. 140.

21. John Alden Williams, *op. cit.*, p. 93.

22. Cf. Sura II/285 in *The Qur'an*, trans. with a critical rearrangement of the Suras by Richard Bell Vol. 1 (Edinburgh: T. & T. Clark, 1960), p. 42; Annemarie Schimmel, "Der Islam," in *op. cit.*, p. 833; and *A Reader on Islam. Passages from Standard Arabic Writings Illustrative of the Beliefs and Practices of Muslims*, ed. by Arthur Jeffrey ('s-Gravenhage: Mouton, 1962), p. 343 (from the Wasiya of Abu Hanifa).

23. Cf. Sura III/145 that seems to imply the notion of free will, while Sura LXXIV/34 speaks of strict determinism. Some Muslims, however, object to a deterministic view of God. Syed Ameer Ali, *The Spirit of Islam. A History of the Evolution and Ideals of Islam.*

With a Life of the Prophet (London: Chatto & Windus, 1964), p. 402, for instance, asserts that in contradiction to the stern fatalism of the pre-Islamite Arabs the teachings of the Islam advocate the idea of liberty of human volition. Yet in the light of the *Qur'an* itself this assertion is difficult to maintain.

24. Cf. Shafik Ghorbal, "Ideas and Movements in Islamic History," in *Islam—The Straight Path*, p. 43.

25. Cf. for the following Shafik Ghorbal, *loc. cit.*, p. 66; cf. also Reynold Alleyne Nicholson, *Studies in Islamic Mysticism* (Cambridge: University Press [1921] 1967), p. 78, who rightly claims that the *wali* or saint bridges the chasm that the *Qur'an* and scholasticism have set between man and an absolutely transcendent God.

26. Shafik Ghorbal, *loc. cit.*, pp. 70f.

27. Annemarie Schimmel, *loc. cit.*, pp. 840f.

28. Cf. Shafik Ghorbal, *loc. cit.*, p. 69; cf. also Karl Heim, "Geschichte des Satzes von der doppelten Wahrheit," in Karl Heim, *Glaube und Leben. Gesammelte Aufsätze und Vorträge*, pp. 73-97.

29. Cf. for the following Annemarie Schimmel, "Ikbal, Muhammad," in *The Encyclopedia of Islam. New Edition*, Vol. 3, p. 1058.

30. We agree with W. Montgomery Watt, *Islamic Revelation in the Modern World* (Edinburgh: University Press, 1969), p. 117, that each religion is valid in a particular cultural region. Yet his conclusion is not convincing that therefore "the religions complement one another in that each in a particular region enables men to live a good life." Our culture, or rather civilization, is no longer particularistic, it is becoming increasingly global. But its dynamic features undeniably contain Judeo-Christian features. Consequently religions not open for or adaptable to these features do not enable men to live a good life. On the contrary they foster an increasing dichotomy between religion and civilization and thereby contribute to the despiritualization of both man and his religion. This does not mean that a mere transplantation of Judeo-Christian faith would provide a panacea. Indigenization of Judeo-Christian faith through transforming indigenous faiths and fostering their Judeo-Christian features is of vital importance, otherwise Judeo-Christian faith will remain a stranger in those cultures.

31. Günter Lanczkowski, "Die Religion der Iranier," in Friedrich Heiler, *Die Religionen der Menschheit in Vergangenheit und Gegenwart*, pp. 422f.; cf. also for the following Hans Schwarz, *On the Way to the Future*, pp. 30ff.

32. Günter Lanczkowski, *loc. cit.*, p. 428, not without justification, talks here about the strictest dualism that is known in the history of religion.

33. Cf. for instance Yasna, 48, 11f., in *Songs of Zarathustra: The Gathas*, trans. from the Avesta by D. F. A. Bode and P. Nanavutty,

foreword by Radhakrishnan (London: George Allen & Unwin, 1952), p. 92.

34. Cf. Geo Widengren, *Die Religionen Irans* (Stuttgart: W. Kohlhammer, 1965), p. 88.

35. Cf. the careful and excellent evaluation of Zoroastrianism by Geo Widengren, *op. cit.*, pp. 355f.

36. So also Günter Lanczkowski, *loc. cit.*, p. 433.

37. James Emerson Whitehurst, in his illustrative article "The Zoroastrian Response to Westernization: A Case Study of the Parsis of Bombay," *Journal of the American Academy of Religion*, XXXVII (September, 1969), pp. 224-236, is very pessimistic about survival of the Parsees in India as a group and as a religious community due to their thorough Westernization for which they were ill-equipped through their religious heritage.

38. Cf. Jagadish Kashyap, "Origin and Expansion of Buddhism," in *The Path of the Buddha. Buddhism Interpreted by Buddhists*, ed. by Kenneth W. Morgan (New York: Roland Press, 1956), pp. 27f.

39. Edward Conze, *Buddhism. Its Essence and Development*, preface by Arthur Waley (New York: Harper Torchbook, 1959), p. 35. Jagadish Kashyap, *loc. cit.*, p. 3, states too that the term "Buddha" is not a proper name but an honorary title applied to one who has reached the very peak of transcendental wisdom through the practice of the ten great spiritual perfections in numberless births during an incomprehensible length of time. "A Buddha is not a person but is rather a personality evolved through the accumulation of spiritual qualities. The cumulative forces of virtues and perfections finally bring forth a Buddha, a superman, in the world."

40. Cf. for the following Beatrice Lane Suzuki, *Mahayana Buddhism. A Brief Outline*, foreword by Ch. Humphreys (New York: Macmillan, 1969), p. 66.

41. Cf. for the following Beatrice Lane Suzuki, *op. cit.*, pp. 21-26.

42. So Beatrice Lane Suzuki, *op. cit.*, p. 49. For a good introduction to Western interpretations of nirvana cf. Guy Richard Welbon, *The Buddhist Nirvana and Its Western Interpreters* (Chicago: University of Chicago, 1968).

43. Edward Conze, *op. cit.*, p. 39.

44. Beatrice Lane Suzuki, *op. cit.*, p. 85.

45. Cf. H. Saddhatissa, *Buddhist Ethics. Essence of Buddhism* (London: George Allen & Unwin, 1970), especially his chapter on "Sanctions of Moral Conduct: The Precepts," pp. 87-112. One cannot but notice the similarity between the Judeo-Christian tradition and Buddhist ethics as far as basic precepts are concerned.

46. So Beatrice Lane Suzuki, *op. cit.*, p. 75. Such aggressive attitude, however, seems to be incoherent with the principles laid out in the four noble truths.

47. Nichiren Shoshu is one of the many sects based on a reinterpretation of Buddhism by the 13th century Japanese religious leader Nichiren. Shoshu means "true religion" or, as the followers of Soka Gakkai prefer to say, "true Buddhism." Adherents of Nichiren Shoshu hold Nichiren to be the true Buddha, replacing Siddharta Gautama. For a good introduction to Soka Gakkai, especially in its social dimension, cf. James Allen Dator, *Soka Gakkai, Builders of the Third Civilization. American and Japanese Members* (Seattle: University of Washington, 1969).

48. Cf. Kiyoaki Murata, *Japan's New Buddhism. An Objective Account of Soka Gakkai,* foreword by Daisaku Ikeda (New York: Walker/ Weatherhill, 1969), p. 17.

49. In our attempt to understand the progressive spirit of Soka Gakkai, we should not forget the special character of Japanese Buddhism as an imported religion. It was amalgamated with native beliefs and initially it was primarily used for practical (ethical) ends (cf. E. Dale Saunders, *Buddhism in Japan. With an Outline of Its Origins in India* [Philadelphia: University of Pennsylvania, 1964], pp. 261ff.). The rise of a number of new syncretistic sects or religions, based on ideas drawn indiscriminately from Christianity, Shinto, and Buddhism also indicates a certain dissatisfaction of society with religion as it attempts to adjust itself to the problems of modern (Western) civilization. We might not be wrong to consider Soka Gakkai with its largely pragmatic and Kantian persuasions (So James Allen Dator, *op. cit.,* p. 9), as an attempt to cope with a foreign civilization while still striving to preserve some of its own cultural and religious heritage. We are surprised to hear Dator, *op. cit.,* pp. 140f., say that in contrast to the "Americans," the Japanese do not seem to be a "religious people." Should this mean that the renunciation of its religious heritage was the price that Japan had to pay to become the most "Western" of all Far Eastern countries?

50. Cf. Edward Conze, *Buddhism,* pp. 21f.

51. Wolfgang Philipp, *Die Absolutheit des Christentums und die Summe der Anthropologie* (Heidelberg: Quelle & Meyer, 1959), pp. 69f.; cf. *Butler's Lives of the Saints,* ed. by Herbert Thurston and Donald Attwater, Vol. 4 (New York: P. J. Kenedy, 1956), pp. 432f., for further information on the historic development of this story.

52. Cf. for the following the penetrating studies by Edward Conze, *Thirty Years of Buddhist Studies. Selected Essays* (Columbia, S.C.: University of South Carolina, 1968), pp. 48ff., who points out these striking phenomena without attempting to draw any conclusions.

53. *Ibid.,* p. 46; and Daisetz Teitaro Suzuki, *Mysticism: Christian and*

Buddhist (New York: Harper, 1957), p. 136, who says: "Christianity, on the other hand, presents a few things which are difficult to comprehend, namely, the symbol of crucifixion. The crucified Christ is a terrible sight and I cannot help associating it with the sadistic impulse of a psychically affected brain." Cf. also for the concept of Amida, Beatrice Lane Suzuki, *Mahayana Buddhism,* pp. 63f.

54. Cf. for the following Edward Conze, *Thirty Years of Buddhist Studies,* pp. 38 and 49f.

55. Daisetz Teitaro Suzuki, *Outlines of Mahayana Buddhism,* prefatory essay by Alan Watts (New York: Schocken, 1963), p. 5, mentions too the external and internal forces acting in the body of Buddhism to produce the Mahayana system by absorbing and assimilating all the discordant thoughts with which it came in contact. Yet he does not elaborate on these forces and influences.

56. Wolfgang Philipp, *op. cit.,* p. 61.

57. Rudolf Otto, *Mysticism East and West. A Comparative Analysis of the Nature of Mysticism,* trans. by B. L. Bracey and R. C. Payne (New York: Collier, 1962), p. 216.

58. Daisetz Teitaro Suzuki, *Mysticism: Christian and Buddhist,* p. 137.

59. The understanding of revelation as God's self-disclosure has especially been emphasized by the neo-Reformation theologians in their attack on moralistic liberalism. Cf. for instance Karl Barth, *Church Dogmatics,* Vol. I/1: *The Doctrine of the Word of God,* pp. 362ff. In recent years this emphasis on understanding revelation as God's self-disclosure has been renewed in somewhat different form by Wolfhart Pannenberg. Cf. *Revelation as History,* ed. by Wolfhart Pannenberg, trans. by D. Granskou (New York: Macmillan, 1968), pp. 4ff.; cf. also H. Richard Niebuhr, *The Meaning of Revelation* (New York: Macmillan 1967), esp. pp. 110ff., who emphasizes that revelation is essentially God's self-disclosure which asks for our own faith commitment.

60. Herbert C. Brichto, in his instructive essay, "On Faith and Revelation in the Bible," *Hebrew Union College Annual,* Vol. XXXIX (Cincinnati, 1968), p. 45, puts the issue very precisely saying: "Every revelation is a human experience; . . . it is a discreet event; it takes place in time. . . . And after the event man is free—to remember or to forget, to formulate in words the impact of the event or the message—if any, to accept it or—yes—to question its reality."

61. Paul Tillich's distinction between the detached objectivity of the philosopher toward being and its structure and the committed and existential attitude of the theologian toward his object is to some extent helpful at this point (cf. Paul Tillich, *Systematic Theology,* Vol. 1, pp. 22f.). Tillich asserts that while the theologian should

attempt to approach his object matter with utmost objectivity, he must always be aware that any claim of "pure objectivity" does injustice to the object of his inquiry. Of course, the question must be raised whether even a philosopher or a scientist can remain absolutely neutral toward his object of inquiry. The scientific observer always seems to play an integral part in the very process of scientific observation. John Macquarrie, *God-Talk. An Examination of the Language and Logic of Theology* (New York: Harper, 1967), pp. 238ff., somewhat influenced by Martin Heidegger, offers a more appropriate distinction when he discriminates between the language of existence, being concerned about the structures of existence, and the language of being, being concerned with the mystery of God or of holy Being. Yet again Macquarrie admits that we cannot really make the transition from the existential to the ontological language on our own, since the language of being gains meaning through the initiative of being by which it discloses itself to us. A decision of acceptance or rejection is required concerning that which discloses itself.

62. Cf. Justin Martyr, *The Second Apology for the Christians. Addressed to the Roman Senate* (VIII), *The Ante-Nicene Fathers. Translations of the Writings of the Fathers down to* A.D. *325*, Vol. 1 (Buffalo: Christian Literature Company, 1885), p. 191.

63. *Ibid.*, (XIII), p. 193.

64. Cf. for further details Jaroslav Pelikan, *The Christian Tradition. A History of the Development of Doctrine*, Vol. 1, pp. 33f.

65. St. Ambrose, *Letters* (XVIII, 8), trans. by M. M. Beyenka, Vol. 26 of *The Fathers of the Church. A New Translation* (New York: Fathers of the Church, 1954), p. 40.

66. Cf. Carl Heinz Ratschow, "IV: Begriff und Wesen der Religion. B: Theologisch," *Religion in Geschichte und Gegenwart*, 3rd ed., Vol. 5, col. 977.

67. Martin Luther, *Der 82 Psalm ausgelegt* (1530), in WA 31, I, 191, 22-31, in his exegesis of Ps. 82:1.

68. Martin Luther, *Wider die himmlischen Propheten, von den Bildern und Sakrament* (1525), in WA 18, 80, 18-23; cf. also Heinrich Bornkamm, *Luther and the Old Testament*, trans. by E. W. and R. C. Gritsch (Philadelphia: Fortress, 1969), 124f., who shows the connection that existed for Luther between Decalogue and natural law.

69. Martin Luther, *Vorlesungen über 1. Mose* (1535-1545), in WA 42, 631, 36f. and 38f., in his exegesis of Gen. 17:7.

70. Paul Althaus, *The Theology of Martin Luther*, trans. by R. C. Schultz (Philadelphia: Fortress, 1966), p. 15.

71. In his famous explanation of the first commandment Luther says: "A god is that to which we look for all good and in which we

find refuge in every time of need" (Martin Luther, *The Large Catechism*, in *The Book of Concord. The Confessions of the Evangelical Lutheran Church*, p. 365). Though according to Luther everything can serve as a god, there is still a fundamental difference between a god and God, since only "if your faith and trust are right, then your God is the true God. On the other hand, if your trust is false and wrong, then you have not the true God" *(ibid.).* Thus trusting and having faith in the right God decides upon our missing or "having" him.

72. Philip S. Watson, *Let God Be God! An Interpretation of the Theology of Martin Luther* (Philadelphia: Muhlenberg, 1947), pp. 80f.

73. Martin Luther, *Vorlesungen über 1. Mose* (1535-1545), in WA 44, 549, 20-28, in his exegesis of Gen. 43:23.

74. Martin Luther, *Praelectiones in prophetas minores* (1524-1526), in WA 13, 246, 11f., in his exegesis of Jona 1:5; and Martin Luther, *Vorlesung über den Römerbrief* (1515/16), in WA 56, 177, 8ff., in a *Scholie* for Rom. 1:20.

75. Martin Luther, *Der Prophet Jona ausgelegt* (1526), in WA 19, 207, 11ff., in his exegesis of Jonah 1:5.

76. Cf. Bernhard Lohse, *Ratio und Fides. Eine Untersuchung über die Ratio in der Theologie Luthers* (Göttingen: Vandenhoeck & Ruprecht, 1958), p. 57, who mentions that Luther always recognized the axiom that equal can only be comprehended by equal. Thus God must grant us knowledge of himself and affect the comprehension of this knowledge so we may know him. Even then, since we are not equal to God, all self-disclosure of God remains disclosure in disguise. Cf. also John Dillenberger, in his important study *God Hidden and Revealed. The Interpretation of Luther's deus absconditus and Its Significance for Religious Thought* (Philadelphia: Muhlenberg, 1953).

77. Cf. Martin Luther, *Von den letzten Worten Davids* (1543), in WA 54, 88, 10-12.

78. Martin Luther, *Sermon von dem Sakrament des Leibes und Blutes Christi; Wider die Schwarmgeister* (1526), in WA 19, 492, 22-26.

79. Otto Weber, *Grundlagen der Dogmatik*, Vol. 1 (Neukirchen, Moers: Buchhandlung des Erziehungsvereins, 1959), at least devotes considerable space to the question of a "natural" theology, whereas Werner Elert, *Der christliche Glaube. Grundlinien der lutherischen Dogmatik* (Hamburg: Furche, 1960), pp. 143ff., sees revelation of God only in the tension between law and gospel and therefore excludes this question almost completely.

80. Cf. for the following Hendrik Kraemer, *The Christian Message in a non-Christian World* (Grand Rapids, Mich.: Kregel, 1956), pp. 136 and 140. In his more recent book, *Religion and the Christian*

Faith (Philadelphia: Westminster, 1956), in which he gives an excellent survey of the different historical and contemporary approaches to the relationship between Christian faith and the world religions, he attempted to modify his approach. Yet his candid and refreshing evaluations of the positions portrayed show that his approach can still hardly be called dialectical.

81. Emil Brunner, *Dogmatics*, Vol. 1: *The Christian Doctrine of God*, p. 135, states that "mankind cannot help producing religious ideas, and carrying on religious activities. It also shows the confusion caused by sin." Man's religious dimension is too quickly connected here with his sinfulness. Yet at least Brunner deems it worthwhile to mention the complexity of man's religious heritage.

82. Cf. for the following Paul Althaus, "Mission und Religionsgeschichte," in *Theologische Aufsätze*, Vol. 1 (Gütersloh: C. Bertelsmann, 1929), esp. pp. 192-194; and Paul Althaus, "Der Wahrheitsgehalt der Religionen und das Evangelium," *ibid.*, Vol. 2 (Gütersloh: C. Bertelsmann, 1935), esp. pp. 68-72.

83. Paul Althaus, *Die christliche Wahrheit. Lehrburch der Dogmatik* (Gütersloh: Gerd Mohn, 1959), p. 93.

84. *Ibid.*, p. 146.

85. Paul Tillich, *Christianity and the Encounter of the World Religions* (New York: Columbia University, 1963), p. 51.

86. *Ibid.*, p. 79.

87. *Ibid.*, pp. 96f.

88. Paul Tillich, *Systematic Theology*, Vol. 1, p. 28.

89. Paul Tillich, *The Future of Religion*, ed. by Jerald C. Brauer (New York: Harper, 1966), p. 81. Tillich does not get tired to emphasize in this essay the importance of the world religions for the systematic theologian. This is a much needed emphasis.

90. Cf. "Declaration on the Relationship of the Church to Non-Christian Religions" (1f.), in *The Documents of Vatican II*, pp. 660ff. A consequence of this sentiment is the significant volume *Religions. Fundamental Themes for a Dialogistic Understanding* (Rome: Editrice Ancora, 1970), ed. by the Secretariate for non-Christian Religions. Specialists of various world religions have contributed to this important book, composed in an appreciative spirit.

91. Cf. for the following Hans Küng, *Freedom Today*, trans. by C. Hastings (New York: Sheed and Ward, 1966), pp. 114-118.

92. *Ibid.*, p. 121.

93. *Ibid.*, pp. 139f.

94. *Ibid.*, p. 147.

95. *Ibid.*, p. 155.

96. *Ibid.*, p. 160.

97. Cf. H. van Straelen, *The Catholic Encounter with World Religions* (Westminster, Md.: Newman, 1966), esp. pp. 95-132.

98. Eugene Hillman, "The Main Task of the Mission," in *Re-thinking the Church's Mission*, Vol. 13 of *Concilium. Theology in an Age of Renewal* (New York: Paulist, 1966), pp. 3-10.
99. Karl Rahner, "Christianity and the non-Christian Religions," in *Theological Investigations*, Vol. 5: *Later Writings*, trans. by K. H. Kruger (Baltimore: Helicon, 1966), pp. 115-134.
100. *Ibid.*, p. 134.
101. *Ibid.*, p. 118.
102. *Ibid.*, p. 121.
103. *Ibid.*, p. 125.
104. *Ibid.*, p. 131; cf. also the vehement objections against Rahner's notion of "anonymous Christians" by H. van Straelen, *op. cit.*, pp. 108f.
105. Karl Rahner, *loc. cit.*, p. 132.
106. Cf. for the following Arnold Toynbee, *Christianity Among the Religions of the World* (New York: Charles Scribner's, 1957), pp. 85-89.
107. *Ibid.*, pp. 92f.
108. Cf. Arnold Toynbee, *A Study of History*, Vol. 7 (London: Oxford University, 1961), pp. 701ff.
109. Karl Löwith, *Meaning in History* (Chicago: Chicago University, Phoenix Book, 1957), p. 19, expresses this point well when he says: "It seems as if the two great conceptions of antiquity and Christianity, cyclic motion and eschatological direction, have exhausted the basic approaches to the understanding of history. Even most recent attempts at an interpretation of history are nothing else but variations of these two principles or a mixture of both of them." Cf. also Hans Schwarz, *On the Way to the Future*, pp. 16ff.
110. Arnold Toynbee, *Christianity Among the Religions of the World*, p. 95.
111. *Ibid.*, p. 100.
112. Arnold Toynbee, *An Historian's Approach to Religion* (London: Oxford University, 1956), p. 276.
113. Cf. for the following Arnold Toynbee, *Christianity Among the Religions of the World*, pp. 103-107.
114. Cf. for the following Ernst Troeltsch, *The Absoluteness of Christianity and the History of Religions*, pp. 111-114.
115. *Ibid.*, p. 126.
116. Cf. for the following Ernst Troeltsch, "The Place of Christianity Among the World Religions," in *Christian Thought. Its History and Application*, pp. 52ff.
117. Cf. for the following Ernst Troeltsch, *loc. cit.*, pp. 55-59.
118. *Ibid.*, p. 61.
119. Cf. the excellent essay by Wolfhart Pannenberg, "Toward a Theology of the History of Religions," in *Basic Questions in Theology*.

Collected Essays, Vol. 2, esp. p. 75, where he states: The more the phenomenology of religion "abstracts from the historical particularity of its material, the less it is able empirically to distinguish between superficial and essential mutualities."

120. Cf. the relationship between Buddhism and Christianity, or even more evident, between Islam and the Judeo-Christian tradition. Wolfhart Pannenberg, *loc. cit.*, pp. 86ff., has shown especially convincingly the influence of other traditions upon the development of Christianity.

121. Cf. Friedrich Heiler, "Versuche einer Synthese der Religionen," in *Die Religionen der Menschheit in Vergangenheit und Gegenwart*, pp. 877-889, who gives a good survey of significant attempts to create one world religion. He realizes that these attempts arise from the feeling of a basic unity of all religions. Yet he does not think that this unity can be attained by man alone.

122. Cf. Anders Nygren, *Commentary on Romans*, trans. by C. C. Rasmussen (Philadelphia: Fortress, 1949), pp. 208ff., in his exegesis of Rom. 5:12-21, in which he demonstrates the antithetical character of Adam and Christ portrayed by Paul.

123. Cf. the thoughtful remarks by Bernard Towers, "The Scientific Revolution and the Unity of Man," in *No Man Is Alien. Essays on the Unity of Mankind*, ed. by J. Robert Nelson (Leiden: E. J. Brill, 1971), esp. pp. 166ff. Though aware that there has been science also in other cultures, Towers shows that "science, as we know it on a world-wide basis, stems directly from the culture of the Christian West." He also points out that mutual suspicion and recrimination between science and the Christian faith, "have resulted from both a betrayal by Christians of their own tradition, and an ignorance on the part of many scientists of what that tradition really has to say about the world and our responsibilities to it."

124. Friedrich Heiler, *Erscheinungsformen und Wesen der Religion*, pp. 563f.; cf. also Nathan Söderblom, *The Living God*, p. 384, who stated that for Christian theology the history of religions is a divine self-communication.

125. Cf. for the following Gustav Mensching, *Die Religion*, pp. 374ff. Martin Buber, *The Eclipse of God: Studies in the Relation between Religion and Philosophy* (New York: Harper, 1952), p. 22, appropriately remarked to this issue: "The great images of God fashioned by mankind are born not out of imagination but of real encounters with the real divine power and glory."

126. Cf. Paul Althaus, *Die christliche Wahrheit*, pp. 37-94, who only arrives at the notion of an *Uroffenbarung*.

127. Cf. Hans Schwarz, *On the Way to the Future*, p. 150.

128. Wilfred Cantwell Smith, *The Faith of Other Men* (New York: Harper Torchbook, 1972), pp. 139f.

129. Cf. the interesting essay by Carl Heinz Ratschow, "Die Religionen und das Christentum," *Neue Zeitschrift für Systematische Theologie und Religionsphilosophie,* IX (1967), p. 126, who mentions that the decisive difference between Christian faith and the non-Christian religions lies in the fact that according to Christian faith mortification of man is *consecutive* to God's offer of salvation, whereas in non-Christian religions mortification is always *constitutive* for obtaining salvation.

130. So Robert D. Young, *Encounter with World Religions* (Philadelphia: Westminster, 1970), p. 164.

131. Donald K. Swearer, *Buddhism in Transition* (Philadelphia: Westminster, 1970), p. 146.

132. Raimundo Pannikkar, "Sunyata and Pleroma: The Buddhist and Christian Response to the Human Predicament," in *Religion and the Humanizing of Man,* ed. by James M. Robinson (Council on the Study of Religion, 1972), p. 77.

133. J. Robert Nelson, "Signs of Mankind's Solidarity," in *No Man Is an Alien,* p. 13.

134. This has been pointed out very well by Owen C. Thomas, ed., *Attitudes toward Other Religions: Some Christian Interpretations* (London: SCM, 1969), p. 2.

135. Contrary to Hendrik Kraemer, *World Cultures and World Religions: The Coming Dialogue* (Philadelphia: Westminster, 1960), pp. 372f. Cf. also the interesting study by Bardwell L. Smith, "Toward a Buddhist Anthropology: The Problem of the Secular," in *Journal of the American Academy of Religion,* XXVI (September, 1968), pp. 203-216, where he shows the dangers of secularization for (Theravada) Buddhism. He points out that traditionally the pursuit of attaining nirvana runs contrary to the involvement in worldly affairs. Thus with the increasing dominance of the worldly immense problems arise for the believer.

136. Hendrik Kraemer, *op. cit.,* p. 347.

137. Arend Th. van Leeuwen, *Christianity in World History. The Meetings of the Faiths of East and West,* foreword by Hendrik Kraemer, trans. by H. H. Hoskins (London: Edinburgh House, 1966), p. 404.

138. *Ibid.,* p. 13.

139. *Ibid.,* p. 419.

140. Wolfhart Pannenberg, "Reden von Gott angesichts atheistischer Kritik," in *Gottesgedanke und menschliche Freiheit,* pp. 35ff. We must also refer here to the important collection of essays, *Religion and Progress in Modern Asia,* ed. by Robert N. Bellah (New York: Free Press, 1965). Especially Robert N. Bellah in his concluding essay, "Epilogue: Religion and Progress in Modern Asia," emphasizes that the influence of Christianity on cultural modernization in Asia is out of all proportion to the small number of people in-

volved (p. 203). He also cautions that progress would be self-defeating if it so interrupts a society's identity pattern as to cause a breakdown in its functioning. As a possible remedy to alleviate this threat he advocates a syncretistic ideology, stressing continuity with the best of the past and progress toward a better future. But then he wonders: "Can such a harmonious combination break the myriad clinging tendrils of tradition that keep society from making any real advance?" (p. 224). We might suggest that to adopt and adapt Christianity would be a better option. This suggestion follows up on Bellah's own discovery that Christianity is concerned with both the identity problem and progress, through criticizing past identities and seeking to mold new cultural identities, "identities by and large more relevant to the modern world" (p. 223).

Chapter 6: From Tribal God to Savior

1. Cf. Gerhard von Rad, *Genesis. A Commentary*, trans. by J. H. Marks (Philadelphia: Westminster, 1961), p. 109, in his exegesis of Gen. 4:26.
2. Martin Noth, *Exodus. A Commentary*, trans. by J. S. Bowden (Philadelphia: Westminster, 1962), p. 43, in his exegesis of Ex. 3:13f.
3. Cf. Gerhard von Rad, *Genesis*, p. 193, in his exegesis of Gen. 17:1, who mentions that, in the theology of P, God's revelation as El Shaddai designates a definite and, moreover, temporary stage of God's revelation to the patriarchs. Cf. also Martin Noth, *Exodus*, p. 61, in his exegesis of Ex. 6:2f.
4. This has been pointed out by Ludwig Köhler, *Old Testament Theology*, trans. by A. S. Todd (Philadelphia: Westminster, 1957), p. 44.
5. We cannot agree here with the otherwise excellent book by Georg Fohrer, *History of Israelite Religion*, p. 36, when he says that "there are no extra-biblical sources." Archeology has provided us with at least modest results in shedding light on this period.
6. Albrecht Alt, "The God of the Fathers," in *Essays on Old Testament History and Religion*, trans. by R. A. Wilson (Oxford: Basil Blackwell, 1966), pp. 3-77; cf. for the following p. 47.
7. *Ibid.*, p. 55.
8. *Ibid.*, p. 62.
9. Cf. Georg Fohrer, *History of Israelite Religion*, pp. 36f., for the contemporary discussion of the God of the Fathers.
10. Georg Fohrer, *op. cit.*, p. 38, appropriately suggests that here "we may be dealing with a mere term for 'God,' with a divine name that is an expression of a nomadic El religion, or with the name of the Canaanite high god El." Frank Moore Cross, Jr., in his careful and convincing study "Yahweh and the God of the Patriarchs," *The Har-*

vard Theological Review, LV (October, 1962), p. 232, argues too that the patriarchal gods were not typically nameless, except for designation by the eponym of the clan and the founders of their cult. Though the patriarchal deities were foreign to the promised land, the god(s) of the Fathers were quickly identified by the features they had in common with the gods worshiped under various liturgical titles in the new land. Cross seems to find the clue for this easy assimilation in the fact that the cult of El, of which even Yahweh is derived as a cultic name of El, is underlying these local and nomadic cults of El Abraham, El Elyon, El Shaddai, and so on *(ibid.*, pp. 256f.).

11. Cf. Hans Wilhelm Hertzberg, *Die Bücher Josua, Richter, Ruth,* (Göttingen: Vandenhoeck & Ruprecht, 1953), p. 133, in his exegesis of Josh. 24:2 and 14f., who emphasizes the significance of the renunciation of other gods.

12. Cf. Gerhard von Rad, *Old Testament Theology,* Vol. 1: *The Theology of Israel's Historical Traditions,* trans. by D. M. G. Stalker (Edinburgh: Oliver & Boyd, 1962), pp. 187f.

13. *Ibid.*, p. 291.

14. Martin Noth, *The History of Israel,* trans. by P. R. Ackroyd (2nd ed.; New York: Harper, 1960), p. 136, n. 2.

15. William Foxwell Albright, *From Stone Age to Christianity. Monotheism and the Historical Process* (Garden City, N.Y.: Doubleday, Anchor Book, 1957), p. 258.

16. Cf for the following the excellent analysis by Gerhard von Rad, *Old Testament Theology,* Vol. 1, pp. 291-296.

17. William Foxwell Albright, *op. cit.*, p. 254.

18. Cf for the following Georg Fohrer, *History of Israelite Religion,* pp. 69f., who argues this point very convincingly. Cf. him also for views other than the one adopted.

19. Cf. Georg Fohrer, *op. cit.*, p. 76, for a list of attempts to explain the meaning of the name "Yahweh."

20. William Foxwell Albright, *op. cit.*, p. 261.

21. Cf. Judges 4:11 and Numbers 10:29, where Moses' father-in-law is described as either a Kenite or a Midianite.

22. So rightly Ludwig Köhler, *Old Testament Theology,* p. 46; and cf. Georg Fohrer, *op. cit.*, p. 72.

23. Cf. William Foxwell Albright, *op. cit.*, pp. 262f. and 270.

24. Deut. 34:10, which could also be cited, does hardly fit here, because the writer emphasizes that Yahweh knew Moses face to face and not vice versa. In other words, Moses was the one with whom God had an exceptionally intimate relationship.

25. William Foxwell Albright, *op. cit.*, p. 265.

26. Martin Noth, *Exodus,* p. 247, in his exegesis of Ex. 32:1-6, comments that the "calf" is explained as a representation of God, "indeed

as an image of the God who had brought Israel up out of Egypt."
Cf. also William Foxwell Albright, *op. cit.*, p. 266, for a slightly
different interpretation of Ex. 32:1-6.

27. The interpretation of the Old Testament meaning of the term "covenant," so central for the Sinai narratives, is highly controversial. We
want to follow here with some modifications Georg Fohrer, *History
of Israelite Religion*, pp. 80f., who rejects the notion that the Sinai
events can be compared with the model of an ancient vassal treaty.
Of course, Dennis J. McCarthy, *Old Testament Covenant. A Survey
of Current Opinions* (Oxford: Basil Blackwell, 1972), p. 58, is right
when he observes "that the apparent sequence of certain ceremonies
reflects in large part the sequence of the elements in the treaty documents." Yet McCarthy also admits that many, if not most, recent
writers are unwilling to assert that the treaty form is to be found
in the Sinai narratives (p. 72). Cf. also Ernst Kutsch, *Verheissung
und Gesetz. Untersuchungen zum sogenannten "Bund" im Alten
Testament* (Berlin: Walter de Gruyter, 1973), who strongly supports
Fohrer at this point.

28. This is especially emphasized by Ludwig Köhler, *Old Testament
Theology*, pp. 61f. One could, however, quote 2 Kings 23:3 as an
exception. But as Lothar Perlitt, *Bundestheologie im Alten Testament*
(Neukirchen-Vluyn: Neukirchener Verlag, 1969), p. 262, has recognized Josiah makes a covenant with his people before Yahweh in
the sense of a pledge or oath of allegiance. Josiah would not dare to
make a covenant with Yahweh.

29. Cf. Georg Fohrer, *History of Israelite Religion*, pp. 63f., who cites
many examples in which a local god El was identified with Israel's
God.

30. Cf. Georg Fohrer, *op. cit.*, pp. 102f. We must agree here with James
Barr, *Old and New in Interpretation. A Study of the Two Testaments* (London: SCM, 1966), p. 72, that gods outside of Israel were
also conceived as acting in history. Barr is right too when he claims
that revelation in history is not at the center of Hebrew thought. Yet
the Old Testament emphasizes on almost every page that Israel enjoys a special relationship with a God who is actively involved in
the history of Israel and who discloses himself through his involvement. Even wisdom literature follows this train of thinking though
it emphasizes more the majesty and ultimate incomprehensibility of
God (cf. Job 26:14).

31. Cf. also William Foxwell Albright, *Yahweh and the Gods of Canaan.
A Historical Analysis of Two Contrasting Faiths* (Garden City, N.Y.:
Doubleday, Anchor Book, 1969), p. 198, who refers to this passage.

32. Cf. William Foxwell Albright, *Yahweh and the Gods of Canaan*, pp.
199-203, in his references to Gideon.

33. Cf. Hans-Joachim Kraus, *Psalmen*, Vol. 1 (Neukirchen/Moers: Neu-

kirchener Verlag, 1960), p. 472, in his exegesis of Ps. 68:5-7. Morton Smith in his provocative book, *Palestinian Parties and Politics that Shaped the Old Testament* (New York: Columbia University, 1971), p. 19, might be right when he claims: "Although the cult of Yahweh is the principle concern of the Old Testament, it may not have been the principle religious concern of the Israelites." While Smith recognizes that by the 10th century B.C. the predominant cult in the hill country of Palestine was that of Yahweh, he asserts that this did not imply a neglect of the other gods of the common religion of the Near East (p. 28f.). In other words, the popular piety was strongly syncretistic. However, Smith argues that a movement existed that wanted Yahweh alone to be worshiped. It gained stronger and stronger influence and finally culminated in the reconstruction and cult of the second temple in Jerusalem. From this movement and its influence does not only stem the highly edited Old Testament, "but Christianity, rabbinic Judaism, and Islam" (p. 30). Though Smith may have overstated his case, it can hardly be doubted that popular pre-exilic piety was much more syncretistic than is commonly assumed.

34. Hans Walter Wolff, *Dodekapropheton (Joel-Amos)* (Neukirchen/Moers: Neukirchener Verlag, 1963), p. 307, in his exegesis of Amos 5:21-27, sees in this passage "an axiomatic assertion of passionate rejection of cultic feasts." Gordon Kaufman, *God the Problem*, p. 164, may have captured the truth well when he said: "The Old Testament is the principal extant record of the tumultuous and painful history of a growing consciousness, unparalleled elsewhere, of one God sovereign over the entire universe."

35. Herbert Braun, "Gottes Existenz und meine Geschichtlichkeit im Neuen Testament," in *Zeit und Geschichte. Dankesgabe an Rudolf Bultmann zum 80. Geburtstag*, ed. by Erich Dinkler (Tübingen: J. C. B. Mohr, 1964), p. 403.

36. For more details cf. Hans Schwarz, *On the Way to the Future*, pp. 47f.

37. Cf. for the following Herbert Braun, *loc. cit.*, pp. 401ff.; cf. also Werner Foerster, "*Kyrios:* The Choice of the Word *kyrios* in the LXX," in *Theological Dictionary of the New Testament*, ed. by Gerhard Kittel, trans. by G. W. Bromiley, Vol. 3 (Grand Rapids, Mich.: Wm. B. Eerdmans, 1965), pp. 1081f.

38. Cf. for the following Hans Schwarz, *op. cit.*, pp. 62f.

39. Cf. Hans Conzelmann, *An Outline of the Theology of the New Testament*, trans. by J. Bowden (New York: Harper, 1969), pp. 145f.

40. Rudolf Bultmann, *Theology of the New Testament*, Vol. 1, trans. by K. Grobel (New York: Charles Scribner's, 1951), p. 43. Bultmann's discovery that "Jesus' call to decision implies a christology," is one

of his great unintentional contributions to unearth the proclamation of Jesus.

41. Cf. for the following Hans Schwarz, *On the Way to the Future,* pp. 59f.; Ethelbert Stauffer, *Jesus and His Story,* trans. by R. and C. Winston (New York: Alfred A. Knopf, 1960), p. 174-195; and Ethelbert Stauffer, *"ego,"* in *Theological Dictionary of the New Testament,* Vol. 2, pp. 343-362.

42. This should not be confused with the *ego eimi* formulas in the Gospel of John (cf. John 6:35) which have a different background. Cf. Eduard Schweizer, *Ego eimi. Die religionsgeschichtliche Herkunft und theologische Bedeutung der johanneischen Bildreden; zugleich ein Beitrag zur Quellenfrage des vierten Evangeliums* (Göttingen: Vandenhoeck & Ruprecht, 1965).

43. Ernst Lohmeyer, *Das Evangelium des Markus* (Göttingen: Vandenhoeck & Ruprecht, 1954), pp. 270f.; and William Manson, *"Ego eimi* of the Messianic Presence in the New Testament," in *Journal of Theological Studies,* XLVIII (1967), pp. 137-145. Cf. also Vincent Taylor, *The Gospel according to St. Mark* (London: Macmillan, 1957), pp. 503ff., who is hesitant to see a theophanic formula contained in this passage. However, he affirms that most can be said for those who interpret it as a Messianic or quasi-Messianic claim.

44. Ernst Haenchen, *Der Weg Jesu: Eine Erklärung des Markus-Evangeliums und der kanonischen Parallelen* (Berlin: Alfred Töpelmann, 1966), pp. 511f., in his discussion with Stauffer rejects the thesis that this passage dates back to Jesus. It simply reflects the expectation of the first Christian community. Since this expectation (the return of Christ before the death of the members of the Sanhedrin) was not fulfilled, the passage was changed in Matthew and Luke. Vincent Taylor, *The Gospel according to St. Mark,* pp. 568f., who admits too that this passage depicts the apocalyptic hopes of the church, comes to the conclusion that it is in every way probable that it is actually the reply of Jesus to the challenge of the high priest. Taylor concludes that in Jesus' reply the emphasis lies on the enthronement, and on the enthronement as the symbol of triumph.

45. Rudolf Bultmann, *The Gospel of John. A Commentary,* trans. by G. R. Beasley-Murray *et al.* (Philadelphia: Westminster, 1971), p. 339, n. 3, in his exegesis of John 9:38.

46. Joachim Jeremias, *Abba. Studien zur neutestamentlichen Theologie und Zeitgeschichte* (Göttingen: Vandenhoeck & Ruprecht, 1966), pp. 16f.

47. Cf. for the following Joachim Jeremias, *op. cit.,* pp. 54ff. There Jeremias still emphasizes the connection of the address *abba* with the way children address their father (pp. 63f.). Later he has tuned down this emphasis by conceding that grown-up sons and daughters too addressed their father as *abba.* Cf. Joachim Jeremias, *New Testa-*

ment Theology. The Proclamation of Jesus, trans. by J. Bowden (New York: Charles Scribner's, 1971), p. 67.

48. Cf. Joachim Jeremias, *The Lord's Prayer*, trans. by J. Reumann (Philadelphia: Fortress, Facet Book, 1969), p. 17.

49. Joachim Jeremias, *New Testament Theology*, p. 197, rightly mentions: "As members of the family of God, they may say 'Father' to God, and ask him for his good gifts. The earliest church right from the beginning regarded it as a great privilege that Jesus in this way gave the disciples a share in his authority as Son." Cf. also Donald Guthrie, *Galatians* (London: Thomas Nelson, 1969), p. 121, who mentions in his exegesis of Gal. 4:6f. "that the apostle assumes that adoption into the status of sons carries with it the full privileges of sonship." He also states that the apostle is strangely attracted to the idea of the connection between sonship and heritage. Yet, we might be safe to assume that Paul only brings to its appropriate conclusion the implications of the newly gained sonship.

50. Cf. for the following Rudolf Bultmann, *The Gospel of John*, pp. 605ff., in his exegesis of John 14:6.

51. Cf. Ernst Haenchen, *Die Apostelgeschichte* (Göttingen: Vandenhoeck & Ruprecht, 1959), p. 177, in his exegesis of Acts 4:12, who has illuminated the Jewish background of this statement.

52. Otto Michel, *Der Brief an die Hebräer* (Göttingen: Vandenhoeck & Ruprecht, 1966), pp. 92f., in his exegesis of Heb. 1:1f., rightly claims that the diversity and multitude of ways and means of God's self-disclosure as recorded in the Old Testament does no longer serve for the writer of this letter as a sign of God's plenitude, but it denotes the incompleteness and non-definity of the prophetic comprehension. Michel also emphasizes the eschatological character of God's self-disclosure in Jesus Christ.

53. Cf. for the messianic leaders of the zealot movement the excellent study by Martin Hengel, *Die Zeloten. Untersuchungen zur jüdischen Freiheitsbewegung in der Zeit von Herodes I. bis 70 n. Chr.* (Leiden: E. J. Brill, 1961). Hengel also demonstrates that Jesus did not associate himself with zealots; he often was critical against them. Nevertheless, the leaders of the Jewish people denounced him to the Roman authorities as an alleged zealot messianic pretender (pp. 385f.).

54. Cf. for the following Hans Schwarz, *On the Way to the Future*, p. 56.

55. Cf. Wolfhart Pannenberg, *Jesus—God and Man*, trans. by L. L. Wilkins and D. A. Priebe (Philadelphia: Westminster, 1968), pp. 67ff., who convincingly asserts that the eschatological character of Christ's resurrection also confirms his pre-Easter activity.

56. Cf. Hans Conzelmann, *Der erste Brief an die Korinther* (Göttingen: Vandenhoeck & Ruprecht, 1969), p. 294, in his explanation of 1

Cor. 15:1-11, where he shows how Paul unmistakably emphasizes that our belief in the resurrection is founded in the Christ event.

57. Of course, we do not want to deny that God is continuously active in the world and thereby continuously disclosing himself. Especially Nathan Söderblom, *The Living God*, pp. 350-386, has stressed the necessity to assert God's continued revelation. He also pointed out that God reveals himself in history and in historic persons, outside the church as well as in it (p. 379). Yet he is quick to admit that "the Church has, in the Scriptures has, in its experience, the means of interpreting God's continued revelation" (p. 378). This statement cannot be overemphasized. A "revelation" is not a means to interpret God's ultimate self-disclosure in Jesus of Nazareth, but God's ultimate self-disclosure enables us to approximately interpret his ongoing activity in the world. To avoid a possible misunderstanding, we would prefer not to talk about God's continued revelation, but rather about his continued and ongoing activity.

58. Council of Chalcedon (451), "Definitions of the Two Natures of Christ" (148), in Heinrich Denzinger, *The Sources of Catholic Dogma*, pp. 60f. Wolfhart Pannenberg, *Jesus—God and Man*, p. 292, is certainly right, when he mentions that the definitions of Chalcedon "accomplish no theological solution for the controversies preceding Chalcedon." Yet we must also listen to Albert C. Outler, "Jesus Christ as Divine-Human Savior," *The Christian Century*, LXXVIII (May 3, 1961), p. 555, when he says that the definitions of Chalcedon are the only place "in the history of Christian thought where the New Testament compound was explicated in exact balance so as to discourage the four favorite ways by which the divine and human 'energies' of the Christ event are commonly misconstrued." Perhaps, because we are always tempted to choose one of those ways, Chalcedon did not have the effect of unification it was intended to have.

59. Cf. Wolfhart Pannenberg, "Dogmatic Theses on the Doctrine of Revelation," in *Revelation as History*, p. 145, where in thesis 5 he makes the same point saying: "The Christ event does not disclose the Godhead of the God of Israel as an isolated event, but rather insofar as it is part of the history of God with Israel." Since the translation of this book is at times rather "free" we usually give our own translation of the German original.

Chapter 7: The Likeness of God

1. Karl Barth, "The Word of God and the Task of the Ministry" (1922), in *The Word of God and the Word of Man*, p. 186. The German original reads "theologians" instead of "ministers." Cf. *Anfänge der*

dialektischen Theologie, ed. by Jürgen Moltmann, Vol. 1 (Munich: Christian Kaiser, 1966), p. 199.

2. Dionysius the Areopagite, *The Divine Names* (VII, 3), Dionysius the Areopagite *On the Divine Names and the Mystical Theology*, trans. by C. E. Rolt (New York: Macmillan, 1951), pp. 151f.

3. This has been pointed out especially well by Gordon D. Kaufman, *Systematic Theology. A Historicist Perspective* (New York: Charles Scribner's, 1968), p. 121; cf. also his book *God the Problem*, p. 113, where he says: "All conceptions of God" . . . , "including that of scripture and faith, must be understood as creations of the human imagination: the 'real God' is never available to us or directly knowable by us."

4. Paul Tillich, *Systematic Theology*, Vol. 1, p. 238.

5. Paul Tillich, *Systematic Theology*, Vol. 2: *Existence and the Christ* (Chicago: University of Chicago, 1957), p. 9.

6. Paul Tillich, *Systematic Theology*, Vol. 1, p. 239.

7. Wolfgang Trillhaas, *Dogmatik* (Berlin: Alfred Töpelmann, 1962), p. 121 (own trans.). However, we wonder if Trillhaas does not overstate his case when he refuses even to list such attributes by claiming that assertions concerning such attributes are a doxological matter and belong to the proclamation. Does not theology fulfill, at least in part, a doxological function too?

8. Cf. for the following Friedrich Schleiermacher, *The Christian Faith* (par. 50), pp. 194f.

9. Cf. Karl Barth, "The Word of God and the Task of the Ministry," p. 196. However, it is difficult to side with Barth and blame Schleiermacher for speaking about God "simply by speaking of man in a loud voice." It seems that especially Schleiermacher attempted to escape from an anthropocentric God language.

10. Martin Luther, *Vorlesungen über 1. Mose* (1535-1545), in WA 42, 11, 19-25, in his exegesis of Gen. 1:2; cf. also Paul Althaus, *The Theology of Martin Luther*, pp. 20-24, in his section on *God in Himself and God as He Reveals Himself*.

11. Martin Luther, *Ennaratio Psalmi LI* (1538), in WA 40, II, 329, 8-12 and 330, 1-7, in his exegesis of Ps. 51:3.

12. Gordon D. Kaufman, *Systematic Theology*, p. 115.

13. Martin Luther, "Vorrede auf die Episteln S. Jakobi and Judä, *Das Neue Testament* (1522), in WA DB 7, 384, 29-32 (DB stands for German Bible).

14. Martin Buber in his classic *I and Thou*, with a postscript by the author added, trans. by R. G. Smith (New York: Charles Scribner's, 1958), p. 135. Karl Barth very rightly reminds us at this point that "the concept of the 'personality' of God" . . . "is a product of the struggle against modern naturalism and pantheism." Cf. Karl Barth, *Church Dogmatics*, Vol. 1/I: *The Doctrine of the Word of God,*

p. 403. Cf. also Harminus Martinus Kuitert, *Gott in Menschenges-talt. Eine dogmatisch-hermeneutische Studie über die Anthropomor-phismen der Bibel* (Munich: Chr. Kaiser, 1967), p. 27, who attempts to show that the anthropomorphisms in the Bible are not human and therefore inadequate concepts projected into God.

15. Cf. Emil Brunner, *Truth as Encounter*, trans. by D. Cairns (Phila-delphia: Westminster, 1964), esp. p. 89, where he asserts: "The re-lation of God to man is always first, that of man to God second and consequent upon the first. Hence, the relation of God to man is wholly other than that of man to God. The relation of God to man is clearly primary, creative, and without presuppositions." . . . "On this point there is basic opposition between the Biblical and the idealist, pantheist, and mystical thought concerning God."

16. Helmut Thielicke in his monumental work *Der evangelische Glaube. Grundzüge der Dogmatik*, Vol. 2: *Gotteslehre und Christologie* (Tübingen: J. C. B. Mohr, 1973), p. 138, appropriately reminds us that understanding of God as person should not be misconstrued as a projection of a human phenomenon unto God. It is rather the other way around: The self-disclosive divine I turns the human thou into a personal counterpart. He concludes: *"When we talk about God as a person, we are not doing this anthropomorphically. We rather intend to do it theomorphically in talking about the human person."* Wolfhart Pannenberg, "The Question of God," in *Basic Questions in Theology*, Vol. 2, pp. 227ff., goes a similar route. Since the idea of a person originates in the phenomenology of religious experience, he argues, one can only talk about man as a person in the full sense, if one recognizes a personal God. The necessity of a religious dimen-sion for recognizing a human being as a person might be further substantiated by Jürgen Moltmann's claim that earthly utopias and revolutions of the future adopt a militant and extortionate attitude to life unless they include certainty in face of death and hope which carries love beyond death (Cf. Jürgen Moltmann, "Hope and Con-fidence: A Conversation with Ernst Bloch," *Dialog*, VII [Winter, 1968], p. 49). We might be safe to assume that the rejection of a dimension above and beyond that of man and his environment im-plies the rejection of man's participation in the inviolable majesty of God. Consequently man can be reduced to a strictly biological phenomenon and treated accordingly.

17. Cf. for the following Gerhard von Rad, *Genesis*, pp. 56ff., in his exegesis of Gen. 1:26ff.

18. The notion of a heavenly court is not uncommon in the Old Testa-ment (cf. Job 1 and Isa. 6).

19. Cf Martin Buber, *I and Thou*, p. 136, and cf. above n. 16.

20. Rudolf Bultmann, *Theology of the New Testament*, Vol. 1, p. 258. Of course, Bultmann's highly present-oriented approach would pre-

vent him from talking about the "ultimate goal" of the Christian's existence.

21. Yehezkel Kaufmann, *The Religion of Israel. From Its Beginnings to the Babylonian Exile,* trans. and abridged by M. Greenberg (Chicago: University of Chicago, 1960), pp. 212f., very interestingly ties up this invitational history with the status of the prophet in Israel. The prophet acts on behalf of God, not of man. He is sent to the people to bring the word of God and his command to the people. But he is not the only one since there is a succession of emissaries of God that come to the people through the centuries. Kaufmann sees here a distinctive difference to the pagan religions. In pagan religions prophets are exceptional figures endowed with a charisma that was theirs alone. Therefore, Buddha, Zoroaster, or Mohammad were exceptional figures whose "mission" ended with them as founders or reorganizers of religions. In Israel, however, there was a continuous commissioning of men of God throughout the ages. In other words, Kaufmann's reference to the succession of prophets as spokesmen of God illustrates what we have called God's invitational history.

22. Cf. for the following Edmond Jacob, *Theology of the Old Testament,* trans. by A. W. Heathcote and Ph. J. Allcock (New York: Harper, 1958), p. 109.

23. Norman H. Snaith, in his helpful book, *The Distinctive Ideas of the Old Testament* (London: Epworth, 1960), p. 95, mentions that *chesed* ("love" or, as we rather say, "faithfulness") is conditional upon there being a covenant. While *'ahabah* (love) is unconditioned love and the very basis and the only cause of the existence of the covenant between God and Israel. "Without the prior existence of a covenant, there could never be any *chesed* at all." Thus Snaith calls *'ahabah* (love) God's election love, while he terms *chesed* (faithfulness) God's covenant love.

24. So Edmond Jacob, *op. cit.,* p. 104.

25. The term "good" that Micah uses here is not a "perfectly general term" *(Allerweltsbegriff* in the German original) as Gerhard von Rad, *Old Testament Theology,* Vol. 2: *The Theology of Israel's Prophetic Traditions,* trans. by D. M. G. Stalker (New York: Harper, 1965), p. 186, assumes. Theodor Lescow, *Micha 6, 6-8. Studien zur Sprache, Form und Auslegung* (Stuttgart: Calwer, 1966), p. 45, rightly objected that doing the good and knowing God is intimately correlated in the Old Testament, since without knowing God one cannot do good and without doing good one does not really express that one knows God. Cf. also Artur Weiser, *Das Buch der Zwölf kleinen Propheten* (Göttingen: Vandenhoeck & Ruprecht, 1959), p. 281, in his exegesis of Mic. 6:8, who emphasizes that communion with God is the deepest root of life as order, envisioned by God *(gottgewollte Ordnung).*

26. Cf. Walter Eichrodt, *Theology of the Old Testament*, Vol. 1, trans. by J. A. Baker (Philadelphia: Westminster, 1961), p. 239, who shows that creation itself is a work of the divine *chesed*. However, in making the covenant relationship the overriding concept of Old Testament theology Eichrodt has to shortchange other equally important concepts in the relationship between God and his people.

27. Cf. Hans Windisch, *Der Zweite Korintherbrief* (1924) (Göttingen: Vandenhoeck & Ruprecht, 1970), p. 121, in his exegesis of 2 Cor. 3:14, where he states that here a Christian theologian had referred to Jer. 31 with the intention to strongly emphasize the preparatory and inadequate character of the Mosaic revelation of God.

28. Johannes Behm, *"diatheke,"* in *Theological Dictionary of the New Testament*, ed. by Gerhard Kittel, Vol. 2, p. 134.

29. Ethelbert Stauffer, *"agapao," ibid.*, Vol. 1, p. 50, esp. n. 140.

30. Cf. Rudolf Bultmann, *"eleos," ibid.*, Vol. 2, pp. 482ff. We find Bultmann's expression of "the divinely required attitude of man" somewhat misleading. "Response" would have been more appropriate than the legalistically sounding term "requirement."

31. Cf. for the following Hans Conzelmann, *"charis,"* in *Theologisches Wörterbuch zum Neuen Testament*, ed. by Gerhard Friedrich, Vol. 9 (Stuttgart: W. Kohlhammer, 1973), esp. pp. 382-386.

32. For a good introduction to the Old Testament understanding of this aspect of God's holiness cf. Norman H. Snaith, *The Distinctive Ideas of the Old Testament*, pp. 40f.

33. Th. C. Vriezen, *An Outline of Old Testament Theology* (2nd ed.; Newton, Mass.: Charles T. Bradford, 1970), p. 298, rightly observes that Yahweh's holiness "first of all involves *unapproachableness,* even for the angels around His throne."

34. Cf. for the following Edmond Jacob, *Theology of the Old Testament*, pp. 87ff.

35. *Ibid.*, p. 89.

36. Norman H. Snaith, *The Distinctive Ideas of the Old Testament*, p. 77.

37. Cf. Edmond Jacob, *op. cit.*, p. 114, who also quotes statistics according to which the most frequently used Hebrew terms for "wrath" are used roughly four times more often for describing a disposition of God than of man.

38. It must be mentioned, however, that the later Chronicles did no longer attribute to Yahweh but to Satan the incitement to number Israel (1 Chron. 21:1). Should this indicate an emerging doubt whether the dreadful feature in God was compatible with his moral integrity? Cf. for further discussion Norman H. Snaith, *op. cit.*, pp. 40f.

39. Artur Weiser, *Das Buch der zwölf kleinen Propheten*, p. 86, comments to this passage that, in contrast to our reasoning, the serious-

ness of God's judgment and his seeking, pedagogical love do not exclude each other. "God's wrath does not suffocate his love; it is only the other side of his same fundamental disposition that Yahweh never abandoned with his people."

40. Cf. for the following Otto Procksch, *"hagios,"* in *Theological Dictionary of the New Testament*, Vol. 1, pp. 103ff.
41. Cf. Gottlob Schrenk, *"dikaiosyne,"* *ibid.*, Vol. 2, pp. 195f., for extensive treatment of this topic.
42. *Ibid.*, p. 198.
43. So Rudolf Bultmann, *Theology of the New Testament*, Vol. 1, pp. 288f.
44. Friedrich Schleiermacher, *The Christian Faith* (par. 109/4), p. 503.
45. Cf. Paul Althaus, *Die christliche Wahrheit*, p. 398.
46. Cf. Gustav Stählin, *"orge,"* in *Theological Dictionary of the New Testament*, Vol. 5, p. 427, who claims that there is only one refuge from the unqualified wrath of God, "namely, Christ and faith in Him."
47. In the New Testament wrath is seen as something bad, if it is just an attitude of man. It is justified only as holy wrath "which hates what God hates and which is seen above all in Jesus Himself" (cf. Gustav Stählin, *loc. cit.*, p. 419).
48. G. Ernest Wright, *God Who Acts. Biblical Theology as Recital* (Chicago: Henry Regnery, 1952), p. 84, has pointed this out very well when he said: "The so-called 'attributes' of God are inferences drawn from the way he has acted. His righteousness, justice, love, grace, jealousy, and wrath are not abstractions with which we are free to deal abstractly—that is, apart from history. They are descriptive of the way God has directed history; and hence it is inferred that they all find their unity in him."
49. This impression is reinforced by Gerhard von Rad's comment, *Old Testament Theology*, Vol. 1, p. 121: "Thus, retelling remains the most legitimate form of theological discourse on the Old Testament." Cf. also Friedrich Baumgärtel, "Gerhard von Rad's 'Theologie des Alten Testaments,' " *Theologische Literaturzeitung*, LXXXVI (November, 1961), col. 803, where he vehemently objects to this comment. However, in his preface to the fourth edition of his *Old Testament Theology von Rad* mentions to his critics that he never thought of separating between the historical and the less or not at all historical (cf. *Theologie des Alten Testaments*, Vol. 1 [4th ed.; Munich: Chr. Kaiser, 1962], pp. 11f.). Evidently this is exactly the point that Baumgärtel attacked. Faith and history seem inextricably interwoven in von Rad's *Old Testament Theology*.

For an excellent introduction to the issue of history and salvation history cf. Carl E. Braaten, *History and Hermeneutics*, Vol. 2 of *New Directions in Theology Today*, ed. by William Hordern (Philadelphia: Westminster, 1966). Braaten himself comes close to Pannenberg in emphasizing the progressive, eschatological character of history of which the Christ event is its proleptically anticipated goal. Cf. his book *The Future of God. The Revolutionary Dynamics of Hope.* (New York: Harper, 1969), in which he characterizes the church as the "prolepsis of a new world."

50. Gerhard von Rad, *Old Testament Theology*, Vol. 1, p. 121.
51. Cf. Gerhard von Rad, *Old Testament Theology*, Vol. 1, p. 121ff., who points out the significance of this creed.
52. G. Ernest Wright, in his instructive essay, "Reflections Concerning Old Testament Theology," in *Studia Biblica et Semitica Theodoro Christiano Vriezen Dedicata* (Wageningen: H. Veenman & Zonen, 1966), p. 382, states the matter very clearly: "The biblical event was a happening in time which was deemed of special importance because God's word was present within it, interpreting its meaning. The historical happening and its interpretation, the deed and the word of God as its commentary, these constitute the biblical event."
53. Cf. Jürgen Moltmann, *Theology of Hope. On the Ground and the Implications of a Christian Eschatology*, trans. by J. W. Leitch (New York: Harper, 1967), p. 109.
54. Jürgen Moltmann, *op cit.*, pp. 137ff., has pointed out especially well the significance of this change for eschatology. Yet the emergence of an outlook comprising the whole universe is equally important for the relationship between salvation history and history.
55. This is especially noticeable in the Gospel of Luke in which God's revelation in Christ is depicted as the center of history. Cf. Hans Conzelmann, in his illustrative study, *The Theology of St. Luke*, trans. by G. Buswell (New York: Harper, 1960), esp. pp. 150f.
56. Johann Gottlieb Fichte, *Die Anweisung zum seligen Leben*, ed. by Fritz Medicus (Hamburg: Felix Meiner, 1954), p. 97, in his sixth lecture. This statement is also quoted by Oscar Cullmann, *Salvation in History*, trans. by S. G. Sowers (London: SCM, 1967), p. 21.
57. Gotthold Ephraim Lessing, *On the Proof of the Spirit and of Power* (1777), in *Lessing's Theological Writings*, trans. with an intr. essay by Henry Chadwick (Stanford, Cal.: Stanford University, 1957), p. 55.
58. Rudolf Bultmann, "Liberal Theology and the Latest Theological Movement" (1924), in *Faith and Understanding*, Vol. 1, ed. with an intr. by Robert W. Funk, trans. by L. P. Smith (London: SCM, 1969), p. 30; cf. also Rudolf Bultmann, "Die Frage der natürlichen Offenbarung," in *Offenbarung und Heilsgeschehen* (Munich: A. Lempp, 1941), p. 22.
59. Cf. for the following Rudolf Bultmann, *Theology of the New Testament*, Vol. 1, esp. pp. 33 and 43.
60. *Ibid.*, pp. 43f.

61. Rudolf Bultmann, *The Presence of Eternity. History and Eschatology* (New York: Harper, 1957), p. 37.

62. Rudolf Bultmann, "New Testament and Mythology," in *Kerygma and Myth. A Theological Debate,* ed. by Hans Werner Bartsch, trans. by R. H. Fuller (London: SPCK, 1953), p. 5.

63. Rudolf Bultmann, *The Presence of Eternity,* p. 151.

64. A good example is Ernst Fuchs' essay, "Christus das Ende der Geschichte," *Evangelische Theologie,* VIII (1948/49), pp. 447-461, written in reply to Oscar Cullmann's book *Christ and Time.*

65. Karl Barth, *Church Dogmatics,* Vol. 3/I: *The Doctrine of Creation,* p. 60.

66. Karl Barth, *Church Dogmatics,* Vol. 4/II: *The Doctrine of Reconciliation,* ed. by G. W. Bromiley and T. F. Torrance (Edinburgh: T. & T. Clark, 1958), p. 806.

67. Oscar Cullmann, *Christ and Time. The Primitive Christian Conception of Time and History,* trans. by F. V. Filson (London: SCM, 1962), p. 83.

68. *Ibid.,* p. 137, where Cullmann also observes that the Christ event as the mid-point is in its part illuminated by the Old Testament preparation. Thus the Old Testament does not become superfluous once we have reached the New.

69. Oscar Cullmann, *Salvation in History,* p. 294.

70. Cf. for the following Oscar Cullmann, *Salvation in History,* pp. 154ff., esp. p. 156.

71. *Ibid.,* p. 166.

72. *Ibid.,* p. 163.

73. *Ibid.,* pp. 151f.

74. Wolfhart Pannenberg, "Redemptive Event and History," in *Basic Questions in Theology. Collected Essays,* Vol. 1, trans. by G. H. Kehm (Philadelphia: Fortress, 1970), p. 41.

75. Wolfhart Pannenberg, thesis 3 of "Dogmatic Theses on the Doctrine of Revelation," in *Revelation as History,* p. 135.

76. *Ibid.,* pp. 136ff.

77. Paul Althaus, "Offenbarung als Geschichte und Glaube. Bemerkungen zu Wolfhart Pannenbergs Begriff der Offenbarung," *Theologische Literaturzeitung,* LXXXVII (May, 1962), cols. 321-330, rightly asks this question and suggests to change the title of Pannenberg's booklet to "Revelation as History and Faith."

78. For the rest of this paragraph cf. Wolfhart Pannenberg's reply to Paul Althaus, reprinted as "Insight and Faith," in *Basic Questions in Theology. Collected Essays,* Vol. 2, pp. 28-45, esp. pp. 28, 33, 36, 40, and 44.

79. *Ibid.,* p. 36.

80. Th. C. Vriezen, *An Outline of Old Testament Theology,* p. 336.

81. Gerhard von Rad, "The Theological Problem of the Old Testament

Doctrine of Creation" (1936), in *The Problem of the Hexateuch and Other Essays,* trans. by E. W. T. Dicken, intr. by Norman W. Porteous (Edinburgh: Oliver & Boyd, 1966), p. 138. Cf. also Th. C. Vriezen, *op. cit.,* p. 334, who remarks: "This linking together of Israel's faith in the God of Salvation and the Creation of the world gives to the Old Testament philosophy of life a clarity, tranquility, warmth, and grandeur not to be found outside the Bible."—It is beyond the scope of our present investigation to render a complete theology of creation. We only want to touch upon the topic of creation as an "attribute" of God.

82. Gerhard von Rad, *loc. cit.,* p. 142.

83. Rudolf Bultmann, *The Gospel of John,* p. 431, in his exegesis of John 12:31. Yet we cannot agree with Bultmann when he continues in the same sentence: "And all apocalyptic pictures of the future are empty dreams." The emphasis on the decisiveness of the now does not render the future meaningless. The judgment taking place in the coming of Jesus does not eliminate all future judgments, including a "final" judgment. The eschatological now occurring in and with the Christ event is only proleptic anticipation. This means it is anticipation of something the realization and ultimate disclosure of which we still expect. Due to this proleptic anticipation we are not left with the all-inclusive present, but we are also looking forward to a meaningful future.

84. R. G. Collingwood, *The Idea of History* (New York: Oxford University, Galaxy Book 1957), p. 41.

85. Cf. for the following Martin E. Marty in his stimulating book *Varieties of Unbelief* (New York: Holt, Rinehart and Winston, 1964), esp. pp. 218-221. It is very difficult for us to agree with F. Gerald Downing, *Has Christianity a Revelation?* (London: SCM, 1964), esp. pp. 282ff., when he advocates to exchange the word "revelation" for "salvation" and in claiming that revelation occurs only in the end. Since the end has occurred in a proleptic way in Jesus the Christ, we can legitimately talk already now about revelation. Even in the Old Testament there is revelation, though indirectly as Pannenberg has shown. Downing may be right when he claims that the insistence on revelation often leads to a static Christianity, detached from the affairs of the day, while salvation calls on our part for commitment to a Christian life style. We wonder, however, whether such life style cannot also be the result of our response to God's self-disclosure in Jesus Christ? As long as the God who acts in history has a people who live in obedience to his word, revelation, salvation, and commitment are not totally unrelated to each other.

Selected Bibliography

1. *Atheism and Secularization (Theological Perspectives):*

Altizer, Thomas J. J. *The Gospel of Christian Atheism.* Philadelphia: Westminster, 1966.

———. *The New Apocalypse: The Radical Christian Vision of William Blake.* Michigan State University, 1967.

———. *Oriental Mysticism and Biblical Eschatology.* Philadelphia: Westminster, 1961.

———. and Hamilton, William. *Radical Theology and the Death of God.* Indianapolis: Bobbs-Merrill, 1966.

Aubrey, Edwin Ewart. *Secularism a Myth. An Examination of the Current Attack on Secularism.* New York: Harper, 1954.

Barth, Karl. *Church Dogmatics.* Vol. 1/I: *The Doctrine of the Word of God.* Translated by G. T. Thomson. Edinburgh: T. & T. Clark, 1936.

———. *Church Dogmatics.* Vol. 1/II: *The Doctrine of the Word of God.* Translated by G. T. Thomson and H. Knight. New York: Charles Scribner's, 1956.

———. *Church Dogmatics.* Vol. 3/I: *The Doctrine of Creation.* Translated by J. W. Edwards *et al.* Edinburgh: T. & T. Clark, 1958.

———. *The Epistle to the Romans.* Translated from the 6th ed. by E. C. Hoskyns. London: Oxford University, 1933.

———. "The Word of God and the Task of the Ministry" (1922). *The Word of God and the Word of Man.* Translated by D. Horton. New York: Harper Torchbook, 1957, pp. 183-217.

Bonhoeffer, Dietrich. *Christ the Center.* Translated by J. Bowden. Introduction by E. H. Robertson. New York: Harper, 1966.

———. *Letters and Papers from Prison.* Edited by Eberhard Bethge. Rev. ed. New York: Macmillan, 1967.

Callahan, Daniel, ed. *The Secular City Debate.* New York: Macmillan, 1966.

Cobb, John B. Jr., ed. *The Theology of Altizer: Critique and Response.* Philadelphia: Westminster, 1970.

Cox, Harvey. *On Not Leaving It to the Snake.* New York: Macmillan, 1967.

———. *The Secular City. Secularization and Urbanization in Theological Perspective.* New York: Macmillan, 1966.

Duquoc, Christian, ed. *Secularization and Spirituality.* Vol. 49 of *Concilium. Theology in the Age of Renewal.* New York: Paulist, 1969.

Gogarten, Friedrich. *Despair and Hope for Our Time.* Translated by Th. Wieser. Philadelphia: Pilgrim, 1970.

———. *The Reality of Faith. The Problem of Subjectivism in Theology.* Translated by C. Michalson *et al.* Philadelphia: Westminster, 1959.

Hamilton, William. *The New Essence of Christianity.* New York: Association, 1966.

Hefner, Philip. "The Relocation of the God-Question." *Zygon,* V (March, 1970) pp. 5-17.

Macquarrie, John. *God and Secularity.* Vol. 3 of *New Directions in Theology Today.* Edited by William Hordern. Philadelphia: Westminster, 1967.

Marty, Martin E. *The Modern Schism. Three Paths to the Secular.* New York: Harper, 1969.

Mascall, Eric L. *The Secularization of Christianity. An Analysis and a Critique.* New York: Holt, Rinehart and Winston, 1966.

Metz, Johannes B., ed. *Is God Dead?* Vol. 16 of *Concilium. Theology in the Age of Renewal.* New York: Paulist, 1966.

———. ed. *New Questions on God.* Vol. 76 of *Concilium. Religion in the Seventies.* New York: Herder and Herder, 1972.

Niebuhr, H. Richard. *Radical Monotheism and Western Culture.* With Supplementary Essays. New York: Harper, 1960.

Ogletree, Thomas W. *Christian Faith and History. A Critical Comparison of Ernst Troeltsch and Karl Barth.* Nashville: Abingdon, 1965.

———, ed. *The Death of God Controversy.* Nashville: Abingdon, 1966.

Pelikan, Jaroslav. *The Christian Tradition. A History of the Development of Doctrine.* Vol. 1: *The Emergence of the Catholic Tradition (100-600).* Chicago: University of Chicago, 1971.

Robinson, John A. T. *Honest to God.* Philadelphia: Westminster, 1963.

Schlitzer, Albert L., ed. *The Spirit and Power of Christian Secularity.* Notre Dame: University of Notre Dame, 1969.

Shiner, Larry. *The Secularization of History. An Introduction to the Theology of Friedrich Gogarten.* Nashville: Abingdon, 1966.

Vahanian, Gabriel. *The Death of God. The Culture of Our Post-Christian Era.* New York: George Braziller, 1961.

van Buren, Paul M. *The Edges of Language. An Essay in the Logic of a Religion.* New York: Macmillan, 1972.

——. *The Secular Meaning of the Gospel. Based on an Analysis of Its Language.* New York: Macmillan, 1963.

——. *Theological Explorations.* New York: Macmillan, 1968.

Vorkink, Peter II, ed. *Bonhoeffer in a World Come of Age.* Foreword by John C. Bennett. Philadelphia: Fortress, 1968.

Weber, Otto. *Karl Barth's Church Dogmatics.* Translated by A. C. Cochrane. Philadelphia: Westminster, 1953.

2. *Atheism and Secularization (Philosophical Perspectives):*

Allison, Henry E. *Lessing and the Enlightenment. His Philosophy of Religion and Its Relation to Eighteenth-Century Thought.* Ann Arbor: University of Michigan, 1966.

Bloch, Ernst. *Atheism in Christianity. The Religion of the Exodus and the Kingdom.* Translated by J. T. Swann. New York: Herder and Herder, 1972.

——. *Man on His Own. Essays in the Philosophy of Religion.* Translated by E. B. Ashlon. New York: Herder and Herder, 1970.

Cantor, Norman F., and Klein, Peter L., eds. *Renaissance Thought: Dante and Machiavelli.* Waltham, Mass.: Ginn-Blaisdell, 1969.

Darwin, Francis., ed. *The Life and Letters of Charles Darwin Including an Autobiographical Chapter.* 2 vols. New York: D. Appleton, 1898.

Fabro, Cornelio. *God in Exile. Modern Atheism. A Study of the Internal Dynamic of Modern Atheism, from Its Roots in the Cartesian Cogito to the Present Day.* Translated and edited by A. Gibson. Westminster, Md.: Newman, 1968.

Feuerbach, Ludwig. *The Essence of Christianity.* Translated by G. Eliot. Introduction by Karl Barth. Foreword by H. Richard Niebuhr. New York: Harper Torchbook, 1957.

Flew, Antony, and MacIntyre, Alasdair, eds. *New Essays in Philosophical Theology.* New York: Macmillan, 1955.

Fromm, Erich. *Beyond the Chains of Illusion. My Encounter with Marx and Freud.* New York: Simon and Schuster, 1962.

Garaudy, Roger. *From Anathema to Dialogue. A Marxist Challenge to the Christian Churches.* Translated by Luke O'Neill. New York: Herder and Herder, 1966.

——. *Marxism in the Twentieth Century.* Translated by R. Hague. New York: Charles Scribner's, 1970.

Haeckel, Ernst. *The Riddle of the Universe at the Close of the Nineteenth Century.* Translated by J. McCabe. New York: Harper, 1900.

Kline, George L. *Religious and Anti-religious Thought in Russia.* Chicago: University of Chicago, 1968.

Kristeller, Paul Oskar. *The Philosophy of Marsilio Ficino.* Translated by V. Conant. Gloucester, Mass.: Peter Smith, 1964.

Lenin, Vladimir Il'ich. *Collected Works.* Moscow: Foreign Languages Publication House, 1960-.

Lochman, Jan Milic. *Church in a Marxist Society. A Czechoslovak View.* New York: Harper, 1970.

Marx, Karl, and Engels, Friedrich. *On Religion.* Introduction by Reinhold Niebuhr. New York: Schocken, 1964.

Masterson, Patrick. *Atheism and Alienation. A Study of the Philosophical Sources of Contemporary Atheism.* Notre Dame: University of Notre Dame: University of Notre Dame, 1971.

Moltmann, Jürgen. "Hope and Confidence: A Conversation with Ernst Bloch." Dialog, VII (Winter, 1968), pp. 42-55.

Novak, Michael. *Belief and Unbelief. A Philosophy of Self-Knowledge.* New York: Macmillan, 1965.

Patterson, Antoinette Mann. *The Infinite Worlds of Giordano Bruno.* Springfield, Ill.: Charles C. Thomas, 1970.

Plato. *The Collected Dialogues of Plato Including the Letters.* Edited by Edith Hamilton and Huntington Cairns. New York: Bollingen Foundation, 1961.

Trinkhaus, Charles. *In Our Image and Likeness. Humanity and Divinity in Italian Humanist Thought,* 2 vols. Chicago: University of Chicago, 1970.

3. Reason and Revelation (Theological Perspectives):

Abbott, Walter M., ed. *The Documents of Vatican II.* Translated by J. Gallagher. New York: Herder and Herder, 1966.

Anselm of Canterbury. *Proslogion with a Reply on Behalf of the Fool by Gaunilo and the Author's Reply to Gaunilo.* Translation, introduction and philosophical commentary by M. J. Charlesworth. Oxford: Clarendon Press, 1965.

Barth, Karl. *Anselm: Fides Quaerens Intellectum. Anselm's Proof of the Existence of God in the Context of His Theological Scheme.* Translated by I. W. Robertson. London: SCM, 1960.

Buber, Martin. *The Eclipse of God. Studies in the Relation between Religion and Philosophy.* New York: Harper, 1952.

Burrill, Donald R., ed. *The Cosmological Arguments. A Spectrum of Opinion.* Garden City, N.Y.: Doubleday, Anchor Book, 1967.

Cobb, John B., Jr. *A Christian Natural Theology. Based on the Thought of Alfred North Whitehead.* Philadelphia: Westminster, 1965.

———. *Living Options in Protestant Theology: A Survey of Methods.* Philadelphia: Westminster, 1962.

———. *The Structure of Christian Existence.* Philadelphia: Westminster, 1967.

Cousins, Ewert H., ed. *Process Theology. Basic Writings.* New York: Newman, 1971.

Denzinger, Heinrich. *The Sources of Catholic Dogma.* Translated by R. J. Deferrari. St. Louis: B. Herder, 1957.

Kierkegaard, Søren. *Concluding Unscientific Postscript.* Translated by D. F. Swenson and W. Lowrie. Princeton: Princeton University, 1941.

Leibrecht, Walter. *God and Man in the Thought of Hamann.* Translated by J. H. Stam and M. H. Bertram. Philadelphia: Fortress, 1966.

Lessing, Gotthold Ephraim. *On the Proof of the Spirit and of Power* (1777). *Lessing's Theological Writings.* Translated with an introductory essay by Henry Chadwick. Stanford, Cal.: Stanford University, 1957.

Macquarrie, John. *God-Talk. An Examination of the Language and Logic of Theology.* New York: Harper, 1967.

Madden, Arthur G., and Weigel, Gustave. *Religion and the Knowledge of God.* Englewood Cliffs, N. J.: Prentice-Hall, 1961.

Marty, Martin E. *Varieties of Unbelief.* New York: Holt, Rinehart and Winston, 1964.

Ogden, Schubert M. *Christ without Myth. A Study Based on the Theology of Rudolf Bultmann.* New York: Harper, 1961.

———. *The Reality of God and Other Essays.* New York: Harper, 1966.

Smith, Ronald Gregor. *J. G. Hamann. 1730-1788. A Study in Christian Existence. With Selections from His Writings.* New York: Harper, 1960.

4. *Reason and Revelation (Philosophical Perspectives):*

Aristotle. *The Basic Works of Aristotle.* Edited and introduction by Richard McKeon. New York: Random House, 1941.

Cleve, Felix M. *The Giants of Pre-Sophistic Greek Philosophy. An Attempt to Reconstruct Their Thoughts,* Vol. 1. The Hague: Martinus Nijhoff, 1969.

Descartes, René *Philosophical Writings.* Selected and translated by N. K. Smith. New York: Random House, Modern Library, 1958.

Hartshorne, Charles. *Anselm's Discovery: A Re-Esamination of the Ontological Proof for God's Existence.* Lasalle, Ill.: Open Court, 1965.

———. *Beyond Humanism. Essays in the Philosophy of Nature* (1937). Lincoln: University of Nebraska, Bison Book, 1968.

———. *The Divine Relativity. A Social Conception of God.* New Haven: Yale University, 1948.

———. *The Logic of Perfection and Other Essays in Neoclassical Metaphysics.* Lasalle, Ill.: Open Court, 1962.

———. *Man's Vision of God and the Logic of Theism.* Chicago: Willett, Clark, & Co., 1941.

———. *A Natural Theology for Our Time.* Lasalle, Ill.: Open Court, 1967.

Hick, John, and McGill, Arthur C., eds. *The Many-Faced Argument.*

Recent Studies on the Ontological Argument for the Existence of God. New York: Macmillan, 1967.

James, Ralph E. *The Concrete God. A New Beginning for Theology— The Thought of Charles Hartshorne.* Indianapolis: Bobbs-Merrill, 1967.

Kant, Immanuel. *Critique of Judgment.* Translated with an introduction by J. H. Bernhard. New York: Hafner, 1951.

——. *Critique of Practical Reason and Other Writings in Moral Philosophy.* Translated, edited and introduction by H. Rackham. London: William Heinemann, 1933.

——. *Critique of Pure Reason.* Translated, with an introduction by N. K. Smith. Abridged edition. New York: Random House, Modern Library, 1958.

——. *Religion within the Limits of Reason Alone.* Translated with an introduction and notes by Th. M. Greene and H. H. Hudson. With a New Essay, "The Ethical Significance of Kant's Religion," by John R. Silber. 2nd ed. Lasalle, Ill.: Open Court, 1960.

La Croix, Richard R. *Proslogion II and III. A Third Interpretation of Anselm's Argument.* Leiden: E. J. Brill, 1972.

Leclerc, Ivor, ed. *The Relevance of Whitehead. Philosophical Essays in Commemoration of the Centenary of the Birth of Alfred North Whitehead.* London: George Allen & Unwin, 1961.

Leibniz, Gottfried Wilhelm. *New System. Leibniz. The Monadology and Other Philosophical Writings.* Translated, introduction and notes by Robert Latta. London: Oxford University, 1951.

Pittenger, Norman. *Alfred North Whitehead.* Richmond, Va.: John Knox, 1969.

Pols, Edward. *Whitehead's Metaphysics. A Critical Examination of Process and Reality.* Carbondale: Southern Illinois University, 1967.

Reese, William L., and Freeman, Eugene, eds. *Process and Divinity. Philosophical Essays Presented to Charles Hartshorne.* Lasalle, Ill.: Open Court, 1964.

Smith, John E. *The Analogy of Experience. An Approach to Understanding Religious Truth.* New York: Harper, 1973.

Smith, Norman Kemp. *New Studies in the Philosophy of Descartes. Descartes as Pioneer.* London: Macmillan, 1952.

Whitehead, Alfred North. *Process and Reality. An Essay in Cosmology.* New York: Macmillan, 1960.

——. *Religion in the Making.* New York: Macmillan, 1926.

——. *Science and the Modern World.* 1925. New York: Macmillan, 1960.

5. *The Search for Ultimates (Theological Perspectives):*

Berger, Peter L. *A Rumor of Angels. Modern Society and the Rediscovery of the Supernatural.* Garden City, N.Y.: Doubleday, 1969.

——. *The Sacred Canopy. Elements of a Social Theory of Religion.* Garden City, N.Y.: Doubleday, 1967.

Brunner, Emil. *Dogmatics.* Vol. 1: *The Christian Doctrine of God.* Translated by O. Wyon. Philadelphia: Westminster, 1950.

——. *Revelation and Reason. The Christian Doctrine of Faith and Knowledge.* Philadelphia: Westminster, 1946.

Burrell, David B. "The Possibility of a Natural Theology." *Encounter,* XXIX (Spring, 1968), pp. 158-164.

Dewart, Leslie. *The Foundations of Belief.* New York: Herder and Herder, 1969.

——. *Religion, Language and Truth.* New York: Herder and Herder, 1970.

Gilkey, Langdon. *Naming the Whirlwind. The Renewal of God-Language.* Indianapolis: Bobbs-Merrill, 1969.

——. *Religion and the Scientific Future. Reflections on Myth, Science, and Theology.* New York: Harper, 1970.

Heim, Karl. *Christian Faith and Natural Science.* Translated by N. H. Smith. London: SCM, 1953.

Herzog, Frederick. *Understanding God. The Key Issue in Present-Day Protestant Thought.* New York: Charles Scribner's, 1966.

Lonergan, Bernard J. F. *Insight. A Study of Human Understanding.* New York: Philosophical Library, 1970.

——. *Method in Theology.* New York: Herder and Herder, 1972.

Mascall, Eric L. *The Openness of Being. Natural Theology Today.* Philadelphia: Westminster, 1972.

Pannenberg, Wolfhart. *What Is Man? Contemporary Anthropology in Theological Perspective.* Translated by D. A. Priebe. Philadelphia: Fortress, 1970.

——. *The Idea of God and Human Freedom.* Philadelphia: Westminster, 1973.

Tillich, Paul. *Systematic Theology.* Vol. 1. Chicago: University of Chicago, 1951.

6. *The Search for Ultimates (Philosophical Perspectives):*

Bellah, Robert N. *Beyond Belief. Essays on Religion in a Post-traditional World.* New York: Harper, 1970.

Brée, Germaine. *Camus and Sartre. Crisis and Commitment.* New York: Delacorte, 1972.

Cumming, Robert Denoon, ed. *The Philosophy of Jean-Paul Sartre.* New York: Random House, 1965.

Camus, Albert. *Exile and the Kingdom.* Translated by J. O'Brien. New York: Alfred A. Knopf, 1958.

——. *The Fall.* Translated by J. O.'Brien. New York: Alfred A. Knopf, 1960.

――. *The Myth of Sisyphus and Other Essays*. Translated by J. O'Brien. New York: Alfred A. Knopf, 1967.

――. *The Rebel. An Essay on Man in Revolt*. Foreword by Sir Herbert Read. Translated by A. Bower. New York: Alfred A. Knopf, 1961.

Comte, Auguste. *Introduction to Positive Philosophy*. Edited with an introduction and revised translation by Frederick Ferré. Indianapolis: Bobbs-Merrill, 1970.

Copi, Irving M., and Beard, Robert W., eds. *Essays on Wittgenstein's Tractatus*. New York: Macmillan, 1966.

Dampier, William Cecil. *A History of Science and Its Relation with Philosophy and Religion*. Cambridge: Cambridge University, 1961.

Driesch, Hans. *The Science and Philosophy of the Organism*. 2 vols. New York: D. Appleton, 1898.

Heidegger, Martin. *Being and Time*. Translated by J. Macquarrie and E. Robinson. London: SCM, 1962.

Heisenberg, Werner. *Physics and Beyond. Encounters and Conversations*. Translated by A. J. Pomerans. New York: Harper Torchbook, 1972.

――. *Physics and Philosophy. The Revolution in Modern Physics*. New York: Harper, World Perspectives, 1958.

Hudson, W. D. *Ludwig Wittgenstein. The Bearing of His Philosophy Upon Religious Belief*. Richmond, Va.: John Knox, 1968.

Hume, David. *Hume on Religion*. Edited with an introduction by Richard Wollheim. Cleveland: World, Meridian Book, 1964.

――. *An Inquiry Concerning Human Understanding. Hume: On Human Nature and the Understanding*. Edited by Antony Flew. New York: Collier, 1962.

Jaspers, Karl. *Reason and Existenz. Five Lectures*. Translated with an introduction by W. Earle. New York: Noonday, 1955.

Jolivet, Régis. *Sartre. The Theology of the Absurd*. Translated by W. C. Piersol. Westminster, Md.: Newman, 1967.

Klemke, E. D., ed. *Essays on Wittgenstein*. Urbana: University of Illinois, 1971.

Locke, John. *An Essay Concerning Human Understanding*. Edited by Alexander C. Fraser, Vol. 1. New York: Dover, 1959.

――. *Locke on Politics, Religion, and Education*. Edited with an introduction by Maurice Cranston. New York: Collier, 1965.

Sartre, Jean-Paul. *The Age of Reason*. Translated by E. Sutton. New York: A. Knopf, 1948.

――. *Being and Nothingness. An Essay on Phenomenological Ontology*. Translated with an introduction by Hazel E. Barnes. New York: Philosophical Library, 1956.

――. *No Exit*, in *No Exit and Three Other Plays*. Translated by L. Abel. New York: Alfred A. Knopf, Vintage Book, 1949.

Scott, Nathan A. *Albert Camus*. New York: Hillary House, 1962.

Simon, Walter. *European Positivism in the Nineteenth Century. An Essay in Intellectual History.* Port Washington, N. Y.: Kennikat, 1972.

Toynbee, Arnold J. *Civilization on Trial.* New York: Oxford University, 1948.

Versényi, Laszlo. *Heidegger, Being, and Truth.* New Haven: Yale University, 1965.

Wittgenstein, Ludwig. *Notebooks. 1914-1916.* Edited by G. H. von Wright and G. E. M. Anscombe. Translated by G. E. M. Anscombe. New York: Harper, 1961.

——. *Tractatus Logico-Philosophicus.* New translation by D. F. Pears and B. F. McGuinness. Introduction by Bertrand Russell. London: Routledge & Kegan Paul, 1961.

7. *Origin and Basic Concepts in Religion:*

Allegro, John M. *The End of a Road.* London: Macgibbon & Kee, 1970.

——. *The Sacred Mushroom and the Cross. A Study of the Nature and Origins of Christianity within the Fertility Cults of the Ancient Near East.* London: Hodder and Stoughton, 1970.

Altizer, Thomas J. J. *Mircea Eliade and the Dialectic of the Sacred.* Philadelphia: Westminster, 1963.

Capps, Walter H., ed. *Ways of Understanding Religion.* New York: Macmillan, 1972.

Eliade, Mircea. *The Quest. History and Meaning in Religion.* Chicago: University of Chicago, 1969.

——. *The Sacred and the Profane. The Nature of Religion.* Translated by W. R. Trask. New York: Harcourt, Brace and Co., 1959.

——. "On Understanding Primitive Religions." *Glaube, Geist, Geschichte. Festschrift für Ernst Benz zum 60. Geburtstage am 17. November 1967.* Edited by Gerhard Müller and Winfried Zeller Leiden: E. J. Brill, 1967, pp. 498-505.

Evans-Pritchard, E. E. *Theories of Primitive Religion.* Oxford: Clarendon Press, 1965.

Frazer, Sir James George. *The Golden Bough. A Study in Magic and Religion.* Abridged Edition. New York: Macmillan, 1958.

Freeman, Kathleen. *Ancilla to the Pre-Socratic Philosophers. A Complete Translation of the Fragments in Diels, 'Fragmente der Vorsokratiker'.* Oxford: Basil Blackwell, 1952.

Freud, Sigmund. *Basic Writings.* Translated, edited and introduction by A. A. Brill. New York: Random House, Modern Library, 1938.

——. *The Complete Introductory Lectures on Psychoanalysis.* Translated and edited by James Strachey. New York: W. W. Norton, 1966.

——. *On Creativity and the Unconscious. Papers on the Psychology of Art, Literature, Love, Religion.* Selected with an introduction by Benjamin Nelson. New York: Harper Torchbook, 1958.

————. *The Future of an Illusion.* Translated by W. D. Robson-Scott. Garden City, N.Y.: Doubleday, Anchor Book, n.d.

Guirdham, Arthur. *Christ and Freud. A Study of Religious Experience and Observance.* Preface by L. Durrell. London: George Allen & Unwin, 1959.

Homans, Peter. *Theology after Freud. An Interpretive Inquiry.* Indianapolis: Bobbs-Merrill, 1970.

James, William. *The Varieties of Religious Experience. A Study in Human Nature.* Enlarged edition with appendices and introduction by Joseph Ratner. New Hyde Park, N.Y.: University Books, 1963.

Jung, Carl Gustav. *Psychology and Religion.* New Haven: Yale University, 1940.

King, John C. *A Christian View of the Mushroom Myth.* London: Hodder and Stoughton, 1970.

Lang, Andrew. *Magic and Religion.* London: Longmans, Green, and Co., 1901.

————. *The Making of Religion.* London: Longmans, Green, and Co., 1898.

Malinowski, Bronislaw. *Magic, Science and Religion; and Other Essays.* Introduction by Robert Redfield. Garden City, N.Y.: Doubleday, Anchor Book, 1954.

Marett, R. R. *The Threshold of Religion.* London: Methuen, 1929.

Meng, Heinrich, and Freud, Ernst L., eds. *Psychoanalysis and Faith. The Letters of Sigmund Freud & Oskar Pfister.* Translated by E. Mosbacher. New York: Basic Books, 1963.

Otto, Rudolf. *The Idea of the Holy. An Inquiry into the Non-rational Factor in the Idea of the Divine and Its Relation to the Rational.* Translated by J. W. Harvey. London: Oxford University, 1957.

Pettazzoni, Raffaele. "The Supreme Being: Phenomenological Structure and Historical Development." *The History of Religions. Essays in Methodology.* Edited by Mircea Eliade and Joseph M. Kitagawa. Preface by Jerald C. Brauer. Chicago: University of Chicago, 1959, pp. 59-66.

————. *The World of Primitive Man.* New York: Henry Schuman, 1953.

Radin, Paul. *Primitive Religion. Its Nature and Origin.* New York: Dover, 1957.

Ricoeur, Paul. *Freud and Philosophy. An Essay on Interpretation.* Translated by D. Savage. New Haven: Yale University, 1970.

Sanders, Benjamin G. *Christianity after Freud. An Interpretation of the Christian Experience in the Light of Psycho-Analytic Theory.* London: Geoffrey Bles, 1949.

Schaer, Hans. *Religion and the Cure of Souls in Jung's Psychology.* Translated by R. F. C. Hull. Vol. 21 of Bollingen Series. New York: Pantheon Books, 1950.

Schleiermacher, Friedrich. *On Religion. Speeches to Its Cultured Despisers.* Translated by J. Oman. New York: Frederick Ungar, 1955.

Schmidt, Wilhelm. *The Origin and Growth of Religion. Facts and Theories.* Translated by H. J. Rose. New York: Lincoln Macveagh, 1931.

Schoeps, Hans-Joachim. *The Religions of Mankind.* Translated by R. and C. Winston. Garden City, N.Y.: Doubleday, 1966.

Söderblom, Nathan. *The Living God. Basal Forms of Personal Religion.* Biographical introduction by Yngve Brilioth. Boston: Beacon, 1962.

Tylor, Sir Edward Burnett. *Religion in Primitive Culture* (Part II of "Primitive Culture"). Introduction by Paul Radin. New York: Harper Torchbook, 1958.

van der Leeuw, Gerhardus. *Religion in Essence & Manifestation. A Study in Phenomenology.* Translated by J. E. Turner. London: George Allen & Unwin, 1938.

8. *Islam, Zoroastrianism, and Buddhism:*

Ali, Syed Ameer. *The Spirit of Islam. A History of the Evolution and Ideals of Islam. With a Life of the Prophet.* London: Chatto & Windus, 1964.

Conze, Edward. *Buddhism. Its Essence and Development.* Preface by Arthur Waley. New York: Harper Torchbook, 1959.

———. *Thirty Years of Buddhist Studies. Selected Essays.* Columbia, S.C.: University of South Carolina, 1968.

Dator, James Allen. *Soka Gakkai. Builders of the Third Civilization. American and Japanese Members.* Seattle: University of Washington, 1969.

Duchesne-Guillemin, Jacques. *Symbols and Values in Zoroastrianism. Their Survival and Renewal.* New York: Harper, 1966.

———. *The Western Response to Zoroaster.* Oxford: Clarendon Press, 1958.

Gibb, H. A. R. *Modern Trends in Islam.* Chicago: University of Chicago, 1950.

Jeffery, Arthur, ed. *A Reader on Islam. Passages from Standard Arabic Writings Illustrative of the Beliefs and Practices of Muslims.* 's-Gravenhage: Mouton, 1962.

MacDonald, Duncan B. *Development of Muslim Theology, Jurisprudence and Constitutional Theory.* New York: Russell & Russell, 1965.

Masani, Rusdom Pestonji. *Zoroastrianism: The Religion of the Good Life.* With a foreword by John McKenzie. New York: Macmillan, 1968.

Morgan, Kenneth W., ed. *Islam—The Straight Path. Islam Interpreted by Muslims.* New York: Roland Press, 1958.

———, ed. *The Path of the Buddha. Buddhism Interpreted by Buddhists.* New York: Roland Press, 1956.

Murata Kiyoaki. *Japan's New Buddhism. An Objective Account of Soka Gakkai*. Foreword by Daisaku Ikeda. New York: Walker/Weatherhill, 1969.

Nicholson, Reynold Alleyne. *Studies in Islamic Mysticism*. Cambridge: University Press, 1967.

Saddhatissa, H. *Buddhist Ethics. Essence of Buddhism*. London: George Allen & Unwin, 1970.

Saunders, E. D. *Buddhism in Japan. With an Outline of Its Origins in India*. Philadelphia: University of Pennsylvania, 1964.

Smith, Bardwell L. "Toward a Buddhist Anthropology: The Problem of the Secular." *Journal of the American Academy of Religion*, XXVI (September, 1968), pp. 203-216.

Swearer, Donald K. *Buddhism in Transition*. Philadelphia: Westminster, 1970.

Suzuki, Beatrice Lane. *Mahayana Buddhism. A Brief Outline*. Foreword by Ch. Humphreys. New York: Macmillan, 1969.

Suzuki, Daisetz Teitaro. *Mysticism: Christian and Buddhist*. New York: Harper, 1957.

———. *Outlines of Mahayana Buddhism*. Prefatory essay by Alan Watts. New York: Schocken, 1963.

Watt, W. Montgomery. *Islamic Revelation in the Modern World*. Edinburgh: University Press, 1969.

Welbon, Guy Richard. *The Buddhist Nirvana and Its Western Interpreters*. Chicago: University of Chicago, 1968.

Whitehurst, James Emerson. "The Zoroastrian Response to Westernization: A Case Study of the Parsis of Bombay." *Journal of the American Academy of Religion*, XXXVII (September, 1969), pp. 224-236.

Williams, John Alden. *Islam*. New York: George Braziller, 1961.

Zaehner, Robert Charles. *The Teachings of the Magi. A Compendium of Zoroastrian Beliefs*. New York: Macmillan, 1956.

9. *Christian Faith and the World Religions:*

Althaus, Paul. *The Theology of Martin Luther*. Translated by R. C. Schultz. Philadelphia: Fortress, 1966.

Bellah, Robert N., ed. *Religion and Progress in Modern Asia*. New York: Free Press, 1965.

Dillenberger, John. *God Hidden and Revealed. The Interpretation of Luther's deus absconditus and Its Significance for Religious Thought*. Philadelphia: Muhlenberg, 1953.

Forman, Charles W., ed. *Christianity in the Non-Western World*. Englewood Cliffs, N. J.: Prentice-Hall, 1967.

Kraemer, Hendrik. *The Christian Message in a non-Christian World*. Grand Rapids, Mich.: Kregel, 1956.

———. *Religion and the Christian Faith*. Philadelphia: Westminster, 1956.

——. *World Cultures and World Religions. The Coming Dialogue.* Philadelphia: Westminster, 1960.

Küng, Hans. *Freedom Today.* Translated by C. Hastings. New York: Sheed and Ward, 1966.

Löwith, Karl. *Meaning in History.* Chicago: University of Chicago, Phoenix Book, 1957.

Nelson, J. Robert, ed. *No Man Is Alien. Essays on the Unity of Mankind.* Leiden: E. J. Brill, 1971.

Otto, Rudolf. *Mysticism East and West. A Comparative Analysis of the Nature of Mysticism.* Translated by B. L. Bracey and R. C. Payne. New York: Collier, 1962.

Pannikkar, Raimundo. "Sunyata and Pleroma: The Buddhist and Christian Response to the Human Predicament." *Religion and Humanizing of Man.* Edited by James M. Robinson. Council on the Study of Religion, 1972, pp. 67-86.

Parrinder, Geoffrey. *Comparative Religion.* London: George Allen & Unwin, 1962.

Pauck, Wilhelm. *Harnack and Troeltsch. Two Historical Theologians.* New York: Oxford University, 1968.

Radhakrishnan, S. *East and West in Religion.* New York: Barnes & Noble, 1958.

Rahner, Karl. "Christianity and the non-Christian Religions." *Theological Investigations.* Vol. 5: *Later Writings.* Translated by K.-H. Kruger. Baltimore: Helicon, 1966, pp. 115-134.

Religions. Fundamental Themes for a Dialogistic Understanding. Edited by the Secretariate for non-Christian Religions. Rome: Editrice Àncora, 1970.

Re-thinking the Church's Mission. Vol. 13 of *Concilium Theology in an Age of Renewal.* New York: Paulist, 1966.

Röper, Anita. *The Anonymous Christian.* Translated by J. Donceel. With an Afterword: "The Anonymous Christian According to Karl Rahner" by Klaus Riesenhuber. New York: Sheed and Ward, 1966.

Smith, Wilfred Cantwell. *The Faith of Other Men.* New York: Harper Torchbook, 1972.

——. *The Meaning and End of Religion. A New Approach to the Religious Traditions of Mankind.* New York: Macmillan, 1963.

Thomas, Owen C., ed. *Attitudes Toward Other Religions. Some Christian Interpretations.* London: SCM, 1969.

Tillich, Paul. *Christianity and the Encounter of the World Religions.* New York: Columbia University, 1963.

——. *The Future of Religion.* Edited by Jerald C. Brauer. New York: Harper, 1966.

Toynbee, Arnold. *Christianity Among the Religions of the World.* New York: Charles Scribner's, 1957.

———. *An Historian's Approach to Religion*. London: Oxford University, 1956.

Troeltsch, Ernst. *The Absoluteness of Christianity and the History of Religions*. Introduction by James Luther Adams. Translated by D. Reid. Richmond, Va.: John Knox, 1971.

———. *Christian Thought. Its History and Application*. Edited with an introduction by Baron F. von Hügel. New York: Meridian, Living Age Book, 1957.

———. *Protestantism and Progress. A Historical Study of the Relation of Protestantism to the Modern World*. Translated by W. Montgomery. Boston: Beacon, 1958.

van Leeuwen, Arend Th. *Christianity in World History. The Meetings of the Faiths of East and West*. Foreword by Hendrik Kraemer. Translated by H. H. Hoskins. London: Edinburgh House, 1966.

van Straelen, H. *The Catholic Encounter with World Religions*. Westminster, Md.: Newman, 1966.

Wach, Joachim. *The Comparative Study of Religions*. Edited with an introduction by Joseph M. Kitagawa. New York: Columbia University, 1958.

Watson, Philip S. *Let God Be God! An Interpretation of the Theology of Martin Luther*. Philadelphia: Muhlenberg, 1947.

Young, Robert D. *Encounter with World Religions*. Philadelphia: Westminster, 1970.

10. God's Self-disclosure in the Judeo-Christian Tradition:

Albright, William Foxwell. *From Stone Age to Christianity. Monotheism and the Historical Process*. Garden City, N.Y.; Doubleday, Anchor Book, 1957.

———. *Yahweh and the Gods of Canaan. A Historical Analysis of Two Contrasting Faiths*. Garden City, N.Y.: Doubleday, Anchor Book, 1969.

Alt, Albrecht. "The God of the Fathers." *Essays on Old Testament History and Religion*. Translated by R. A. Wilson. Oxford: Basil Blackwell, 1966, pp. 1-77.

Baillie, John. *The Idea of Revelation in Recent Thought*. New York: Columbia University, 1964.

Barr, James. *Old and New in Interpretation. A Study of the Two Testaments*. London: SCM, 1966.

Barth, Karl. *Church Dogmatics*. Vol. 4/II: *The Doctrine of Reconciliation*. Edited by G. W. Bromiley and T. F. Torrance. Edinburgh: T. & T. Clark, 1958.

Braaten, Carl E. *The Future of God. The Revolutionary Dynamics of Hope*. New York: Harper, 1969.

———. *History and Hermeneutics*. Vol. 2 of *New Directions in Theology Today*. Edited by William Hordern. Philadelphia: Westminster, 1966.

Brichto, Herbert C. "On Faith and Revelation in the Bible." *Hebrew Union College Annual*, XXXIX (Cincinnati, 1968), pp. 35-53.

Brunner, Emil. *Truth as Encounter*. Translated by D. Cairns. Philadelphia: Westminster, 1964.

Buber, Martin. *I and Thou*. Added postscript by the author. Translated by R. G. Smith. New York: Charles Scribner's, 1958.

Bultmann, Rudolf. *The Gospel of John. A Commentary*. Translated by G. R. Beasley-Murray *et al.* Philadelphia: Westminster, 1971.

———. "New Testament and Mythology." *Kergyma and Myth. A Theological Debate*. Edited by Hans Werner Bartsch. Translated by R. H. Fuller. London: SPCK, 1953, pp. 1-44.

———. *The Presence of Eternity. History and Eschatology*. New York: Harper, 1957.

———. *Theology of the New Testament*. Vol. 1. Translated by K. Grobel. New York: Charles Scribner's, 1951.

Collingwood, R. G. *The Idea of History*. New York: Oxford University, Galaxy Book, 1957.

Conzelmann, Hans. *An Outline of the Theology of the New Testament*. Translated by J. Bowden. New York: Harper, 1969.

Cross, Frank Moore, Jr. "Yahweh and the God of the Patriarchs." *The Harvard Theological Review*, LV (October, 1962), pp. 225-259.

Cullmann, Oscar. *Christ and Time. The Primitive Christian Conception of Time and History*. Translated by F. V. Filson. London: SCM, 1962.

———. *Salvation in History*. Translated by S. G. Sowers. London: SCM, 1967.

Dionysius the Areopagite. *On the Divine Names and the Mystical Theology*. Translated by C. E. Rolt. New York: Macmillan, 1951.

Downing, F. Gerald. *Has Christianity a Revelation?* London: SCM, 1964.

Eichrodt, Walter. *Theology of the Old Testament*. Vol. 1. Translated by J. A. Baker. Philadelphia: Westminster, 1961.

Fohrer, Georg. *History of Israelite Religion*. Translated by D. E. Green. Nashville: Abingdon, 1972.

Jacob, Edmond. *Theology of the Old Testament*. Translated by A. W. Heathcote and Ph. J. Allcock. New York: Harper, 1958.

Jeremias, Joachim. *New Testament Theology*. Vol. 1: *The Proclamation of Jesus*. Translated by J. Bowden. New York: Charles Scribner's, 1971.

Kaufman, Gordon D. *God the Problem*. Cambridge, Mass.: Harvard University, 1972.

———. *Systematic Theology. A Historicist Perspective*. New York: Charles Scribner's, 1968.

Kaufmann, Yehezkel. *The Religion of Israel. From Its Beginnings to the Babylonian Exile*. Translated and abridged by M. Greenberg. Chicago: University of Chicago, 1960.

Kitamori, Kazoh. *Theology of the Pain of God.* Richmond, Va.: John Knox, 1965.

Köhler, Ludwig. *Old Testament Theology.* Translated by A. S. Todd. Philadelphia: Westminster, 1957.

Labuschagne, C. J. *The Incomparability of Yahweh in the Old Testament.* Leiden: E. J. Brill, 1966.

McCarthy, Dennis J. *Old Testament Covenant. A Survey of Current Opinions.* Oxford: Basil Blackwell, 1972.

Moltmann, Jürgen. *Theology of Hope. On the Ground and the Implications of a Christian Eschatology.* Translated by J. W. Leitch. New York: Harper, 1967.

Niebuhr, H. Richard. *The Meaning of Revelation.* New York: Macmillan, 1967.

Pannenberg, Wolfhart. *Basic Questions in Theology. Collected Essays.* 2 vols. Translated by G. H. Kehm. Philadelphia: Fortress, 1970/71.

———. *Jesus—God and Man.* Translated by L. L. Wilkins and D. A. Priebe. Philadelphia: Westminster, 1968.

———, ed. *Revelation as History.* Translated by D. Granskou. New York: Macmillan, 1968.

von Rad, Gerhard. *Old Testament Theology.* Vol. 1: *The Theology of Israel's Historical Traditions.* Translated by D. M. G. Stalker. Edinburgh: Oliver & Boyd, 1962.

———. *Old Testament Theology.* Vol. 2: *The Theology of Israel's Prophetic Traditions.* Translated by D. M. G. Stalker. New York: Harper, 1965.

———. "The Theological Problem of the Old Testament Doctrine of Creation" (1936). *The Problem of the Hexateuch and Other Essays.* Translated by N. W. Porteous. Edinburgh: Oliver & Boyd, 1966, pp. 131-143.

Schleiermacher, Friedrich. *The Christian Faith.* Edited by H. R. Mackintosh and J. S. Stewart. Edinburgh: T. & T. Clark, 1960.

Schwarz, Hans. *On the Way to the Future. A Christian View of Eschatology in the Light of Current Trends in Religion, Philosophy, and Science.* Minneapolis, Minn.: Augsburg, 1972.

Smith, Morton. *Palestinian Parties and Politics that Shaped the Old Testament.* New York: Columbia University, 1971.

Snaith, Norman H. *The Distinctive Ideas of the Old Testament.* London: Epworth, 1960.

Tillich, Paul. *Systematic Theology.* Vol. 2: *Existence and the Christ.* Chicago: University of Chicago, 1957.

Vriezen, Th. C. *An Outline of Old Testament Theology.* 2nd ed. Newton, Mass.: Charles T. Bradford, 1970.

Wright, G. Ernest. *God Who Acts. Biblical Theology as Recital.* Chicago: Henry Regnery, 1952.

Index of Names

278

Index of Subjects

Index of Biblical References